The Best of Mayberry

The Best of the Best — Home Economists Tested Recipes

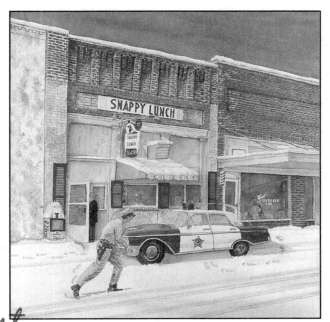

Janet,

By Betty Conley Lyerly

God's Blessings!

Betty C. Lyerly

Mount Airy, North Carolina

Christmas 2006

Honored as
"America's Best"
The Oxmoor House

The Best of Mayberry

The Best of the Best, Home Economists Tested Recipes

by Betty Conley Lyerly

A portion of the profits from the sale of these books will go for Lions Club projects. The purpose of the Lions Club is service to the blind, visually handicapped, Lion-Quest (drug and alcohol youth program), Sight First dedicated to eradicating preventable and reversible blindness worldwide, and other sight-related activities.

Additional copies of *The Best of Mayberry* may be obtained at the cost of $19.95, plus $4.00 postage and handling, each book. North Carolina residents add $1.40 sales tax, each book.

Send to:

Betty Conley Lyerly
125 Taylor Street
Mount Airy, North Carolina 27030

First Printing	May, 1996	4,074 copies
Second Printing	June, 1997	4,200 copies
Third Printing	June, 1998	3,138 copies
Fourth Printing	April, 1999	4,308 copies
Fifth Printing	April, 2000	4,032 copies
Sixth Printing	June, 2001	3,260 copies
Seventh Printing	November, 2001	4,266 copies
Eighth Printing	May, 2003	4,302 copies
Ninth Printing	July, 2004	4,223 copies
Tenth Printing	July, 2005	4,223 copies
Eleventh Printing	September, 2006	6,000 copies

ISBN Number: 0-9650515-0-1
Library of Congress Card Catalog Number: 94-12045

PUBLISHED BY: Betty Conley Lyerly

SKETCHES BY: Betty Conley Lyerly

PHOTOGRAPHY BY: Betty Conley Lyerly

FRONT COVER – WATER COLOR PAINTING: *Snappy Lunch And Floyd's Barber Shop*, by Betty Conley Lyerly

WIMMER
COOKBOOKS

A CONSOLIDATED GRAPHICS COMPANY

800.548.2537   wimmerco.com

Dedication

In honor of my mother,
Bessie Lee Spake Conley

In loving memory of my father,
Hugh Grady Conley,
who was called to his heavenly home on
Dec. 24, 1990.

In loving memory of my dearly beloved husband,
The Reverend John Wilford Lyerly, D.D., Ph.D.
He was called to his heavenly home on
January 7, 2003.

Without their love, support, and encouragement, this book would not have been possible.

Many thanks to Duke Power Company employees who taste-tested many thousands of our favorite recipes.

About The Author

Betty Jane Conley Lyerly, daughter of Bessie Lee Spake Conley and the late Hugh Grady Conley, comes to you as chef extraordinaire from Shelby, North Carolina. She learned Reading, Writing, and Arithmetic at Shelby High School, but learned to cook at home with her mother.

Her first experiences in the kitchen centered around cakes. As any good cook knows, good cooking comes with experience, with trial and error—more often error in the beginning days in the kitchen. So it was with Betty. She specialized in layered cakes with Seven Minute Frosting. She would color the frosting a different color each week: one week, a lemony yellow; another week, cotton-candy pink; and then one week, she tried the blue food coloring on a pineapple cake.

Betty never used blue food coloring in a cake again. She suggests that you don't either. She also recommends that you test the oven temperature to make sure it works and, more specifically, to make sure it cuts off. Betty trusted her oven timer…but that's a whole other story.

After years of home cooking, Betty decided to pursue a degree in Home Economics and General Science from Appalachian State University, Boone, North Carolina. With her Bachelor of Science degree, she found a job in 1958 in Consumer Education at Duke Power Company, an electric utility company, in Wilkes, Yadkin, and Surry Counties, North Carolina. In this position, she promoted the use of electricity, energy conservation, and demonstrated electric appliances for home economics classes and various clubs. To this day, among Betty's best friends are electricity, the microwave oven, and her freezer. She made guest appearances on television and has been featured in numerous food columns in local newspapers.

Betty's favorite season is Christmas. In conjunction with her work at Duke Power, she presented Christmas programs and special Christmas goodies to her many consumer students. In addition, Duke Power published a collection of recipe booklets each year for the past thirty-eight years. Betty spent much of her time with the publication of these collectible booklets.

These holiday booklets are the inspiration behind this book, *The Best of Mayberry*. Betty has gone through her own flour-and-egg splattered collections to compile a "Best of the Best" cookbook, complete with her photographic collection of Andy Griffith's "Mayberry". When you have the opportunity to visit our lovely town and know its wonderful people, you will know why Betty and her husband, The Reverend Doctor John Wilford Lyerly, love calling "Mayberry" Home.

About The Book

The Best of Mayberry, a collector's edition of 616 recipes, is the best of the best, home economists tested recipes. From 1957 to 1996, Duke Power Company's home economists selected their favorite recipes. They were printed in small booklets and later as calendars as handouts at special holiday programs. For thirty-eight years, these recipes have been recognized as pace-setters for the best recipes, and the best in foods in Piedmont North and South Carolina.

The Best Of Mayberry is an extraordinary treasure of homespun recipes to make everyday a festive occasion.

The Best of Mayberry reflects rich flavor, traditions, life styles of the people of "Mayberry" and the Piedmont Carolinas.

The Best of Mayberry offers you a unique opportunity to experience the very best from "Mayberry". Recipes were selected to bring you the most delicious and widest variety; easy to prepare recipes; reliable home economists tested; and favorite recipes of Donna Fargo and Tommy Jarrell, plus Snappy Lunch's Famous Pork Chop Sandwich, a "Mayberry" favorite.

The Best of Mayberry provides special hints for food preparation and special recipe poems. As we say in "Mayberry", *"Eat til it ouches you"* and other comments highlight some of the favorite recipes.

The Best of Mayberry, truly a "Mayberry" souvenir, features a special photographic collection with a brief history of each to help you discover the real "Mayberry", the mythical name of Mount Airy, North Carolina, home-town of Andy Griffith. You will not want to miss these special places, traditions, and events on your visit to Mount Airy, the 1994 All America City.

Whether you enjoy the simplicity of "Mayberry" foods or that of a gourmet chef, we are pleased to offer this unique collection—the best of the best, *The Best of Mayberry*.

It Is The Real Snappy Lunch

(shown on the front cover)

Since 1923, Snappy Lunch, circa 1896, originally served as the Mount Airy Post Office, has been a famous landmark at 125 North Main Street, Mount Airy, North Carolina. The small diner, right out of the "Good Ole Days", is the oldest continuous eating establishment in the same location, and is one of the Mount Airy businesses made famous on "The Andy Griffith Show" and it exists today. The walls are decorated with memorabilia of "The Andy Griffith Show" and other celebrities.

Our special friend, Charles Dowell, is owner of the world famous Snappy Lunch and creator of the famous Snappy Lunch Pork Chop Sandwich, a "Mayberry" favorite. Charles Dowell remembers when Andy Griffith would walk about a block from his school on Rockford Street to have a 5 cent bologna sandwich, a moon pie, and a drink at Snappy Lunch.

Dowell came to Snappy Lunch when he was fourteen years old. In the early days, most people stood to eat as it was too crowded to be seated. People would gather there before and after theater performances. Later tables, booths, and "ole timey" school desks were added to create more places for customers to sit and enjoy their meals.

Locals, visitors, and motorcoaches flock to Snappy Lunch to enjoy the mouth-watering Pork Chop Sandwich, and people are going out of their way to meet friendly Charles Dowell. His trademark is his white paper envelope cap. You will find Charles at his grill in Snappy Lunch's front window, keeping an eye on Main Street, and greeting passers-by while cooking. Famous people, TV cameras, and visitors making pictures are frequently seen at Snappy Lunch.

Many visitors are disappointed when they arrive to find Snappy Lunch closed. Snappy Lunch serves breakfast and lunch. Don't miss Snappy Lunch! It's a real treat right out of "Mayberry" and provides what everyone wants: delicious foods, fast service, affordable prices, and homespun friendliness. There's nothing like it anywhere.

In 2000, Charles Dowell purchased the Snappy Lunch Building. The Snappy Lunch building's recent makeover takes it back in time with the restoration of the three original stained glass windows. They are beautiful in the morning sun. Snappy Lunch with the stained glass windows restored stands as a piece of Mount Airy's history.

Snappy Lunch's Famous Pork Chop Sandwich

I am grateful to Charles Dowell for sharing his Pork Chop Sandwich recipe with us. The real treat comes when Charles prepares a Pork Chop Sandwich, "fully dressed" (hot bun, battered pork chop, mustard, homemade chili, homemade slaw, sliced tomato, and chopped onion), at Snappy Lunch just for you. It's a meal in itself.

Pork Chops, boneless
BATTER
2 cups plain flour   **Salt to taste**
2 eggs, beaten   **About 1 cup milk**
2 tablespoons sugar

Place flour in mixing bowl, add sugar and salt. Add eggs and gradually add milk. Beat mixture until the batter is completely smooth, not lumpy or watery. The batter should run off the spoon without being watery and stick to the pork chop and not run off.

Remove the bone and fat from the pork chop. Pound the pork chop to tenderize. Wash pork and dry pork chop. Dip the PORK CHOP in the BATTER. Place in greased hot skillet, but not too hot. The pork chop needs to cook done, brown, and not burn the batter. Turn and brown on the other side. Yield: enough batter for 12 large pork chops. NOTE: For onion rings, slightly thin batter by adding more milk.

Floyd's Barber Shop

(shown on the front cover)

A touch of Mayberry! Floyd's Barber Shop advertises "Two Chairs, No Waiting". It's next door to Snappy Lunch, and just a block away from the elementary school, now the Andy Griffith Playhouse, circa 1920, where Andy Griffith was smitten with the urge to be an actor. Floyd's Barber Shop has been operating since 1929 at 129 North Main Street, Mount Airy, North Carolina.

Friendly Russell Hiatt will welcome you with a smile. Russell looks and sounds a lot like the original Floyd Lawson on the "Andy Griffith Show". Russell snaps photos of visitors in Andy Griffith's famous barber chair and plasters them on Floyd's Barber Shop's "Wall of Fame". There are some four to five thousand pictures in the collection and other memorabilia. He is constantly adding new pictures.

Russell worked in the barber shop before Andy left Mount Airy. Although Russell was not Andy's regular barber, he gave Andy Griffith a hair cut at the shop several times during his Mount Airy days.

Here you will find ornate old-fashioned barber chairs, the small army of bottles filled with hairstyling solutions, the low-tech cash register, the smell of freshly cut hair, and Vitalis.

The red and white barber shop logo, located outside, represents blood and bandages. During the early barber shop days, warts were removed with an electric machine that gave a (lightning) blue light-like flame with a needle point. In a few days the wart would fall off.

Table of Contents

FAVORITE RECIPES
FROM MY COOKBOOK

Recipe Name	Page Number

Appetizers

*Pilot Mountain
State Park*

PILOT MOUNTAIN STATE PARK

In 1662, Surry County in North Carolina began as a gift from King Charles II of England who gave his eight Lords Proprietors the gift of land which we call Carolina. The majestic Blue Ridge Mountains and Foothills are dominated by the incomparable Pilot Mountain.

Pilot Mountain is a touch of the real "Mayberry". Take a stroll just 14 miles south of Mount Airy off U. S. Hwy. 52 to Pilot Mountain State Park, a national, natural landmark. From the summit, view the spectacular countryside of Surry County, Sauratown Mountain, and Winston-Salem. Overlooks on the mountain give a view of the countryside said to be unexcelled in the eastern United States. On a clear day you can see forever, over 3,000 square miles.

Pilot Mountain is a geologic wonder, with two distinctive pinnacles. According to geologists, it is a mountain of resistant rock, (quartzite monadnock), so rugged that it has survived millions of years, while the elements were eroding the foothills around it. The mountain pinnacle rises 2,421 feet above sea level and 1,400 feet above the surrounding countryside.

A tribe of Indians, called the Saura, roamed the area before the arrival of the white man. The mountain was used as a landmark. They called it "Jo-me-o-kee" meaning "great guide" or "Pilot". In the past, the mountain has been called Mount Ararat and Stonehead, but in 1753, the Moravians coined the word Pilot and it has been known by that name ever since. In 1751, it was mapped by Joshua Frye and Peter Jefferson, father of President Thomas Jefferson, who fought in the American Revolution. The mountain was owned by Andre Mathieu, a French soldier who fought in the American Revolution. In 1857, William Gilliam and Andre Mathieu's son-in-law, inherited the mountain after Mathieu's death at the age of 97. The mountain was sold to Gerald Bernard and then to McDonald Boyd about 1870. The Boyd heirs became involved in a suit over the property, which lasted for 20 years.

About 1923, W. L. Spoon, an engineer-geologist, acquired the mountain and built the road to the summit and constructed ladders to the top of the pinnacle. In 1944, J. W. Beasley bought the mountain from the Spoon's estate. Mr. Beasley paved the road to the summit and rebuilt the steps to the Big Pinnacle. In 1968, it became North Carolina's fourteenth state park. In an effort to protect the pinnacle, the steps were removed in 1970. Also in 1970, 1400 acres along the Yadkin River were added to the state park, giving the park a total of 3,700 acres.

The remains of the Bean Shoals Canal wall are located in the Yadkin River section of Pilot Mountain State Park. Between 1820 and 1825, a three mile long canal was to be constructed around the Bean Shoals. After two miles were built, considerable cost forced the company into bankruptcy. Remnants of the Bean Shoals Canal remain today. It is the most extensive contiguous canal remaining in North Carolina.

Cheese Log

½ pound sharp cheese, grated
1-2 tablespoons onion, minced
3 tablespoons green pepper, minced
3 stuffed olives, chopped
2 tablespoons pickle, chopped
1 tablespoon pimento, chopped
1 hard-cooked egg, chopped
½ cup saltines, finely crushed
¼ cup mayonnaise
½ teaspoon salt

Combine cheese with rest of ingredients; form into long roll; wrap in waxed paper. Refrigerate until firm. Serve surrounded by crackers and stuffed olives. Yield: 1½ cups.

Ginger Cheese Apple

*Place 5-6 apples in a wicker basket with the
Ginger Cheese Apple for a lovely hostess gift.*

8 ounces cream cheese, softened
4 ounces Cheddar cheese, shredded
1 tablespoon honey
8¼ ounces crushed pineapple, well drained
½ teaspoon ginger, ground
¼ cup wheat germ
Bay Leaf
Cinnamon stick
Fresh apple slices

Combine cream cheese, cheddar cheese, and honey in large mixing bowl; beat until blended. Stir in pineapple and ginger. Cover bowl with plastic wrap; chill several hours or overnight. Shape mixture into a ball, roll in wheat germ. On a sheet of plastic wrap, press and mold ball into an apple shape. Coat with additional wheat germ, if necessary. Insert a bay leaf and cinnamon stick in top. Wrap in plastic wrap; refrigerate until serving. Serve with fresh apple slices. Yield: 1 cheese ball.

Herbed Boursin

2 (8 ounces) cream cheese
1 clove garlic, crushed
2 teaspoons caraway seeds
2 teaspoons basil
2 teaspoons dill weed
2 teaspoons chives, chopped
Lemon pepper
Assorted crackers

Blend softened cream cheese with all ingredients except lemon pepper. Pat into a round flat shape. Roll on all sides (lightly) in lemon pepper. Make a few days ahead. Serve with assorted crackers. Yield: 2 cups.

Moss Ball

A lovely presentation for the holidays!

8 ounces cream cheese
¼-½ pound bleu cheese, crumbled
¼ pound sharp Cheddar cheese, grated
1 small onion, minced

1 tablespoon Worcestershire sauce
½ cup pecans, chopped
Parsley, finely snipped

Beat softened cheeses on medium speed until well mixed. Add onion and Worcestershire sauce. Stir in pecans. Chill 3-4 hours. Roll cheese mixture into one large ball; chill 2 hours. Roll cheese ball in fresh parsley. Serve with crackers. Yield: 1 large cheese ball.

Pickle-Cheese Pineapple

2 (8 ounces) cream cheese, softened
½ cup Swiss cheese, grated
½ cup cheddar cheese, grated

½ cup peanut butter
½ cup sweet pickle relish
Sweet gherkins

Combine cheeses, peanut butter, and pickle relish; blend; chill. Shape into ball. Garnish with sweet gherkins slices and strips to resemble a pineapple. Serve on rye bread. Yield: 1 cheese ball.

Pineapple Cheese Ball

Eat til it ouches you!

2 (8 ounces) cream cheese, softened
8 ounces crushed pineapple, drained

¼ cup green pepper, chopped
2 tablespoons onion, chopped
1 tablespoon seasoned salt
2 cups pecans, chopped

Cream softened cream cheese. Add pineapple to cheese. Mix pepper, onion, and salt into cheese mixture. Add ½ cup nuts. Form into 2 large balls, cover each with remaining nuts. Chill in refrigerator. Yield: 2 large balls.

Cheese Beef Balls

½ cup cream cheese, softened
¼ cup mayonnaise
¼ cup dried beef, minced

¼ teaspoon Worcestershire sauce
1 teaspoon onion, finely minced
½ cup dried beef, shredded

Cream softened cream cheese and gradually add mayonnaise. Add finely minced dried beef, Worcestershire sauce, and onion. Shape into 24 small balls and roll in shredded dried beef. Chill and serve on food picks. Yield: 24 balls.

Plain And Fancy Cheese Wreath

1 pound sharp cheddar cheese,
    grated
¼ teaspoon pepper
Dash cayenne pepper
2 tablespoons milk

¼ cup mayonnaise
1 cup pecans, chopped
2 tablespoons onion, grated
1 cup strawberry preserves
Crackers

Cream together cheese, peppers, milk, and mayonnaise until smooth. Add pecans and onion. Mix well. On serving plate, spoon cheese mixture into wreath shape, leaving a hole in center of wreath. Chill. Add strawberry preserves in hole left in cheese. Serve with assorted crackers.

Snappy Cheese Balls

8 ounces cream cheese
1 small package bleu cheese
½ pound sharp cheese, grated
½ cup mayonnaise

½ teaspoon onion, grated
¼ teaspoon paprika
Few drops Worcestershire sauce
1 cup nuts, chopped

Mix all ingredients well, except nuts. Shape into two balls and roll in nuts. Yield: 2 balls.

Be sure to read your recipes through before you begin to cook. It saves time and lots of mistakes.

"Porcupine" Cheese Ball

An elegant cheese ball with quills!

4 ounces bleu cheese
8 ounces cream cheese
1 pound sharp cheddar cheese, shredded
1 tablespoon onion, minced

1 teaspoon Worcestershire sauce
½ cup walnuts, finely chopped
Green olives
Paprika

Allow cheese to soften at room temperature. Mix well with onion, Worcestershire sauce, and nuts. On waxed paper form mixture into oval shape. Refrigerate 2 hours. Roll "Porcupine" in paprika. Let stand at room temperature ½ hour before serving. Garnish with green olives on wooden picks for "quills". Serve with crisp crackers.

Ribbon Cheese Square

A stunting presentation with very colorful cheese layers!

4 ounces cream cheese
2 tablespoons butter or margarine
½ teaspoon basil or dry mustard
3 slices Colby cheese, (3½x3½-inch each)

3 slices brick cheese, (3½x3½-inch each)
2 slices salami
2 tablespoons fresh parsley, snipped
Crackers

To soften cream cheese and butter, place in small bowl, MICROWAVE, MEDIUM-LOW, 30 seconds. Blend in basil. On serving plate, layer cheese slices and salami, spreading about 2 teaspoons of cream cheese mixture between each layer. Use remaining cream cheese mixture to spread on top and sides. Sprinkle with parsley, pressing gently to coat loaf. Refrigerate 3 hours. Serve with crackers. Yield: 1 loaf.

Margarine has 80% or more of oil. A vegetable oil spread contains less than 80% oil and more water and can be used instead of margarine. The water content results in a softer dough, but do not add more flour.

Salmon Ball

7¾ ounces can red salmon,
    drained and flaked
8 ounces cream cheese, softened
1 tablespoon lemon juice
2 teaspoons onion, grated

1 teaspoon horseradish
¼ teaspoon salt
¼ teaspoon liquid smoke
Parsley, chopped

Combine all ingredients except parsley. Shape into a ball; roll ball in parsley. Yield: 1 salmon ball.

Deviled Ham Rolls

An appetizer that scores big!

2 cups flour, sifted
2 teaspoons baking powder
½ teaspoon salt

4 tablespoons butter or margarine
¾ cup milk (about)
1 cup deviled ham

Sift flour once, measure, add baking powder and salt, sift again. Cut butter into dry ingredients, add milk, gradually stirring until a soft dough is formed. Turn out on slightly floured board and knead 30 seconds, or enough to shape. Roll ⅛-inch thick and cut in 2-inch squares. Place about 1 tablespoon deviled ham in center of each square, fold over ham and pinch edge together and shape into roll, then seal ends. Preheat oven. Place seam side down on ungreased baking sheet. Bake. Temperature: 450 degrees. Baking Time: 12-15 minutes. Yield: about 16.

Miniature Ham And Cheese Rolls

Eat til it ouches you!

2 packages small tea rolls
8 ounces ham, sliced
6 ounces Swiss cheese slices
1 stick margarine, melted

1½ tablespoons poppy seeds
½ teaspoon Worcestershire sauce
1½ tablespoons prepared mustard
1 tablespoon onion flakes

Do not break rolls apart but slice lengthwise through center. Layer ham and cheese between layers of bread. Replace rolls in foil tray. Mix remaining ingredients and pour over rolls. Leave uncovered until butter sets, then cover. Preheat oven. Bake covered. Rolls can be refrigerated 24 hours or frozen until ready for baking. Temperature: 350 degrees. Baking Time: 15 minutes. Yield: 24 servings.

Fancy Franks

A taster's choice!

½ cup chili sauce
½ cup currant jelly
1½ tablespoons lemon juice
1½ teaspoons prepared mustard

13½ ounces pineapple chunks, drained
2 (7 ounces) cocktail franks

Combine all ingredients in a saucepan. Simmer 15 minutes. Serve warm on cocktail picks. Half a lime on small dish makes a colorful holder for picks.

Red And Green Pinwheels

3 ounces cream cheese, softened
6 thin slices boiled ham (6x4-inch)

6 medium-sized asparagus spears, cooked and chilled

Cut cream cheese into 6 slices and spread one piece on each slice of ham. Trim asparagus spears to a length of 4 inches and place asparagus spear on each ham slice. Roll ham tightly around asparagus spear. Chill well. Slice each roll into ½ inch pieces. Place on toothpicks. Yield: 42.

Sweet And Sour Meatballs

Makes a great appetizer.

1 pound lean ground beef
½ medium potato, grated
1 small onion, grated

½ teaspoon salt
⅛ teaspoon garlic powder
2 tablespoons raisins

SWEET AND SOUR SAUCE
6 ounces chili sauce
½ cup catsup

¼ cup lemon juice
6 ounces grape jam

Mix first five ingredients. Shape into 1-inch balls. Mix sauce ingredients together. Gently stir meat balls and raisins into boiling SWEET AND SOUR SAUCE. Simmer 30 minutes in saucepan. For slow cooker, cook 3 hours on medium setting.

Burgerettes

¾ pound ground beef
1 teaspoon steak sauce
½ teaspoon salt
1 can flaky rolls

Chili sauce
12 very small white onions, thinly
    sliced
12 cherry tomatoes, thinly sliced

Mix ground beef with steak sauce and salt lightly. Shape into 48 balls; place without touching in a shallow baking pan. Preheat oven. Place the 12 rolls, flat side down, on an ungreased cookie sheet. Cut each into quarters, but do not separate. Bake rolls until golden brown and meat balls are done. Separate rolls into quarters, then split open. Put together in this order: bottom of roll, chili sauce, meat ball, onion slice, tomato slice, top of roll; hold in place with wooden pick. Temperature: 375 degrees. Baking Time: 14 minutes. Yield: 48.

Hot Asparagus Canapés

20 thin slices white bread
3 ounces bleu cheese
8 ounces cream cheese

1 egg
20 asparagus spears, canned
½ pound butter, melted

Trim crusts and flatten slices with rolling pin. Blend cheeses and egg and spread evenly on each slice of bread. Roll 1 asparagus spear in each slice. Fasten with toothpick and dip in melted butter to thoroughly coat. Place rolls on baking sheet to freeze. When frozen, slice into 3 equal parts. You can put them back in the freezer, then bake in preheated oven just before serving. Temperature: 400 degrees. Baking Time: 15 minutes until lightly brown. Yield: 60 pieces.

Hot Corned Beef Delights

1 can corned beef, flaked
1 cup American cheese, diced
½ cup olives, diced
¼ cup green onion or chives,
    chopped

½ cup catsup
2 tablespoons Worcestershire
    sauce
3 packages Pepperidge Farm
    party rolls

Preheat oven. Mix all ingredients well. Spread on rolls, wrap in foil and bake. Temperature: 325 degrees. Baking Time: 25 minutes, or Microwave in waxed paper for 5-6 minutes.

Party Reubens

6 ounces corned beef, cut in pieces
8 ounces sauerkraut, drained
½ cup Thousand Island salad
   dressing

30 slices party rye bread
2 ounces Swiss cheese, torn in
   pieces

Place half the corned beef in blender container; blend till chopped. Remove chopped meat to bowl; repeat with remaining corned beef. Put drained sauerkraut and Thousand Island dressing in blender container; blend until sauerkraut is chopped and mixture is blended. Combine with corned beef in bowl. Lightly toast one side of rye bread under broiler, about 3-4 inches from heat. Spread corned beef mixture on untoasted side of rye bread. Top each sandwich with Swiss cheese. Broil 3-4 inches from heat for about 1-2 minutes or until cheese melts and corned beef is heated through. Temperature: Broil. Yield: 30 appetizers.

Sausage Balls In Cheese Pastry

1 pound mild or hot pork sausage
¾ cup dry bread crumbs
⅓ cup chicken broth
⅛ teaspoon nutmeg, ground
¼ teaspoon poultry seasoning
1½ cups flour

¼ teaspoon salt
¼ teaspoon paprika
8 ounces sharp cheddar cheese,
   shredded
½ cup margarine, softened

Combine first 5 ingredients, mixing well. Shape into 1-inch balls. Cook over low heat until done. Brown on all sides. Drain; combine remaining ingredients; cut in butter with pastry blender. Mix with hands until dough is smooth. Shape 1 tablespoon dough around each sausage ball, covering sausage completely. Place on greased baking sheets in preheated oven. Note: They may be frozen. To serve, thaw and bake. Temperature: 350 degrees. Baking Time: 15-20 minutes. Yield: 4 dozen.

"Today's favorite recipes shared will be tomorrow's memories and treasures."

Brown 'n Serve Sausage With Hot Mustard Dip

3 (8 ounces) sausage links
2 tablespoons sugar
1½ tablespoons dry mustard
1 teaspoon salt
¼ cup milk

1 cup mayonnaise
2 teaspoons horseradish
1 tablespoon vinegar
1 tablespoon sweet pickle relish

Cut sausage links in half and brown. Place on electric griddle to keep warm for serving. Prepare mustard dip by combining sugar, dry mustard, and salt in saucepan. Add milk, mayonnaise, and horseradish. Beat until smooth. Blend in vinegar and pickle relish. Serve hot. Yield: 60.

Saucy Ham Nibbles

1 egg, slightly beaten
¾ cup soft bread crumbs
1 teaspoon dry mustard
2 (6¾ ounces) chunk ham,
    drained and flaked

2 tablespoons cooking oil
1 cup cranberry-orange relish
½ cup dry white wine
2 tablespoons parsley flakes
2 teaspoons Worcestershire sauce

In bowl, combine egg, bread crumbs, and mustard. Add ham, mix well and shape into 1-inch balls. In skillet, quickly brown balls in hot oil. Combine cranberry-orange relish, wine, parsley flakes, and Worcestershire sauce. Pour over ham balls, cover and simmer 10 minutes or until hot. Transfer to chafing dish; place over burner. Serve warm with wooden picks. Yield: 36.

Jalapeño Dip

Make in advance and allow flavors to blend.

2 tablespoons oil
2 tablespoons flour
½ teaspoon salt
1 cup milk
½ pound cheese, grated

8 ounces tomatoes, canned
¼ cup onion, chopped
¼ teaspoon garlic salt
2-3 pickled chili jalapeño peppers

In saucepan, mix oil, flour, salt, milk, and cheese. Heat slowly over low heat until blended. In blender, mix tomatoes, onion, garlic salt, and peppers. Add to cooked mixture. Serve warm or cold with chips or crackers. NOTE: This is very runny when warm. Yield: 2 cups.

Bacon Crunchy Chip Dip

½ cup cream cheese
2 teaspoons catsup
1 teaspoon prepared mustard
⅛ teaspoon ginger, ground

¼ cup sour cream
½ cup cooked bacon, chopped
Potato chips or crackers

Soften cream cheese. Add catsup, mustard, ginger, sour cream, and bacon. Blend well. Serve with potato chips or crackers. Yield: 1 cup.

Company Cheese Dip

⅓ cup cream
8 ounces cream cheese
1½ teaspoons anchovy paste
1 teaspoon parsley, finely chopped

1 teaspoon onion
Dash fresh pepper, ground
Crackers

Blend the cream into the cheese. Add remaining ingredients. Mix well. Serve with crackers. Yield: 1⅓ cups.

Creamy Beef And Cheese Dip

8 ounces cream cheese
2½ ounces sliced dried beef, finely chopped
¼ cup walnuts, chopped
¼ cup sour cream
2 tablespoons onion, finely chopped

2 tablespoons green pepper, finely chopped
2 tablespoons milk
½ teaspoon pepper
Melba toast rounds

MICROWAVE OVEN: Unwrap and place cream cheese in 1 quart casserole. MICROWAVE, ¾-1 minute until softened. Add all other ingredients and stir until blended, cover. MICROWAVE, 3-5 minutes, stirring once during cooking. Serve with melba toast rounds or assorted crackers.

CONVENTIONAL OVEN: Let cream cheese soften at room temperature. Mix remaining ingredients. Bake. Temperature: 350 degrees. Baking Time: 30 minutes. Yield: about 2 cups.

Deviled Ham Dip

Use the electric mixer.

2 (3 ounces) cream cheese
⅓ cup evaporated milk
2 teaspoons horseradish, drained
2 tablespoons pickle relish

1 teaspoon Worcestershire sauce
2 teaspoons onion, grated or ½
   teaspoon onion powder
4½ ounces deviled ham

Let cream cheese soften. Add milk about 2 tablespoons at a time, mixing until smooth each time. Mix in remaining ingredients. Yield: 2 cups.

Dill Weed Vegetable Dip

A divine dip for veggies!

1 cup mayonnaise
1 cup sour cream
1 teaspoon dried onion flakes

1 tablespoon parsley, snipped
1 tablespoon (heaping) dill weed
1 teaspoon seasoning salt

Mix ingredients together. Make the day before serving and refrigerate. Serve as a dip for fresh raw vegetables. Yield: 2 cups.

Fiesta Salsa

Colorful and favorful!

1½ pounds tomatoes, very ripe
½ cup onion, finely chopped
½ cup celery, finely chopped
¼ cup green pepper, finely
   chopped
¼ cup olive or cooking oil
2-3 tablespoons green chili
   peppers, canned and finely
   chopped

2 tablespoons red wine vinegar
1 teaspoon mustard seeds
1 teaspoon coriander seeds,
   crushed
1 teaspoon salt
Dash pepper

To peel tomatoes, dip them in boiling water for 30 seconds; plunge into cold water. Slip skins off; chop tomatoes. Combine all ingredients. Cover and refrigerate several hours or overnight, stirring occasionally. Serve as a relish or with chips. Yield: 3 cups.

Hot Vegetable Dip

May be used as a vegetable salad. HOT!

7 ounces Jalapeño pepper relish
6 ounces pitted black olives,
   chopped
¼ teaspoon garlic powder
1 large onion, chopped

4 green peppers, chopped
4 large tomatoes, diced
1 tablespoon vinegar
1 tablespoon oil (optional)
Triscuit crackers

Mix all ingredients. Refrigerate overnight to marinate. Serve with crackers. Yield: 50 servings.

Liptauer (Cheese Spread)

3 ounces cream cheese
½ cup butter or margarine
1 small can rolled anchovies with
   caper, chopped

2 teaspoons prepared mustard
1 tablespoon onion, minced
1 teaspoon paprika
1 tablespoon caraway seeds

Cream cheese and butter until fluffy. Add remaining ingredients and beat until blended. Place in covered container and store in refrigerator about one hour before serving. Serve with crisp assorted crackers.

Peppy Cheese Dip

⅔ cup evaporated milk
½ pound process American
   cheese, grated
2 teaspoons prepared mustard

1 teaspoon Worcestershire sauce
1 teaspoon barbecue sauce
4 ounces pimento, drained and
   diced

Put all the above ingredients, except pimento, into a 1-quart saucepan and cook over low heat, stirring occasionally, until cheese melts and mixture is smooth. Remove from heat and stir in pimento. Keep warm to serve. Yield: about 2 cups.

Spinach Dip

A healthy way to eat more vegetables!

⅝ ounces dried vegetable soup
   mix
10 ounces frozen spinach,
   chopped, thawed, and drained
1 onion, chopped

1 cup mayonnaise
1 cup sour cream
8 ounces water chestnuts, chopped
Raw vegetables

Mix together all ingredients. Chill. Serve with raw vegetables. Yield: 1 quart.

Spring Garden Dip

This makes a fine salad dressing for wedges of lettuce.

1 cup sour cream
½ cup mayonnaise
1 teaspoon salt
Dash of pepper sauce
Sugar to taste
½ cup green onion, minced
¼ cup radishes, minced

¼ cup cucumber, minced and well
   drained
¼ cup green pepper, minced
1 clove garlic, crushed
Carrots, celery, zucchini, squash,
   white turnip sticks, broccoli,
   or cauliflowerets, uncooked

Blend ingredients and pour into a small bowl. Place in the center of a large serving plate and surround with arrangements of crisp fresh vegetables. Garnish with radish roses, parsley, or sprigs of watercress. Yield: 2½ cups.

Sombrero Dip

½ pound ground beef
¼ cup onion, chopped
¼ cup catsup
1½ teaspoons chili powder
½ teaspoon salt
1 cup red kidney beans with
   liquid, canned

Cheese (optional)
¼ cup onion, chopped
¼ cup stuffed green olives,
   chopped
Corn chips

Brown meat and ¼ cup onion in skillet. Place catsup, chili powder, salt, and beans in blender. Turn blender on high for 30 seconds. Add mixture to ground meat and heat. Garnish with the cheese, ¼ cup onion, and olives. Serve hot as a dip for corn chips. Yield: 1½ cups.

Fruit Dip

8 ounces cream cheese, softened
4 ounces coconut cream, if desired
8 ounces crushed pineapple,
   undrained

1 tablespoon rum flavoring
5 tablespoons instant vanilla dry
   pudding mix

In blender, thoroughly process first four ingredients. Add pudding mix and lightly blend. Pour into a small bowl and chill. Serve with fresh fruits. Yield: 2½ cups.

Tangy Vegetable Dip

2 cups mayonnaise or salad
   dressing
1 cup cottage cheese
¾ cup green onions, chopped
1 tablespoon plus 1½ teaspoons
   horseradish
1 tablespoon plus 1½ teaspoons
   Worcestershire sauce

1½ teaspoons caraway seeds
1½ teaspoons celery seeds
1 teaspoon garlic salt
1 teaspoon salt
1 teaspoon hot pepper sauce
½ teaspoon seasoned salt
Green onion, sliced
Assorted vegetables

Measure all ingredients except sliced green onions and vegetables into large bowl. Beat until smooth. Garnish with sliced green onion. Serve with vegetable dippers. Yield: 4 cups.

Vegetable Dip

1 cup mayonnaise
2 teaspoons tarragon vinegar
½ teaspoon salt
⅛ teaspoon thyme

¼ teaspoon curry powder
2 tablespoons catsup
¾ teaspoon chives
2 tablespoons onion, grated

Mix all ingredients. Let stand 24 hours and serve with fresh vegetables dippers. Yield: 1¼ cups.

Arrange your kitchen so that you never waste a minute searching for something. Store items in the cabinets where they are used. Everything has a place and is in its place.

Tuna Dip

½ cup sour cream
7 ounces can tuna
1 tablespoon horseradish
1 teaspoon Worcestershire sauce
8 ounces cream cheese
½ small onion, sliced

1 clove garlic
½ teaspoon salt
Dash pepper
½ teaspoon monosodium
  glutamate

Place all ingredients in blender container. Blend until smooth. Chill for several hours. Serve with crisp crackers. Yield: 3 cups.

"The Works" Crab Dip

4 ounces cream cheese, softened
½ cup sour cream
¼ cup mayonnaise
1 tablespoon sherry (optional)
1 cup fresh or imitation crabmeat,
  drained

2 tablespoons water chestnuts,
  chopped
2 tablespoons onion, minced
1 clove garlic, minced
½ teaspoon dill weed
2 tablespoons pecans, finely
  chopped

Beat cream cheese until light and fluffy. Blend in sour cream, mayonnaise, and sherry. Stir in next 5 ingredients. Cover and refrigerate until serving time. Before serving, stir in pecans. Serve with crackers and/or vegetables. Yield: 2 cups.

Deep Fried Dill Pickles

Vegetable oil for deep frying
1 egg, beaten
1 cup milk
1 tablespoon Worcestershire
  sauce

5-6 drops red pepper sauce
2 cups plus 1 tablespoon flour
Salt and pepper to taste
10 medium dill or garlic pickles,
  sliced

In deep fryer, heat oil to 350 degrees. In shallow bowl, combine egg, milk, Worcestershire sauce, pepper sauce, flour, and 1 tablespoon flour. Season with salt and pepper. In another bowl, combine remaining flour with salt and pepper to taste. Dip pickle slices in egg mixture, then in flour. Repeat. Fry until golden brown. Drain on paper towels and serve hot.

Olive Puffs

A great hit!

½ cup margarine or butter
1¼ cups flour
2 cups sharp cheese, grated

1 teaspoon paprika
48 stuffed olives, drained and dry

Mix margarine into flour; add cheese and paprika until well blended. Chill dough 15-20 minutes. Put flour on hands, if needed. Mold ½ teaspoon dough around dry olive. Chill overnight. Preheat oven. Bake. Temperature: 400 degrees. Baking Time: 10-12 minutes. Yield: 4 dozen.

Pickled Shrimp

Eat til it ouches you!

2½ pounds shrimp
½ cup celery tops
¼ cup mixed pickling spices
3½ teaspoons salt
2 cups onion, sliced
7-8 bay leaves

1¼ cups salad oil
¾ cup white vinegar
2½ tablespoons capers and juice
2½ teaspoons celery seeds
Dash Tabasco sauce
1½ teaspoons salt

Cover shrimp with boiling water; add celery tops, pickling spices, and salt. Cover and simmer five minutes. Drain, cool, peel, and clean shrimp. Alternate layers of shrimp and onion rings in shallow dish. Add bay leaves and cover with sauce made from salad oil, vinegar, capers, celery seeds, Tabasco sauce, and salt. Marinate in refrigerator at least 24 hours. Drain and serve. Yield: 2½ pounds.

Frozen Cucumber Pickles

The pickles can be made and stored in the refrigerator
for a month without freezing. Use immediately.

7 cups cucumbers, thinly sliced
1 cup onions, sliced
¼ cup noniodized salt
2 cups sugar

1 cup white vinegar
1 teaspoon mustard seeds
1 teaspoon celery seeds

Mix cucumbers, onion, and salt together and let stand for 1 hour; rinse. Bring to boil sugar, vinegar, mustard, and celery seed. Pour mixture over cucumbers, let stand overnight. Put in freezer container. Freeze. Thaw before serving. Yield: 6 pints.

Squash Pickles

Pack in fancy canning jars and give as gifts all year long.

8-10 cups squash, sliced thin
2 cups onions, sliced
2 green peppers, sliced
2 red peppers, sliced
Salt to taste

2 cups white vinegar
3 cups sugar
2 teaspoons white mustard seeds
2 teaspoons celery seeds

Mix together the first five ingredients. Let stand 1½ hours. Mix together all the remaining ingredients. Bring to a boil. Pour squash into this mixture and bring to a boil again. Pack in sterilized jars, seal.

Pickled Garden Relish

½ small head cauliflower, cut in flowerettes, sliced
2 carrots, pared, cut in 2-inch strips
2 stalks celery, cut in 2-inch strips
4 ounces pimento, cut in strips and drained
2 tablespoons sugar

3 ounces pitted olives, drained
¾ cup wine vinegar
½ cup salad oil
½ teaspoon oregano
¼ teaspoon pepper
1 teaspoon salt
¼ cup water

In electric skillet, combine all ingredients. Bring to boil, stirring constantly. Reduce heat, simmer covered for 5 minutes. Cool. Then refrigerate 24 hours. Drain well. Yield: 4-6 servings.

Tomato Relish

Some like it HOT! Tomato Relish is a real favorite on hot dogs and beans. If tomatoes and apples are not ripe at the same time, freeze tomatoes until the apples are in season, then make the relish.

1 gallon ripe tomatoes, peeled and chopped
10 Golden Delicious apples, peeled and chopped
4 cups onions, chopped
6 pods hot pepper, chopped

4 sweet peppers, chopped
6 cups sugar
3 tablespoons black pepper
4 tablespoons salt
2 cups vinegar

Mix and cook to the thickness you like. Pack in hot jars, seal. It is HOT. You can cut down on hot pepper and black pepper.

Old-fashioned Corn Relish

A colorful and interesting combination!

¼ cup sugar
½ cup vinegar
½ teaspoon salt
¼ teaspoon Tabasco sauce
½ teaspoon celery seeds
¼ teaspoon mustard seeds

12 ounces whole kernel corn
2 tablespoons green pepper,
    chopped
1 tablespoon onion, minced
1 tablespoon pimento, chopped

Combine first six ingredients in saucepan. Bring to a boil, boil two minutes. Remove from heat. Combine with remaining ingredients and chill. Yield: 1⅔ cups.

Hot Pepper Jelly

*May be served as an accompaniment with meat
or with cream cheese on crackers.*

¾ cup hot peppers, chopped
    (about 20 red or green)
¾ cup green pepper
1½ cups vinegar (never more than
    10% acidity)

6½ cups sugar
6 ounces liquid pectin
Red or green food coloring

Remove seeds from peppers and chop. Place vinegar and peppers in blender and chop fine. Place in saucepan and bring mixture to a boil. Stir in sugar until dissolved. Remove from heat and strain through a mesh sieve. Let stand 5 minutes. Add pectin and food coloring. Stir. Pour into jars and cover with wax.

Red Deviled Eggs

Makes a great meal accompaniment!

6 hard-cooked eggs
2 tablespoons mayonnaise
1 teaspoon onion, grated
1 teaspoon prepared mustard

½ teaspoon Worcestershire sauce
2½ ounces deviled ham
Salt and pepper to taste

Halve eggs lengthwise. Combine yolks with mayonnaise, onion, mustard, Worcestershire sauce, and deviled ham. Add salt and pepper. Fill egg cups with deviled mixture. Chill. Yield: 12.

Sausage And Cheese Balls

May be frozen. Eat til it ouches you!

1 pound hot sausage
8 ounces extra sharp cheese,
    grated

3 cups biscuit mix
Dash cayenne pepper, if desired

Preheat oven. Mix above ingredients and roll into small balls. Bake. Temperature: 375 degrees. Baking Time: 15 minutes.

Shell Hors D'oeuvres

¼ pound large shell macaroni
    (Maruzze)

Salt to taste
Oil for deep frying

ASSORTED FILLINGS
Shrimp salad
Deviled ham moistened with
    relish spread

Egg salad
Cream cheese with olives,
    moistened with mayonnaise

Cook shells in about 2 quarts boiling, salted water until tender about 10-15 minutes. Drain, rinse with cold water, drain well. Arrange on absorbent paper on tray and allow to dry thoroughly. Fry about 8-10 at a time in deep fat, 375 degree, for 5-8 minutes until golden brown. Drain on absorbent paper; sprinkle with salt. Cool and fill. Yield: 4-5 dozen.

Nutty Cheese Gems

8 ounces cream cheese, softened
7 ounces coconut, flaked
3 ounces lemon-flavored gelatin

1 tablespoon sugar
1 cup blanched pistachio nuts,
    finely chopped

In large bowl, thoroughly combine first 4 ingredients. Chill until firm. Roll into 1-inch balls. Coat balls with pistachio nuts. Chill in a single layer until firm. Cover lightly and store in refrigerator. Yield: 40 balls.

Dried Beef Fingers

Eat til it ouches you! Beautiful and easy!

1 package dried beef, refrigerated

FILLING
8 ounces cream cheese, softened
½ cup Miracle Whip salad
    dressing
1 teaspoon horseradish

2 teaspoons Worcestershire sauce
Dash garlic salt
Dash onion salt

Whip cheese until fluffy. Add all filling ingredients. Mix well. Place small amount of FILLING in center of dried beef slice. Roll and chill. Yield: 24 beef fingers.

Cheez-its

Eat til it ouches you!

½ pound Cheddar cheese, grated
½ cup Parmesan cheese
1 stick butter, soft
Salt to taste

Cayenne pepper to taste
Worcestershire sauce to taste
2 cups self-rising flour
2 cups Rice Krispies

Preheat oven. Cream together cheeses and butter. Season with salt, cayenne pepper, and Worcestershire sauce. Knead in flour, add Rice Krispies (whole—not crushed). Pinch into small balls. Bake on greased baking sheet. Temperature: 350 degrees. Baking Time: 30 minutes. Yield: 60-75.

Cheese Dreams

2 cups sharp cheese, grated
1 cup butter or margarine
3 cups flour

¾ teaspoon salt
¾ teaspoon paprika
4 dozen pecan halves

Cut cheese and margarine into flour. Add seasonings. Shape into ball; place in bowl and chill. Roll thin and cut with small cutter working with small amount of dough each time. Place pecan half on top of each biscuit. Bake in preheated oven until lightly browned. Temperature: 400 degrees. Baking Time: 8-10 minutes. Yield: 4 dozen.

A bright shiny baking sheet reflects heat and gives bread a golden brown color on both top and bottom. A black bottom pan absorbs more heat and burns bread on the bottom.

Biscuit Crisps

1 can biscuits
2 tablespoons butter or
margarine, melted

Sesame seeds
Parmesan cheese

Preheat oven. Separate biscuits; press out each into a 5-inch round on an ungreased baking sheet. Brush lightly with melted butter; sprinkle with sesame seeds and Parmesan cheese and cut each round into eighths. Bake until golden; remove from baking sheet at once. Cool completely on wire racks, store in airtight container. Temperature: 400 degrees. Baking Time: 5 minutes. Yield: 6½ dozen.

Party Snack Mix

Great nibbles!

½ cup butter or margarine
½ cup soy sauce
2 cups blanched almonds, slivered
4 cups salted Spanish peanuts

2 cups golden raisins
3 ounces chow mein noodles
¼ cup sesame seeds
3½ ounces coconut, flaked

Heat butter and soy sauce in electric skillet over low heat. Add almonds; cook, stirring constantly, 5 minutes. Add peanuts, raisins, noodles, and sesame seeds, stirring constantly, 10 minutes. Stir in coconut. Spread half the mixture in 15½x10½x1-inch jelly roll pan. Bake. Cool on paper toweling. Repeat with remaining mixture. Store in airtight container at room temperature up to 1 month. Temperature: 350 degrees. Baking Time: 8-10 minutes. Yield: 10 cups.

Whamits

2 cups Cheerios
2 cups Rice Chex
2 cups Wheat Chex
2 cups Corn Chex
½ pound cashew nuts
⅙ ounce salted almonds

1 stick margarine
1 teaspoon garlic salt
1 teaspoon celery salt
1 teaspoon Worcestershire sauce
2 beef bouillon cubes
1 teaspoon onion salt

Preheat oven. Mix together all cereals and nuts in large baking pan. In heavy saucepan, melt butter with all remaining ingredients. The liquid should be sprinkled over the top of the cereal mixture a few spoonfuls at a time. Stir liquid well and dip from the bottom of the pan. When top of cereal is evenly coated with liquid, mix well and repeat until all liquid is used and all cereal evenly coated. Bake, stirring several times to be sure all cereal is evenly baked. These keep well in tightly covered jar. Temperature: 250 degrees. Baking Time: 2 hours. Yield: 10 cups.

Popcorn Medley

6 tablespoons butter or margarine	1 quart popped popcorn, unsalted
1 tablespoon Worcestershire sauce	1½ cups chow mein noodles
1 teaspoon seasoned salt	1½ cups bite-size shredded wheat biscuits
½ teaspoon garlic powder	1 cup pecan halves

Melt butter in skillet; add Worcestershire sauce, seasoned salt and garlic powder. Add popcorn, chow mein noodles, wheat biscuits, and pecan halves. Toss gently until well coated. Place in broiler pan and heat, stirring occasionally. Cool. Temperature: 250 degrees. Baking Time: 45 minutes. Yield: 2 quarts.

Spiced Walnuts

A perfect homemade gift!

1 egg white	¼ teaspoon cloves, ground
1 tablespoon water	¼ teaspoon nutmeg, ground
2 cups nuts	½ teaspoon salt
½ cup sugar	2 tablespoons butter
1 teaspoon cinnamon, ground	

Preheat oven. Blend egg white and water. Add nuts. Be sure to coat each piece of nut. Add other ingredients. Place nuts in shallow buttered pan and bake. Stir a time or two while nuts are baking. Temperature: 300 degrees. Baking Time: 30 minutes. Yield: 2 cups.

Summer Sausage (Beef Stick)

This makes a lovely gift!

5 pounds hamburger, very lean	2 tablespoons hickory smoke salt
5 rounded teaspoons curing salt (Morton's Tender Quick)	1 teaspoon monosodium glutamate
1 tablespoon garlic salt	1 teaspoon liquid smoke
4 teaspoons mustard seeds	½ teaspoon cayenne pepper
5 teaspoons pepper, coarsely ground	

Mix together all ingredients. Cover and refrigerate 3 days. On the 4th day form into rolls the diameter of Ritz crackers. Put on rack of broiler pan. Preheat oven. Bake. Cool and refrigerate. This freezes well. Serve with your favorite crackers. Temperature: 175 degrees. Baking Time: 8 hours. Yield: 5 pounds.

North Carolina
Granite Corporation

NORTH CAROLINA GRANITE CORPORATION

Mount Airy, the Granite City, and the Mount Airy quarry are recognized as having the largest open-faced granite quarry in the world. Open-face means open, on which a person can walk or drive.

Back in 1872, a farmer named John Gilmer purchased several thousand acres of farm and woodlands in Mount Airy and the Flat Rock community. One of his friends learned that the tract of land contained 40 acres of bare rock. Mr. Gilmer immediately went to the seller and threatened to back out on the deal because of the "worthless" 40 acres. The seller is supposed to have agreed to deduct that 40 acres of "worthless" rock in calculating the dollar value of the whole tract. Therefore, the story goes of the world's finest natural quarry changing hands for nothing.

About seventeen years later when the old Cape Fear and Yadkin Valley Railroad was built from Greensboro to Mount Airy, a firm of builders, Thomas Woodruff & Sons, recognized the potential value of a granite quarry and they bought John Gilmer's "worthless" rock for $5,000.00 and built a railroad spur from Mount Airy over to the foot of Flat Rock.

The quarry is in the shape of an enormous oyster shell and covers approximately 90 acres under operation. The deposits are approximately one mile long and one-third mile wide. The granite deposit is a homogeneous mass (solid Mass) free from natural bed planes and vertical cracks. Since 1899, quarrying has been in full operation and according to tests (depth) the surface has only been scratched. Geologists informed the company that there is enough granite to quarry for approximately 500 more years without exhausting the supply. The granite quarried today is guaranteed a perfect match for granite taken 100 years ago or quarried hundreds of years from now.

The North Carolina Granite Corporation has four departments: Cut stone or Building stone; Curbing; Crusher; and Quarry Departments. At the quarry, there is practically no loss. Products produced are small enough to feed canaries and large enough to construct a huge building.

The magnificent workmanship of the skilled craftsmen of the North Carolina Granite Corporation can be seen and appreciated in many beautiful granite banks, churches, homes, walls, memorials, municipal buildings, which are located in the historic district on Main Street. Travel from the Central Methodist Church, 1909 North Main Street, to view the Chancel windows, by Grace Moravian Church, Holy Angels Catholic Church, First Baptist Church, Trinity Episcopal Church, First Presbyterian Church, to the Mount Airy Friends Meeting, at the corner of South Main Street and 109 West Wilson Street, to view these excellent examples of exquisite structures made of Mount Airy Granite.

Banana Punch (yellow)

A real favorite! Serve as a slush.

8 cups water
4 cups sugar
2 (12 ounces) frozen orange juice
6 (12 ounces) water

2 (46 ounces) pineapple juice
½ cup fresh lemon juice
5 ripe bananas
2 (28 ounces) ginger ale

Bring water and sugar to boil. Allow to boil 15 minutes. Cool. Add juices and water. Place bananas in blender and liquify. Add to juices. Mix well, freeze for at least 3 hours. Freeze in plastic milk jugs. Note: If frozen solid, remove from freezer 1 hour before serving. Beat punch frozen in plastic jugs with a hammer to break into a slush. Pour ginger ale in punch bowl and add frozen slush. Yield: 50 servings.

Berry Loving Cup (pink)

6 cups cranberry apple drink,
    chilled
1 liter lemon-lime soda, chilled

Ice cubes
Orange slices

In a large 2-quart punch bowl, mix cranberry drink and soda. Add ice cubes and orange slices. Yield: 16 servings.

Christmas Punch (pink)

1 quart pineapple juice
1 quart cranberry juice
½ cup sugar

½ teaspoon almond flavoring
28 ounces ginger ale

Mix all ingredients except ginger ale. Chill. Add ginger ale before serving. Yield: 24 servings.

Temper glass punch bowl and glass ladle gradually with cold punch. Never add ice to an empty punch bowl.

Christmas Wreath Punch (yellow)

13 red maraschino cherries, drained
13 green maraschino cherries, drained
½ cup boiling water (about)
1 quart cold boiled water
2 (6 ounces) frozen limeade concentrate
2 (6 ounces) frozen lemonade concentrate
2 (20 ounces) unsweetened grapefruit juice
2 (20 ounces) pineapple juice
3 quarts ginger ale
1 quart water
3 quarts ice, crushed

WREATH: Wash excess color from cherries. Arrange, alternating colors, in bottom of 1¼ quart ring mold. Pour on just enough boiling water to cover cherries; freeze solid. Then fill mold to top with cold boiled water; freeze solid. (Wreath may be made day before the party.)

PUNCH: In punch bowl, blend undiluted juices. Just before serving, stir in ginger ale, 1 quart water, ice. Then unmold wreath on top of punch. Yield: 50 punch cups servings.

Cherry Punch (pink)

Recipe may be halved and served as a slush.

6 ounces cherry flavored gelatin
3 cups sugar
12 ounces frozen orange juice
12 ounces frozen lemonade
46 ounces pineapple juice
6 (28 ounces) ginger ale

Dissolve cherry gelatin and sugar in 1 quart boiling water. Add the fruit juices. Freeze. Take out of freezer one hour before serving time. Just before serving, add 6 (more if desired) bottles ginger ale. Yield: 60 servings.

Evergreen Punch (green)

$ Saver.

3 ounces lime flavored gelatin
46 ounces pineapple juice
8 ounces lemon juice
2½ cups sugar
1 quart ginger ale

Mix gelatin according to package directions. Mix prepared gelatin, pineapple juice, lemon juice, and sugar until sugar is dissolved. Pour over crushed ice. Then pour ginger ale over ice and punch mixture. Serve. Yield: about 20 punch cup servings.

Floating Island Punch (yellow)

½ cup sugar
2 cups water
6 ounces frozen lemon juice
3 (6 ounces) frozen orange juice
1 quart ginger ale
1 quart sparkling water or white grape juice

4 ounces maraschino cherries and juice
1 orange, sliced thin
Ice cubes
1 pint lemon or orange sherbet

Heat sugar and water until sugar dissolves, cool and combine with fruit juices, ginger ale, sparkling water, and fruit. Pour into punch bowl. Add ice cubes. Drop in sherbet by spoonfuls or in small balls using an ice cream dipper. Yield: 25-30 servings.

Fruit Frost (yellow)

12 ounces frozen orange juice
6 ounces frozen limeade
6 ounces frozen lemon juice

46 ounces pineapple juice
1 gallon vanilla ice cream
1 quart ginger ale

Mix juices and add ice cream; beat until just blended and then pour ginger ale over it. Garnish with thin slices of oranges, limes, and lemons. Yield: 50 (4 ounce) servings.

Golden Medley (gold)

2 (46 ounces) apricot nectar
16 ounces orange juice
20 ounces pineapple juice

6 ounces lemon juice
1 quart ginger ale
3 quarts cracked ice

Mix in order given. Add to punch bowl, fill with ice. Yield: approximately 100 (6 ounce) cups.

Empty plastic milk jugs are great to freeze punch and can be cut away from frozen punch.

Golden Slush (gold)

12 ounces frozen lemonade
12 ounces frozen orange juice
6 (12 ounces) water

½ cup sugar
46 ounces pineapple juice
2 (28 ounces) ginger ale

Mix first five ingredients. Freeze. Two to three hours before serving time remove from freezer. Just before serving, add frozen slush to cold ginger ale. Do not add ice to the punch. Yield: 40 servings.

Hawaiian Christmas Punch (red)

2 (46 ounces) red fruit punch
12 ounces frozen lemonade
    concentrate

12 ounces water
2 liters orange soda

Mix first three ingredients together. Chill. Just before serving, add orange soda and ice. Yield: 30 servings.

Luscious Slush (red)

2 packages strawberry or cherry
    Kool-aid
2 cups sugar
2 quarts water

46 ounces pineapple juice,
    unsweetened
2 quarts ginger ale

Mix Kool-aid, sugar, water, and juice. Divide mixture in half. Pour each half in a plastic gallon jug. Freeze. About 2 hours before serving, remove from freezer. Thaw at room temperature. Just before serving, break ice mixture apart, add ginger ale. Serve. It will be a slushy ice punch. Yield: 35 cups.

Mint Sparkle (green)

10 ounces mint jelly
1 cup water
24 ounces pineapple juice,
    unsweetened

1 cup water
½ cup lemon juice
12 ounces ginger ale, chilled

Combine mint jelly and 1 cup water in saucepan. Place over low heat and stir until jelly is melted. Cool. Add pineapple juice, remaining 1 cup water, and lemon juice, chill thoroughly. Place ice cubes in tall chilled glasses; fill ½ full with fruit mixture. Tilt each glass and pour ginger ale down side to fill. Garnish with lemon slices and sprig of fresh mint. Yield: 10-12 servings.

Merry Christmas Punch (red)

1 pound jellied cranberry sauce
¾ cup orange juice
½ cup lemon juice

2 teaspoons almond extract
1 quart ginger ale

Break up jellied cranberry sauce with a fork; beat with electric mixer. Add orange and lemon juice; continue beating. Pour into punch bowl and add almond extract, ice cold ginger ale, and ice. Stir gently. Yield: about 15 punch cup servings.

Orange Smoothee

Use the blender.

1½ cups milk
6 ounces frozen orange
    concentrate juice, softened

1½ cups water
1½ teaspoons vanilla extract
    (optional)

Pour milk in blender container. Add the other ingredients. Mix well until the mixture is foamy. Serve at once. Yield: 6-8 servings.

Paradise Island Punch (pink)

1 cup water
1 cup sugar
1 quart pineapple juice
Juice of 2 oranges
Juice of 1 lemon
Juice of ½ grapefruit

½ cup crushed pineapple
⅓ cup strawberries, crushed
2 quarts cranberry juice
1 quart apple juice
1 quart ginger ale

Dissolve 1 cup sugar in 1 cup hot water. Add all other ingredients and mix. Do not add ginger ale until ready to serve. Yield: 50 servings.

Piña Colada Slush (yellow)

1 cup sugar
3 cups water
6 ripe bananas, mashed
12 ounces frozen pineapple juice
    concentrate

12 ounces frozen orange juice
    concentrate
30 ounces cream of coconut
4 liters ginger ale, chilled

Dissolve sugar in water, add fruit, and fruit juices. Freeze until slushy, about 6 hours, stirring once. If mixture freezes solid MICROWAVE, HIGH, 2-3 minutes until softened. To serve, combine slush and ginger ale. Yield: 32 (one cup) servings.

Raspberry Punch (red)

4 (3 ounces) raspberry gelatin
1 cup sugar
4 (46 ounces) pineapple juice

3 (6 ounces) frozen limeade
3 quarts ginger ale

Prepare gelatin as directed on package. Add water as directed on limeade cans. Mix all ingredients together except ginger ale. Add ginger ale just before serving. Yield: 100 servings.

Red Satin Punch (red)

Simple to make! Beautiful served over the frozen 7-Up cubes.

1 quart apple juice   10 bottles 7-Up
1 quart cranberry juice

Fill two ice trays with 7-Up and freeze until firm. Chill all ingredients before mixing. Mix together apple juice and cranberry juice cocktail. Just before serving, add the remainder of the 7-Up. Pour over frozen 7-Up. Yield: 35 servings.

Rosy Sherbet Punch

46 ounces orange juice   1 pint cranberry juice cocktail
46 ounces pineapple-grapefruit   1 quart orange sherbet
   drink   1 quart ginger ale

Chill juices and ginger ale thoroughly. Mix liquids in punch bowl and add sherbet. Yield: about 35 servings.

Santa-Tang Punch

⅔ cup Tang (powdered)   3 cups water
½ cup sugar   ¼ teaspoon almond extract
1 pint cranberry juice or No. 2   1 quart ginger ale
   can pineapple juice

Combine all ingredients except ginger ale. Add ginger ale just before serving. Serve iced. Yield: about 25 punch cups.

Do not add carbonated beverages until ready to serve, then pour the carbonated beverage down the side of the punch bowl.

Coffee Cream Punch

1 quart brewed coffee, very strong   1 quart vanilla ice cream

Make coffee and allow to cool. Blend ice cream and coffee. Yield: ½ gallon.

Plantation Coffee Punch

¼ cup sugar   **5 cups milk**
⅓ cup instant coffee   **1 pint vanilla or coffee ice cream**
Dash salt   **Whipped cream**
1 teaspoon vanilla extract   **Dash nutmeg, ground**

Combine sugar, coffee, salt, vanilla, and milk; stir until sugar dissolves. Chill until serving time. Then ladle ice cream, by large spoonfuls, into punch bowl; pour coffee mixture over. Top with puffs of whipped cream and sprinkle with a little nutmeg. Serve in punch cups. Yield: 12 servings.

Cranberry Cooler Punch (pink)

1 quart cranberry juice cocktail
6 ounces frozen tangerine juice, thawed
1 cup apple juice
1 quart ginger ale

Mix together fruit juices. Add water to tangerine juice as directed on can. Chill. Just before serving, add ginger ale. Yield: 10 servings.

Hanging Of The Greens Punch (green)

3 ounces lime flavored gelatin
46 ounces pineapple juice
1 small real lemon juice
1 ounce almond flavoring
2½ cups sugar

Prepare gelatin as directed on package. Mix ingredients thoroughly. Stir until sugar dissolves. Pour over ice. Yield: about 18 punch cups.

Racy Red Punch (red)

46 ounces pineapple-grapefruit drink
¼ cup red hot cinnamon candies
⅓ cup sugar
1 quart ginger ale

Heat 1 cup of juice, add cinnamon candies, and sugar. Stir until dissolved. Combine with the rest of the juice and chill mixture thoroughly. Add the ginger ale just before serving for sparkle. Yield: 2½ quarts.

"The Modhouse" (green)

6 ounces lime gelatin
2 cups hot water
2 (12 ounces) frozen limeade
½ cup lime juice
1 teaspoon almond extract
90 ounces lemon-lime carbonated beverage

Dissolve gelatin in hot water. Stir in frozen limeade. Add lime juice and extract. Add ice to punch. Add carbonated beverage, just before serving. Yield: 25 punch cups.

Tutti-frutti Punch (yellow)

12 ounces frozen orange
    concentrate
6 ounces frozen lemon
    concentrate

6 ounces frozen lime concentrate
46 ounces pineapple juice
⅓ cup sugar
1 quart ginger ale

Place all ingredients in gallon container and complete filling with water. Mix well. Just before serving, add ginger ale and cracked ice. Yield: 25 punch cups.

White Sparking Punch

48 ounces white grape juice
46 ounces pineapple juice

2 liters ginger ale, chilled

Mix above ingredients; add ginger ale just before serving. Yield: 20-25 servings.

Cider-Citrus Punch

1 gallon apple cider
6 ounces frozen lemonade
    concentrate
6 ounces frozen orange juice
    concentrate

½ cup brown sugar, packed
1 tablespoon whole cloves
1 tablespoon whole allspice

In large percolator, combine cider, concentrates, and brown sugar. Tie cloves and allspice in cheesecloth bag; add to cider mixture. Perk in percolator. Remove spice bag and discard. Serve punch hot. Yield: 20 cups.

Cranberry Wassail

½ teaspoon nutmeg
½ teaspoon cinnamon
½ teaspoon allspice
¼ cup orange Pekoe tea
2 quarts boiling water

1½ cups sugar
1 cup orange juice
½ cup lemon juice
2 pints cranberry juice cocktail
Red coloring, if desired

Tie spices and tea loosely in a cheesecloth bag. Put bag into boiling water. Turn heat off. Cover and let steep for 10-15 minutes. Remove spice bag. Add sugar and juices. Reheat and serve hot. Yield: 3½ quarts.

Friendship Tea Mix

18 ounces orange-flavored instant breakfast drink
1 cup sugar
½ cup pre-sweetened lemonade mix

½ cup instant tea
3 ounces apricot-flavored gelatin
2½ teaspoons cinnamon, ground
1 teaspoon cloves, ground

Mix ingredients well. Store mixture in an air-tight container. To serve, place 1½ tablespoons mixture in a cup and fill cup with hot water and stir well. Yield: 50 servings.

Hot Buttered Tomato Juice

Use a slow cooker.

2 (46 ounces) tomato juice
1 tablespoon Worcestershire sauce
1 teaspoon salt

1 teaspoon oregano
½ cup butter or margarine
Chunks of cheese (optional)
Pretzel sticks (optional)

In pot, combine all ingredients. Cover. Heat at high setting for about 2 hours or until temperature reaches 180 degrees. Reduce to low setting to keep warm for serving. Serve in cups and garnish with chunks of cheese pierced with long pretzel sticks, or with celery hearts. Yield: 16-20 servings.

Hot Chocolate Mix

2 pound chocolate flavored drink
mix
8 quart package instant non-fat
dry milk

½ cup confectioner's sugar
8 ounces powdered coffee creamer

Mix all ingredients well. Keep in air-tight container. Use ⅓ cup of mix and fill with hot water for each serving.

Raspberry Cocoa Mix

Raspberry adds a unique flavor to cocoa!

3 cups instant hot cocoa mix

.15 ounce unsweetened raspberry
flavored soft drink mix

Combine ingredients in a medium bowl. Stir until well blended. Store in an airtight container. To serve. stir 2 heaping tablespoons into 8-ounce hot water.

French Chocolate

3 squares unsweetened chocolate
½ cup water
¾ cup sugar

Dash salt
½ cup heavy cream
6 cups hot milk

Combine chocolate and water in saucepan; cook over low heat, stir until chocolate is melted and mixture is blended. Add sugar and salt; bring to boiling point; boil 4 minutes, stirring constantly. Remove from heat; cool. Whip cream; fold into chocolate mixture. Place one tablespoon mixture in each cup; add hot milk to fill cup; blend. Fold in additional whipped cream, if desired. Yield: 8-12 servings.

"The greatest refreshment in life is love."

Hot Pineapple-Cranberry Punch

Use the slow cooker.

46 ounces pineapple juice
1 quart cranberry juice
3 cups water
½ teaspoon salt

1 cup brown sugar, packed
2 tablespoons whole cloves
1 tablespoon whole allspice
6 cinnamon sticks

Pour pineapple juice, cranberry juice, and water into pot. Add salt and brown sugar. Stir until sugar is dissolved. Tie cloves, allspice and cinnamon sticks in cheesecloth and drop into liquid. Cover pot. Simmer on high setting for about 2 hours or until temperature reaches 170 degrees. Remove spice bag. Keep warm for serving at low setting. Yield: 25 (4 ounce) punch cup servings.

Hot Cranberry Punch

2 (1 pound) jellied cranberry
    sauce
4 cups water
¾ cup brown sugar, packed
¼ teaspoon salt
¼ teaspoon nutmeg

¼ teaspoon cloves
½ teaspoon cinnamon
½ teaspoon allspice
1 quart pineapple juice
Small amount margarine
    (optional)

Crush sauce with 3 cups water. With other cup of water, dissolve brown sugar, salt, and add spices. Simmer for a few minutes. Combine the two mixtures. Add pineapple juice and serve hot. The margarine may be dotted over the top. Yield: about 20 punch cups.

Golden Wassail

4 cups pineapple juice,
    unsweetened
12 ounces apricot nectar
4 cups apple cider
1 cup orange juice

¼ teaspoon salt
6 inches cinnamon stick
1 teaspoon whole cloves
¼ teaspoon whole cardamom
    seeds, crushed

Pour juices into electric percolator. Place remaining ingredients in basket. Allow to go through perk cycle. Serve piping hot. Yield: 20 (½ cup) servings.

Hot Mulled Apple Juice

Juice of 1 lemon
Juice of 2 oranges
4 whole cloves
2-inch stick cinnamon
3 whole allspices

2 cups water
¼ cup brown, packed, or white
sugar (to taste)
Pinch salt
1 quart apple juice

Squeeze lemon and oranges, reserving juices. Place rinds in a saucepan with spices and water. Bring to boil—simmer 5 minutes. Strain; add sugar, salt, and juices. Heat. May be made ahead and reheated for servings. Yield: 12 servings.

Mulled Cider

2 quarts apple juice or cider
½ cup light brown sugar, packed
⅛ teaspoon ginger, ground
(optional)

2 cinnamon sticks
1 teaspoon whole cloves
2 whole oranges, sliced

Combine all ingredients in a crockpot. Slice oranges and add to liquid. Simmer on low for 6-8 hours. Yield: about 2 quarts.

Spiced Tea

16 cups water
3 family-size tea bags
1½ cups sugar
3-4 cinnamon sticks
1 tablespoon whole cloves

12 ounces frozen orange juice
concentrate
2 cups pineapple juice
4 tablespoons lemon juice

In large pot, bring 8 cups water to a boil. Add tea bags and remove from heat. Steep for 5 minutes. Remove tea bags. In a separate pot, bring 8 cups water, sugar, cinnamon sticks, and cloves to a boil and continue to boil for 5 minutes. Pour mixture through strainer into tea. Add orange juice concentrate, pineapple juice, and lemon juice. Allow to cool, then store in refrigerator. Reheat individual servings in microwave oven. Yield: 18-20 servings.

Hot Spiced Lemonade Tea Punch

1 teaspoon whole cloves
4 cinnamon sticks
4 quarts water
⅓ cup loose tea or 15 tea bags

1¼ cups sugar
1 cup orange juice
1 cup pineapple juice
¾ cup fresh lemon juice

Add spices to cold water, bring to rolling boil, remove from heat, and add tea. Brew 5 minutes. Strain, add sugar, stir until dissolved. Add fruit juices. Yield: 25-30 servings.

Peppermint Tea

This makes a wonderful hot beverage for any meal or party.

6 cups water
4 small tea bags
12 whole cloves
2 cups sugar

1 cup pineapple juice
1 cup orange juice
¾ cup lemon juice
1-2 drops oil of peppermint

Bring water to boil. Add tea bags and cloves. Steep 5 minutes. Strain in gallon jar, combine all ingredients. Finish filling gallon jar with water. Serve hot. Reheat individual servings in microwave oven. Yield: 1 gallon.

Spiced Viennese Coffee

4 tablespoons instant coffee
7 whole cloves
1 cinnamon stick
3½ cups boiling water

¼ cup sugar
¼ cup whipping cream
Dash cinnamon, ground

Place instant coffee in coffee pot or saucepan. Put cloves and cinnamon stick in cheesecloth bag and place in coffee pot. Pour boiling water over coffee and spices. Cover; bring to boil. Remove from heat and let stand 5-8 minutes. Remove spice bag; add sugar and stir until dissolved. Whip cream and garnish coffee with whipped cream. Sprinkle with cinnamon and serve at once. Yield: 3-4 servings.

_____

"A friend is the first person who comes in when the whole world has gone out."

Hot Spiced Percolator Punch

Has a wonderful welcoming aroma.

2¼ cups pineapple juice
1¾ cups water
2 cups cranberry juice
1 tablespoon whole cloves

½ tablespoon whole allspice
3 cinnamon sticks, broken
¼ teaspoon salt
½ cup brown sugar, packed

Put pineapple juice, water, and cranberry juice in bottom of an 8 cup electric percolator and the rest of ingredients in the basket in the top. Perk for 10 minutes or until spices permeate. Serve hot. Yield: 8-10 servings.

Percolator Wassail

2 quarts apple cider
½ cup brown sugar
½ teaspoon whole allspice
1 teaspoon whole cloves

1 cinnamon stick
Dash nutmeg
¼ teaspoon salt
1 orange, cut in wedges, with peel

Pour apple cider into lower part of 10-12 cup electric coffee maker. Place basket in coffee maker and put all remaining ingredients in basket. Cover and perk. Yield: 2 quarts wassail.

Wassail Bowl

Whole cloves
3 oranges
2 quarts apple cider or juice

½ cup sugar
Cinnamon sticks
½ cup lemon juice

Preheat oven at 350 degrees. Push cloves, about ¼-inch apart, into oranges. Place in shallow pan. Bake 30 minutes. Heat apple cider or juice, sugar, and several cinnamon sticks until small bubbles show around edge. Remove from heat and stir in lemon juice. Pour into heatproof punch bowl. With ice pick pierce oranges in several places; add to cider. Serve in mugs and use cinnamon sticks to stir, if desired. Yield: 10-12 servings.

Breads

*Boyhood Home of
Andy Griffith*

1935
to
1966

BOYHOOD HOME OF ANDY GRIFFITH

On June 1, 1926, a beautiful blue eyed-baby boy, Andrew Samuel Griffith, one of America's best loved actors, entertainers, and comedians, was born to Carl and Geneva Griffith. At that time, the family lived at 131 South Street with other members of their family. The birthplace does not exist.

It was depression times and the family was very poor. With limited space and no crib, Andy slept in a bureau drawer until he outgrew it. For a few years, the family moved away to Ohio and later to High Point, before coming back to Mount Airy.

His $435.00 boyhood home, circa 1927, is located at 711 Haymore Street, where he lived until he attended the University of North Carolina at Chapel Hill.

He apparently got his humor and wit from his father, Carl. He was known by the locals around Mount Airy as the "great joker". Carl loved woodwork and was a furniture craftsman with the local furniture company. Andy worked there for a while, but hated every minute of it.

Andy was an only child and was very protected. Andy's love of music came from his mother, Geneva. She taught him to play the guitar and simple chords. The family enjoyed listening to the radio. Andy's mother's family came from Mayberry, a little Virginia community to the north near the Blue Ridge Parkway.

The family garden was always bountiful with fresh vegetables, from which the family canned foods for the winter months. Recipes in that era were limited and everyone used the same recipes. Geneva's specialties were homemade pickles and canned half-runner green beans.

Andy wanted to be a preacher, next a singer, but ended up as a comic actor. He hated being laughed at, but ended up doing what really came naturally for him. He provided wonderful entertainment for the whole family.

Carl and Geneva Griffith lived in their Mount Airy home until 1966 when Andy moved them to California.

Andy Griffith's Homeplace was purchased by Gary York on Saturday, June 27, 1998 at a public auction. The house was previously owned by the Hattie Hale Estate. Mr. York's intent is to preserve the history the homeplace brings to the Mount Airy area. Today it is a successful bed and breakfast that tourists from across the country can enjoy.

The City of Mount Airy proclaimed October 16, 2002 as Andy Griffith Day. Thousands gathered to honor Andy Griffith by renaming part of U.S. Hwy. 52, The Andy Griffith Parkway. "This is the biggest day of my life," Andy said. He promised, "I won't be a stranger from here out."

September 24, 2004, the City of Mount Airy and thousands of fans welcomed Andy Griffith and Larry Jones, President of *TV Land* and *Nick at Nite* for the dedication of the statue of Andy and Opie Taylor donated by *TV Land*. The statue is located in a beautiful fishing hole setting in front of The Andy Griffith Playhouse.

Broccoli Bread

10 ounces frozen broccoli,
   chopped, thawed and drained
1 large onion, chopped
6 ounces cottage cheese
½ cup margarine, melted
4 eggs, beaten
1 teaspoon salt
1 Jiffy cornbread mix

Preheat oven. Mix all ingredients except cornbread mix. Add cornbread mix last. Pour into greased 9x13-inch casserole dish. Bake. Temperature: 400 degrees. Baking Time: 25 minutes. Serve hot. Yield: 24 squares.

Monkey Bread

1¼ teaspoons cinnamon, ground
1 cup sugar
3 cans butter biscuits, quartered
1 stick margarine, melted

Preheat oven. Combine cinnamon and sugar; toss biscuits in mixture a few at a time. Place sugared biscuits in greased bundt pan. Combine margarine and leftover sugar mixture. Pour over biscuits. Bake. Remove from oven and turn into serving plate. Simply pull off pieces and enjoy. Temperature: 350 degrees. Baking Time: 40 minutes or until brown. Yield: 10-15 servings.

Onion-Cheese Bread

½ cup onion, minced
1 tablespoon shortening, melted
1½ cups biscuit mix
¼ cup dry milk solids
1 egg
½ cup water
1 cup American cheese, grated
2 teaspoons poppy seeds
1 tablespoon butter or margarine,
   melted

Preheat oven. Cook onion until tender in melted shortening. Meanwhile, mix in a 1½ quart bowl the biscuit mix and milk solids. Add to dry ingredients the cooked onion, egg, water, and ½ cup grated cheese. Mix well. Spread mixture in greased 8-inch round baking pan. Top with ½ cup grated cheese, poppy seeds, and melted butter or margarine. Bake near center of oven until top is golden brown. Cut in wedges and serve hot. Temperature: 425 degrees. Baking Time: about 20 minutes. Yield: 4-6 servings.

Pepperoni Bread

2 loaves frozen white bread dough
   or 2 cans refrigerator pizza
   dough
1 pound pepperoni, sliced

2-3 green peppers, chopped
1 onion, chopped
16 ounces mozzarella cheese,
   shredded

Let bread loaves thaw out about 2 hours. Roll out with rolling pin one bread loaf into a rectangle shape about 18x24-inches. Place half of pepperoni slices all over dough (like pizza). Sprinkle half of chopped vegetables on dough. Sprinkle ½ of cheese evenly on top of vegetables. Start at one long side and roll up into a loaf. Repeat with second loaf. Preheat oven. Make sure oven rack is in center. Transfer to baking sheet and bake. Slice and serve. Temperature: 350 degrees. Baking Time: 20-25 minutes. Yield: 2 loaves.

Petite Party Cream Puffs

½ cup water
¼ cup butter

½ cup flour, sifted
2 eggs

Heat water and butter to boiling point in saucepan. Mix in flour all at once. Stir constantly until mixture leaves sides of pan and forms into a ball, about 1 minute. Remove from heat. Cool about 5 minutes. Beat in eggs, one at a time, beating until smooth after each addition. Whip mixture until velvety. Drop by leveled teaspoon in small mounds on lightly greased baking sheets. Bake. Cool puffs and cut off tops. Fill with chicken salad, tuna salad, your favorite filling or spread. Temperature: 400 degrees. Baking Time: about 20 minutes. Yield: 40.

Skillet Cheese Bread

Use your food processor, mixer, and electric skillet.

½ cup shortening
2 eggs, beaten
1 cup milk
3 cups biscuit mix

½ pound cheddar cheese, grated
2 tablespoons poppy seeds
2 tablespoons dried onion, minced

Melt shortening in electric skillet. Add eggs, milk, and melted shortening to biscuit mix, cheese, poppy seeds, and onion. Mix until dry ingredients are moistened. If electric skillet is not Teflon, line with double layer of waxed paper and spread dough in skillet. Turn out and serve. Temperature: 300 degrees, electric skillet or 375 degrees, oven. Baking Time: 25 minutes. Yield: 12-16 servings.

Butterflake Herb Loaf

¼ cup butter, melted
½ teaspoon instant onion, minced
½ teaspoon sweet basil
¼ teaspoon caraway seeds

¼ teaspoon oregano
2 tablespoons parsley, minced
2 cans butterflake dinner rolls or
similar

Preheat oven. Combine butter and seasonings; spread each butterflake roll with seasoned butter. Stand on edge in greased 9x5x3-inch pan making two rows. (Extra seasoned butter may be poured over the top of the unbaked rolls). Bake until deep golden brown. Carefully remove from pan. Serve warm. Temperature: 375 degrees. Baking Time: 30-35 minutes. Yield: 1 loaf.

Cheesy Bread Sticks

½ cup corn meal
1½ cups flour, sifted
1 teaspoon salt
⅔ cup shortening

½ cup water
Butter, melted
⅔ cup sharp cheese, grated

Sift together corn meal, flour, and salt; cut in shortening until mixture resembles coarse crumbs, add water a little at a time mixing lightly until mixture can be formed into a ball. Let rest 5 minutes. Divide into 6 parts. Roll 1 part at a time on lightly floured board to form a rectangle about 4x20 inches. Brush with melted butter and sprinkle with grated cheese. Roll up as jelly roll, cut in 4 sticks, each about 5 inches long. Repeat for other 5 parts. Preheat oven. Place on ungreased baking sheet, bake. Temperature: 425 degrees. Baking Time: 15-20 minutes. Yield: 2 dozen.

Parmesan Toast Rings

A great treat with salads.

6 slices white bread
Butter, melted

Parmesan cheese

Cut white bread into rings with a 2¾-inch doughnut cutter. Brush rings with melted butter and sprinkle both sides with Parmesan cheese. Place on a greased baking sheet. Toast in oven to a rich golden brown. Serve with salads. Temperature: 450 degrees. Baking Time: about 5 minutes.

Angel Biscuits

This is a good bread to store in refrigerator for several days.

1 package yeast
2 tablespoons warm water
5 cups self-rising flour

¼ cup sugar
¾ cup shortening
2 cups buttermilk

Dissolve yeast in 2 tablespoons warm water. Sift flour, add sugar, cut in shortening, add yeast and buttermilk. Knead and place in refrigerator. Make out as biscuits and do not allow to rise before baking. Preheat oven. Bake until brown. Temperature 400-425 degrees. Baking Time: 15 minutes.

Caraway Wheat Biscuits

¾ cup flour
¾ cup whole wheat flour
2 teaspoons baking powder
½ teaspoon salt

1 teaspoon caraway seeds
⅓ cup shortening
½ cup milk

Preheat oven. Stir together flours, baking powder, salt, and ½ teaspoon caraway seeds. Cut in shortening until mixture resembles coarse crumbs. Make a well in the center. Add milk all at once. Stir just until dough clings together. Knead dough gently on lightly floured surface for 10-12 strokes. On greased baking sheet roll or pat dough to an 8-inch round. Prick surface with tines of a fork, scoring into 8 wedges. (Can also be cut with a biscuit cutter.) Brush top of round with a little additional milk. Sprinkle with remaining caraway seeds. Bake until golden brown. Temperature: 400 degrees. Baking Time: 20-25 minutes. Yield: 8 servings.

Sour Cream Drop Biscuits

2 cups self-rising flour
4 tablespoons shortening
⅔ cup sour cream

½-¾ cup milk to make spooning
consistency

Preheat oven. Mix all ingredients well; drop onto greased pan using teaspoon or tablespoon according to size desired. Bake. Serve immediately. Also good toasted the following day. Temperature: 450 degrees. Baking Time: 8-10 minutes.

For best baking results, bake all foods near the center of the oven unless the recipes state otherwise.

Cheese Curry Biscuits

¾ cup flour, sifted
1 tablespoon curry powder
1 teaspoon baking powder
¼ teaspoon salt
¼ teaspoon dry mustard

¼ cup butter
¾ cup cheese, grated
1 egg yolk
3 tablespoons milk

Preheat oven. Mix dry ingredients by sifting. Cut in butter. Stir in grated cheese. Combine egg yoke and milk; add to the dry mixture. Continue stirring until a stiff dough forms. Turn out on lightly floured board and roll out until ⅛-inch thick. Cut into shape desired. Bake. Remove from oven when they start to brown. Cool. Temperature: 450 degrees. Baking Time: 10-12 minutes. Yield: 1 dozen.

Cherry Coffee Cake

2 sticks margarine
1½ cups sugar
4 eggs
2 cups flour

1 teaspoon vanilla extract
1 teaspoon almond extract
1 can cherry pie filling

Preheat oven. Cream margarine and sugar. Add eggs, one at a time, beating well after each one. Stir in flour. Add vanilla and almond. Spread batter into well greased 15½x10½-inch pan. Mark imaginary squares with spatula in batter and fill with pie filling. Bake. Temperature: 350 degrees. Baking Time: 45 minutes. Yield: 16 servings.

Merry Berry Coffee Cake

2 cups biscuit mix
⅔ cup sugar
¼ cup instant nonfat dry milk
⅔ cup water
1 egg

1½ cups blueberries
⅓ cup sugar
2 tablespoons soft butter
¼ cup instant nonfat dry milk
¼ cup flour

Preheat oven. Combine biscuit mix, sugar, and nonfat dry milk. Stir in water and egg until well blended. Spoon into a buttered 9-inch pan and top with berries. Combine ⅓ cup sugar and butter together. Mix in dry milk and flour until mixture is crumbly; sprinkle over berries. Bake. Serve hot with plenty of butter. Temperature: 350 degrees. Baking Time: 45 minutes. Yield: 1 cake.

Pecan Vienna Dream Coffee Cake

Great for freezing!

TOPPING
1 cup flour, sifted
¾ cup light brown sugar, packed
4 teaspoons cinnamon, ground
½ cup butter or margarine
2 cups pecans, chopped

Combine flour, sugar, cinnamon, and butter or margarine; blend until mixture is crumbly. Add pecans; mix well.

CAKE
4 cups flour, sifted
4 teaspoons baking powder
1 teaspoon salt
1 cup butter or margarine
1¾ cups sugar
3 eggs
1 cup milk
1 teaspoon vanilla or lemon
   extract

Preheat oven. Sift together flour, baking powder, and salt. Cream butter or margarine and sugar. Add eggs, one at a time, and beat until light and creamy after each addition. Add dry ingredients alternately with milk and flavoring, blending well after each addition. Divide batter equally between three greased 9-inch round cake pans. Cover each evenly with an equal amount of TOPPING. Bake until done and browned. Temperature: 350 degrees. Baking Time: 35 minutes. Yield: 3 (9-inch) coffee cakes.

Apple Coffee Cake

1 cup butter
2 cups sugar
2 eggs
1 teaspoon vanilla extract
8 ounces sour cream
2 cups flour
½ teaspoon salt
1 teaspoon baking powder
1 cup cooking apples, pared and
   sliced

TOPPING
1 cup nuts, finely chopped
5 tablespoons brown sugar,
   packed
1 teaspoon cinnamon, ground

Preheat oven. All ingredients should be room temperature. Cream butter and sugar until light and fluffy. Fold in eggs, vanilla, and sour cream; mix well. Add flour, salt, and baking powder, mix well on low speed. Fold in apples. Spoon batter into greased 9x13-inch pyrex dish. Combine topping ingredients; sprinkle TOPPING over batter. Bake until center springs back when pressed. Temperature: 325 degrees. Baking Time: 40-50 minutes. Yield: 15 servings.

Apricot Almond Coffee Cake

¾ cup dried apricots, snipped
1 cup water
¼ cup shortening
¾ cup sugar
1 egg
1½ cups flour, sifted
2 teaspoons baking powder

¾ teaspoon salt
½ teaspoon cinnamon, ground
⅔ cup milk
½ cup brown sugar, packed
⅓ cup flour
4 tablespoons butter
⅓ cup almonds, chopped

Preheat oven. In saucepan, combine apricots and water, simmer, uncovered 15 minutes. Cool, drain, adding enough liquid to make ½ cup. Cream together shortening and sugar. Add egg and beat well. Sift together flour, baking powder, salt, and cinnamon. Add to creamed mixture alternately with milk mixture, beginning and ending with dry ingredients, stir in apricots. Turn into greased 9-inch layer cake pan. Combine brown sugar and ⅓ cup flour, cut in butter until crumbly; add almonds. Sprinkle over batter in pan. Bake. Serve warm. Temperature: 350 degrees. Baking Time: 40-45 minutes. Yield: 6 servings.

Christmas Coffee Cake

¾ cup sugar
¼ cup shortening
1 egg
1 cup milk

1½ cups flour, sifted
2 teaspoons baking powder
½ teaspoon salt

Preheat oven. Mix together sugar, shortening, and egg. Stir in milk. Sift together and stir in flour, baking powder, and salt. Pour in greased and floured 9-inch pan. Sprinkle with TOPPING. Bake. Serve warm. Temperature: 375 degrees. Baking Time: 25-35 minutes. Yield: 6 servings.

TOPPING

½ cup brown sugar, packed
2 tablespoons flour
2 teaspoons cinnamon, ground

2 tablespoons butter, melted
½ cup nuts, chopped
⅓ cup candied fruit, cut up

Mix together all ingredients and set aside.

The air should circulate evenly in the oven for best baking results. DO NOT COVER THE RACKS IN YOUR OVEN WITH ALUMINUM FOIL.

Coffee Cake

Use the mixer and electric frypan.

BATTER
1 small yellow cake mix or ½ the
    batter from a regular size
    cake mix

TOPPING

½ cup brown sugar, packed
4 tablespoons graham cracker
    crumbs, fine

2 tablespoons butter, melted
1½ teaspoons cinnamon, ground
½ cup nuts, chopped

Preheat covered electric skillet to 280 degrees. Prepare yellow cake mix as directed on package. Pour batter into skillet. (If skillet does not have nonstick surface, lightly grease the skillet with one tablespoon of oil.) Cover with lid and open air vent. Bake about 25 minutes or until cake is done. Turn heat to OFF. Mix topping ingredients together and sprinkle TOPPING evenly over cake. Replace lid and let stand about 10 minutes before cutting. Yield: 8-10 servings.

Danish Coffee Cake

1⅓ cups biscuit mix
2 tablespoons sugar
3 ounces cream cheese
2 tablespoons butter

½ cup almonds, slivered
¼ cup milk
½ cup red raspberry preserves

Combine biscuit mix and sugar in mixing bowl. With pastry blender or two knives, cut in cream cheese and butter until crumbly. Stir in nuts, add milk, stir until blended. Turn out onto lightly floured board or pastry cloth and knead 8-10 strokes. On waxed paper, roll dough into a 12x8-inch rectangle. Carefully turn onto greased baking sheet and remove paper. Spread preserves lengthwise down center third of dough. Cut 1-inch strips along long side of dough, cutting from filling out to edges. Beginning at one end, fold strips at angle across filling, alternating from side to side. Chill in refrigerator 30 minutes.

Preheat oven. Bake until golden brown. Drizzle GLAZE over cake. Temperature: 400 degrees. Baking Time: 20-25 minutes. Yield: 6 servings.

GLAZE

1 cup confectioner's sugar   1½-2 tablespoons milk

Mix all ingredients.

Quick Coffee Cake

1½ cups flour, sifted
2 teaspoons baking powder
½ teaspoon salt
½ cup sugar

1 egg, beaten slightly
½ cup milk
3 tablespoons shortening, melted

Preheat oven. Sift together flour, baking powder, salt, and sugar. Combine egg, milk, and shortening. Add to flour mixture, stirring until mixture is smooth. Pour into greased 8-inch square or 9-inch round pan. Bake. Temperature: 400 degrees. Baking Time: 25 minutes. Yield: 1 cake.

Honey Crisp Brunch Cake

1 recipe QUICK COFFEE CAKE
    BATTER
3 tablespoons butter or margarine
⅓ cup honey

¼ cup coconut, shredded
½ cup Corn Flakes, crushed
½ cup crushed pineapple, drained

Preheat oven. Cream together butter or margarine and honey until light and fluffy. Add coconut, Corn Flakes, and pineapple and mix thoroughly. Spread over quick coffee cake before baking. Bake. Temperature: 400 degrees. Baking Time: 25 minutes. Yield: 1 coffee cake.

Pineapple Swirl Coffee Cake

8 ounces crushed pineapple
⅓ cup shortening
½ cup sugar
1 egg
1 teaspoon vanilla extract
1¼ cups flour, sifted

1½ teaspoons baking powder
¼ teaspoon salt
⅓ cup brown sugar, packed
3 tablespoons butter or margarine
½ cup coconut, flaked
⅓ cup walnuts, chopped

Preheat oven. Drain pineapple, reserving ½ cup syrup. Cream shortening and sugar. Add egg and vanilla; beat until light. Sift together next 3 ingredients; add to creamed mixture alternately with reserved syrup, beginning and ending with flour mixture. Spread half in greased 8x8x2-inch baking pan; spread with pineapple. Top with remaining butter. Combine remaining ingredients; sprinkle over all. Bake. Temperature: 350 degrees. Baking Time: 35 minutes. Yield: 1 cake.

Sour Cream Coffee Cake

1 cup butter
1¼ cups sugar
2 eggs
1 cup sour cream
2 cups flour
½ teaspoon baking soda

1½ teaspoons baking powder
1 teaspoon vanilla extract
¾ cup nuts, chopped
2 teaspoons cinnamon, ground
2 tablespoons sugar

In a large mixing bowl, combine butter, 1¼ cups sugar, and eggs. Beat until fluffy. Blend in sour cream. Sift flour with soda and baking powder. Add to creamed mixture. Add vanilla and blend well. Mix nuts, cinnamon, and 2 tablespoons sugar in a small bowl. Spoon half of batter into a well greased and floured bundt pan. Spoon nut filling over batter. Spoon remaining batter on top. Place in cold oven and bake. Serve warm or cold. Temperature: 350 degrees. Baking Time: 55 minutes. Yield: 8-10 servings.

"If you must doubt, never doubt your beliefs."

Angel Corn Sticks

1½ cups corn meal
1 cup flour
1 package yeast
1 tablespoon sugar
1 teaspoon salt
1½ teaspoons baking powder

½ teaspoon baking soda
Sage to taste
2 eggs, beaten
2 cups buttermilk
½ cup vegetable oil

Combine dry ingredients in a large bowl. Combine eggs, buttermilk, and oil; add to dry ingredients, stirring until smooth. Spoon the batter into well-greased cast iron corn stick pans, filling half full. Bake. Temperature: 450 degrees. Baking Time: 12-15 minutes. Yield: 3 dozen.

Corn Bread Special

2 eggs, beaten
1 cup sour cream
½ cup corn oil

1 cup corn meal
1 tablespoon baking powder
½ teaspoon salt

Beat eggs until thick. Blend together sour cream and oil. Fold into eggs. Mix corn meal, baking powder, and salt. Add to egg mixture. Pour into a greased 8x8-inch pan. Preheat oven. Bake. Temperature: 375 degrees. Baking Time: 30-40 minutes. Yield 8 servings.

Corny Corn Bread

12 ounces corn muffin mix
8½ ounces whole kernel corn,
    drained
8½ ounces cream style corn

2 eggs
½ cup butter, melted
8 ounces sour cream

Preheat oven. Mix all ingredients until well blended. Pour into a greased 9x13-inch pan. Bake. Temperature: 400 degrees. Baking Time: 30 minutes. Yield: 24 squares.

Mexican Corn Bread

1 cup self-rising corn meal
½ cup self-rising flour
½ cup oil
1 cup milk
1 cup cream-style corn, canned

1 cup onion, chopped
½ cup cheddar cheese, grated
3 eggs, beaten
3 pods Mexican pepper, chopped

Preheat oven. Mix all ingredients together. Pour into 9x9-inch greased pan. Bake. Temperature: 350 degrees. Baking Time: 45 minutes to 1 hour. Yield: 16 servings.

Favorite Bread Dressing

1 cup onion, minced
1 quart celery, diced
1 cup margarine
1 tablespoon salt
½ teaspoon pepper
2 teaspoons poultry seasoning

Sage to taste
4 quarts small day old bread
    cubes, firmly packed: loaf
    bread, biscuit, and corn bread
1½-2 cups broth, milk, or water

Cook onion and celery in margarine over low heat until onion is soft but not brown, stirring occasionally, Meanwhile blend seasoning with bread crumbs. Add the onion, celery, and margarine. Blend. Pour the broth gradually over surface, stirring lightly. Add more seasoning as desired. Stuffing for 14-18 pound turkey.

When baking in glass dishes, lower oven temperature 25 degrees.

Pecan Waffles

2 cups flour, sifted
1 tablespoon baking powder
¼ teaspoon salt
¾ cup pecans, chopped

2 eggs, separated
1½ cups milk
6 tablespoons shortening, melted

Sift together dry ingredients and add pecans. Beat egg yolks until light. Combine with milk and melted shortening and add to dry ingredients, mixing just until smooth. Beat egg whites until stiff and fold into batter. Preheat waffle iron. Bake.

Cranberry Waffle Sauce

16 ounce cranberry sauce
¼ cup butter

¼ cup brown sugar

Combine cranberry sauce, butter, and brown sugar. Heat to boiling and serve with PECAN WAFFLES.

Stuffed French Toast

8 ounces cream cheese, softened
1 teaspoon vanilla extract
½ cup walnuts, chopped
16 ounces loaf French bread,
    unsliced
4 eggs

1 cup whipping cream
½ teaspoon vanilla extract
½ teaspoon nutmeg, ground
12 ounces preserves, any flavor
½ cup orange juice

Beat together the cream cheese and ½ teaspoon vanilla until fluffy; stir in nuts. Set aside. Cut bread into ten or twelve 1½-inch slices, cut a pocket in the top of each. Fill each with 1½ tablespoons of the cheese mixture. Beat together eggs, whipping cream, the remaining ½ teaspoon vanilla, and nutmeg. Using tongs, dip the filled bread slices in egg mixture, being careful not to squeeze out the filling. Cook on a slightly greased griddle until both sides are golden brown. (Keep warm in a warm oven until all are finished.) Meanwhile, heat together the preserves and orange juice. To serve, drizzle the mixture over hot French toast. Yield: 6-8 servings.

Pineapple Muffins

1 stick margarine, softened
1 cup plus 2 tablespoons sugar
2 large eggs
3 cups flour
½ teaspoon salt
1 tablespoon baking powder

⅛ teaspoon baking soda
1 cup pineapple juice,
   unsweetened
1 teaspoon vanilla extract
8 ounces crushed pineapple, well
   drained

Cream together the margarine and 1 cup sugar until the mixture is light and fluffy and beat in the eggs, one at a time. Sift together flour, salt, baking powder, and baking soda. Combine the pineapple juice and the vanilla. Stir the flour mixture into the butter mixture alternately with the juice mixture, beginning and ending with the flour mixture, and stir in the pineapple. Spoon the batter into 24 paper-lined ⅓ cup muffin pans, sprinkle with the remaining 2 tablespoons sugar, and bake the muffins in a preheated oven until a wooden pick comes out clean. Temperature: 400 degrees. Baking Time: 20 minutes. Yield: 24 muffins.

Lemon Poppy Seed Muffins

Lemon and poppy seeds make this muffin a gourmet's choice.

1 cup sugar
1½ sticks butter
2 eggs
⅔ cup milk
⅓ cup lemon juice

3 cups flour
4 teaspoons baking powder
1 teaspoon salt
¼ cup poppy seeds
4 teaspoons lemon rind, grated

Preheat oven. Cream sugar and butter together. Combine eggs, milk, and lemon juice. Mix flour with baking powder and salt. Alternately add wet and dry ingredients to the butter-sugar mixture. Stir in poppy seeds and lemon rind. Place cupcake papers inside muffin pans, divide batter evenly among the cups. Bake. Cool muffins 10 minutes on rack, then dip each into GLAZE. Set back on racks to dry. Temperature: 350 degrees. Baking Time: 25 minutes. Yield: 2 dozen muffins.

GLAZE
2 cups confectioner's sugar
1 teaspoon vanilla extract

¼ cup lemon juice

Mix all ingredients together.

Banana-Carrot Muffins

¼ cup margarine
½ cup brown sugar
1 large egg
2 medium bananas, mashed
2 cups whole-wheat flour
2 teaspoons baking powder

¼ teaspoon salt
¼ teaspoon baking soda
3 medium carrots, grated
1 teaspoon vanilla extract
½ cup walnuts, chopped

Preheat oven. Grease muffin pans. In a mixing bowl, cream margarine and brown sugar until fluffy. Add egg and beat well. Stir in bananas. In a small bowl, mix together flour, baking powder, salt, and baking soda. Add flour mixture to banana mixture. Do not overmix. Add carrots, vanilla, and nuts, and combine carefully. Fill muffin pans two-thirds full and bake until an inserted toothpick comes out clean. Temperature: 350 degrees. Baking Time: 20-25 minutes. Yield: 12 muffins.

Six-Weeks Muffins

6 cups All-Bran cereal
2 cups boiling water
1 cup shortening, melted
3 cups sugar
4 eggs, beaten

1 quart buttermilk
5 cups flour, unsifted
5 teaspoons baking soda
2 teaspoons salt

Put 2 cups of bran into large bowl; pour over it the boiling water and let stand while assembling other ingredients. Mix in shortening. Mix the remainder of bran with sugar, eggs, and buttermilk. Sift together flour, soda, and salt. Combine all ingredients. Cover and store in refrigerator overnight. Batter will keep six weeks or longer in refrigerator. Preheat oven. Bake as many muffins as desired. Temperature: 400 degrees. Baking Time: 20 minutes. Yield: 5 dozen.

Buttermilk Blueberry Muffins

1 egg, separated
¾ cup buttermilk
¼ cup butter, melted
2 cups flour
½ cup sugar

1 teaspoon salt
¼ teaspoon baking soda
2 teaspoons baking powder
1 cup blueberries

Preheat oven. Sift dry ingredients together. Beat egg white until stiff. Place egg yolk and buttermilk in small bowl and beat lightly with fork to blend; add butter. Stir egg mixture into dry ingredients just enough to moisten ingredients. Fold in blueberries and egg white. Spoon into greased muffin pans and bake. Temperature: 400 degrees. Baking Time: 20-25 minutes. Yield: 15 medium muffins.

Fresh Orange Muffins

2 tablespoons butter
¼ cup sugar
1 egg
2 tablespoons orange rind, grated
¼ cup orange juice

¼ cup milk
1 cup flour
1½ teaspoons baking powder
¼ teaspoon salt

Preheat oven. Cream butter and sugar until light and fluffy. Add egg, beat well. Stir in orange rind, orange juice, and milk. Combine flour, baking powder, and salt. Add to creamed mixture; stirring just enough to moisten dry ingredients. Fill greased muffin pans two-thirds full and bake. Temperature: 400 degrees. Baking Time: 20 minutes. Yield: 6 muffins.

"O Lord, Thou art our Shepherd, and we shall not want. Thou openeth Thy hand and satisfieth the needs of every living being. We thank Thee for the gifts of Thy bounty which we have enjoyed at this table. As Thou hast provided for us hitherto, so mayst Thou sustain us throughout our lives. Thy kindness endureth forever, and we put our trust in Thee."

"While we enjoy Thy gifts may we never forget the needy, nor allow those who want, to be forsaken. May our table be an altar of living kindness, and our home a temple in which Thy spirit of goodness dwells."

GRACE AFTER MEALS—JEWISH

Hidden Treasure

Discover the secret!

2 cups flour, sifted
½ teaspoon salt
1 tablespoon baking powder
2 tablespoons sugar

1 egg
1 cup milk
3 tablespoons shortening, melted
Jelly, raisins, nuts, or dried fruit

Preheat oven. Oil muffin pans including sides of the cups. Measure and sift together all dry ingredients. Beat the egg until foamy and add the milk and melted shortening. Stir only until all the flour is dampened. Fill muffin pans two-thirds full. For the treasure, spoon ½ teaspoon of your favorite jelly, raisins, nuts, or dried fruit into the muffin batter before baking. Bake. Temperature: 425 degrees. Baking Time: 20-25 minutes. Yield: 1 dozen muffins.

Oatmeal Surprise Muffins

1¼ cups quick-cooking rolled oats
1¼ cups milk
1 egg
½ cup vegetable oil
¾ cup brown sugar, firmly
    packed

¾ cup semisweet chocolate chips
1 cup pecans, chopped and
    divided
1¼ cups flour
4 teaspoons baking powder
1 teaspoon salt

Lightly grease 12 cup muffin pan. In a medium bowl, combine oats and milk. Allow to stand 15 minutes. Preheat oven. Stir egg, oil, ½ cup brown sugar, chocolate chips, and ½ cup pecans into oat mixture. In a large bowl, combine flour, baking powder, and salt. Add oat mixture to flour mixture, stirring just until all dry ingredients are moistened. Fill each cup of muffin pan two-thirds full with batter. Sprinkle tops with remaining brown sugar and pecans. Bake until the top of a muffin springs back when lightly touched. Temperature: 400 degrees. Baking Time: 20-25 minutes. Yield: 12 muffins.

Over-mixing causes tunnels in muffins.

Peanut Butter Muffins

2 cups flour, sifted
½ cup sugar
2½ teaspoons baking powder
½ teaspoon salt
½ cup chunk-style peanut butter
2 tablespoons butter or margarine

2 eggs, well beaten
¾ cup milk
¼ cup currant jelly, melted
⅓ cup peanuts, finely chopped
    and toasted

Preheat oven. Sift together dry ingredients. Cut in peanut butter and butter until mixture resembles coarse crumbs. Add eggs and milk, all at once, stirring just until flour is moistened. Grease 2-inch muffin pans or line with paper baking cups; fill two-thirds full. Bake. Immediately brush tops of muffins with melted jelly; dip tops in peanuts. Serve warm. Temperature: 400 degrees. Baking Time: 15-17 minutes. Yield: 20.

Black Cherry Almond Muffins

This recipe may be used for making a coffee cake.

2 cups flour
½ cup sugar
1 tablespoon baking powder
½ teaspoon salt
½ teaspoon nutmeg, ground
1 cup black cherries, fresh or
    canned, pitted, chopped, and
    drained

2 eggs, beaten
½ cup milk
½ cup margarine, melted
½ cup almonds, slivered
2 tablespoons sugar

In a large bowl, mix flour, ½ cup sugar, baking powder, salt, and nutmeg. Add cherries; toss to coat. Mix egg, milk, and margarine. Add to flour mixture, stir until blended. Fill greased muffin pan two-thirds full. Sprinkle tops with almonds and 2 tablespoons sugar. Bake in preheated oven. Temperature: 400 degrees. Baking Time: 20-25 minutes for muffins, 30-35 minutes for 9-inch square coffee cake. Yield: 12 muffins or 1 coffee cake.

Date Nut Tea Bread

This bread freezes nicely. Great for parties. Serve with cream cheese.

8 ounces pitted dates
1¼ cups boiling water
1½ cups brown sugar, packed
6 tablespoons butter or margarine
1 egg, beaten

¾ cup walnuts, chopped
2¼ cups flour, sifted
1½ teaspoons baking soda
1½ teaspoons salt

Cut dates in small pieces into medium-size bowl; pour boiling water over; stir in sugar and butter or margarine; cool to room temperature. Stir in beaten egg and walnuts. Sift flour, soda, and salt onto waxed paper; stir quickly into date mixture just until blended; pour into greased and waxed-paper lined 9x5x3-inch loaf pan; let stand 15 minutes. Preheat oven. Bake until center is firm; cool 5 minutes; turn on wire rack; cool completely. Temperature: 350 degrees. Baking Time: 1 hour 10 minutes. Yield: 1 loaf.

Orange Poppy Seed Loaf

The three flavorings create a taster's choice.

3 cups flour
1½ teaspoons salt
1½ teaspoons baking powder
3 eggs
1½ cups milk
1⅛ cups cooking oil

2¼ cups sugar
1½ tablespoons poppy seeds
1½ teaspoons vanilla extract
1½ teaspoons almond flavoring
1½ teaspoons butter flavoring

Preheat oven. Put all ingredients into mixing bowl and beat for 2 minutes. Pour into greased and floured 9x5x3-inch loaf pan. Bake until toothpick inserted into center is clean and top is cracked. Cool in pan for 5 minutes. Remove from pan. Pour GLAZE over bread. Temperature: 350 degrees. Baking Time: 1 hour. Yield: 1 loaf.

GLAZE

¼ cup orange juice
¾ cup sugar
½ teaspoon butter flavoring

½ teaspoon almond flavoring
½ teaspoon vanilla extract

Stir (DON'T COOK) all glaze ingredients together. Delicious served while warm, but may be prepared ahead and frozen.

Fresh Cranberry Nut Bread

2 cups flour, sifted
1 cup sugar
1½ teaspoons baking powder
½ teaspoon baking soda
1 teaspoon salt
¼ cup shortening

¾ cup orange juice
1 tablespoon orange rind, grated
1 egg white, well beaten
½ cup nuts, chopped
1 cup cranberries, chopped

Preheat oven. Sift together flour, sugar, baking powder, soda, and salt. Cut in shortening until mixture resembles coarse corn meal. Combine orange juice and grated rind with well beaten egg white. Pour all at once into dry ingredients, mixing just enough to dampen. Carefully fold in chopped nuts and cranberries. Spoon into greased 9x5x3-inch loaf pan. Spread corners and sides slightly higher than the center. Bake until crust is golden brown and toothpick inserted comes out clean. Remove from pan, cool. Store overnight for easy slicing. Temperature: 350 degrees. Baking Time: about 1 hour. Yield: 1 loaf.

Peanut Butter Apple Bread

2 cups flour, sifted
½ cup dark brown sugar
1 tablespoon baking powder
½ teaspoon salt
1 teaspoon cinnamon, ground
⅛ teaspoon nutmeg, ground

½ cup nuts, chopped
½ cup golden raisins
½ cup creamy peanut butter
2 eggs
1 cup applesauce

Preheat oven. Combine dry ingredients, nuts, and raisins. Set aside. Beat peanut butter, eggs, and applesauce. Mix well. Pour over dry ingredients, stir until moistened. Pour into greased 9x5x3-inch loaf pan. Bake. Cool in pan 30 minutes. Temperature: 350 degrees. Baking Time: 40-50 minutes. Yield: 1 loaf.

"God is great. God is good. Let us thank Him for our food.
By his hands we all are fed, give us Lord our Daily Bread. Amen."

Strawberry Bread

*Flavor improves if loaves are wrapped tightly
and allowed to sit overnight before slicing.*

3 cups flour
2 cups sugar
1 tablespoon cinnamon, ground
1 teaspoon baking soda
1 teaspoon salt

1¼ cups salad oil
4 eggs, beaten
20 ounces frozen sweetened
    strawberries, thawed
1¼ cups nuts, chopped

Preheat oven. Combine flour, sugar, cinnamon, soda, and salt in large bowl. Add salad oil and eggs. Mix thoroughly. Stir in strawberries and nuts. Pour batter into 2 greased and floured 9x5x3-inch loaf pans and bake. Temperature: 350 degrees. Baking Time: 1 hour. Yield: 2 loaves.

Strawberry Butter

Use the electric blender or food processor.

10 ounces frozen strawberries
1 cup butter

1 cup confectioner's sugar, sifted

Blend all ingredients on high until completely smooth. Yield: 2 cups.

Apple Butterscotch Bread

2 cups biscuit mix
1 cup quick oats
¾ cup sugar
¼ teaspoon salt
1 teaspoon baking powder
½ cup butterscotch pieces

½ cup nuts, chopped
½ cup raisins (optional)
1 egg
¼ cup milk
1 cup applesauce

Preheat oven. Stir together first five ingredients. Add butterscotch pieces, nuts, and raisins. Combine egg and milk; stir in oat mixture. Add applesauce; beat mixture vigorously by hand for 30 seconds. Spoon into greased and floured 9x5x3-inch loaf pan. Bake. Cool before slicing. Temperature: 350 degrees. Baking Time: 50-60 minutes. Yield: 1 loaf.

Bishop Bread

2½ cups flour
1 tablespoon baking powder
1 teaspoon salt
4 ounces German sweet chocolate
2 cups pecans, finely chopped

1 cup dates, chopped
1 cup maraschino cherries,
   chopped and well drained
4 eggs
1¼ cups sugar

Preheat oven. Sift flour, baking powder, and salt. Cut chocolate into small pieces. Add chocolate, nuts, dates, and cherries to flour mixture. Stir to coat pieces with flour. Beat eggs with electric mixer until foamy. Add sugar gradually and continue beating until eggs are thick and light. Add flour mixture, mixing thoroughly. Turn batter into greased 9x5x3-inch pan. Bake. Cool and slice. Temperature: 325 degrees. Baking Time: 1½ hours. Yield: 1 loaf.

Holiday Banana Bread

1¾ cups flour, sifted
2¾ teaspoons baking powder
½ teaspoon salt
½ cup nuts, chopped
⅓ cup shortening
⅔ cup sugar

2 eggs, slightly beaten
1 cup (3-4) bananas, mashed
1 cup mixed candied fruits and
   peels
½ cup raisins

Preheat oven. Sift together flour, baking powder, and salt. Add nuts. Blend. Place shortening in mixing bowl and beat until creamy. Gradually add sugar to shortening, beating well. Add eggs and beat. Add flour mixture and bananas alternately. Blend thoroughly after each addition. Fold in fruits, peels, and raisins. Grease bottom only of 9x5x3-inch loaf pan. Turn batter into pan. Bake. Let bread partially cool in pan 20-30 minutes before turning out on a rack. Cool thoroughly before wrapping for storage. Temperature: 350 degrees. Baking Time: 60-70 minutes. Yield: 1 loaf.

"To love and to be loved is life's greatest joy."

Holiday Slices

Add an extra touch to a mix for something extra special.

1 orange muffin mix
¾ cup whole cranberry sauce

1 cup walnuts, chopped
1 tablespoon orange rind

Preheat oven. Prepare batter from muffin mix according to package directions. Fold in cranberry sauce, nuts, and orange rind. Spoon into 6 greased (6 ounce) frozen juice concentrate cans, filling two-thirds full. Bake until done. Cool about 5 minutes, then ease out of cans with spatula (cut end of can if necessary). For dainty, thin slices, wait till second day to slice, or freeze and slice when ready to serve. Temperature: 375 degrees. Baking Time: 30-35 minutes. Yield: 6 small round loaves.

Magic Bread

2¼ cups flour, sifted
1 cup sugar
1 teaspoon ginger, ground
1 teaspoon cinnamon, ground
½ cup soft shortening

1 egg, beaten
⅓ cup molasses
1 cup buttermilk
1 teaspoon baking soda
¼ teaspoon salt

Preheat oven. Grease and flour a 9-inch square pan. Sift together flour, sugar, and spices. Cut in shortening to size of large peas. In another bowl, mix egg, molasses, buttermilk, soda, and salt. Add to dry mixture; stir only until flour is damp. Mixture will be lumpy. Pour into pan. Bake. Serve plain or warm with softened cream cheese and lemon sauce. Temperature: 350 degrees. Baking Time: about 40 minutes. Yield: 16 squares.

Pineapple Loaf Bread

2 cups flour, sifted
1 tablespoon baking powder
½ teaspoon salt
½ cup shortening

¾ cup sugar
2 eggs
1 cup crushed pineapple
1 teaspoon vanilla extract

Preheat oven. Sift together flour, baking powder, and salt. Cream shortening and sugar together until light and fluffy. Add eggs and beat well. Add flour mixture to creamed mixture alternately with pineapple and vanilla. Pour into greased 9x5x3-inch loaf pan. Bake. Temperature: 350 degrees. Baking Time: about 1 hour. Yield: 1 loaf.

Pumpkin Bread

3 cups sugar
1 cup cooking oil
4 eggs
2 cups pumpkin, canned
⅔ cup water

1½ teaspoons salt
1 teaspoon nutmeg, ground
3½ cups flour
2 teaspoons baking soda

Preheat oven. Mix all ingredients. Pour into two greased 9x5x3-inch loaf pans. Bake. Temperature: 350 degrees. Baking Time: 1 hour. Yield: 2 loaves.

Quick Raisin Bread

2 cups flour
4 teaspoons baking powder
½ teaspoon salt
1 teaspoon cinnamon, ground
    (optional)

⅓ cup butter
½ cup sugar
2 eggs
¾ cup milk
1 cup raisins

Preheat oven. Mix flour, baking powder, salt, and cinnamon. Set aside. Cream butter and sugar until smooth. Add eggs and beat well. Alternately stir in dry ingredients and milk into egg mixture until dough is smooth. Stir in raisins. Pour into greased 9x5x3-inch loaf pan. Bake. Cool in pan for 10 minutes. Temperature: 350 degrees. Baking Time: 40 minutes. Yield: 1 loaf.

Sweet Tater Bread

1½ cups sugar
½ cup oil
2 eggs, well beaten
1½ cups sweet potatoes, cooked
1½ cups self-rising flour
½ teaspoon cinnamon, ground

½ teaspoon baking powder
1 teaspoon baking soda
1 teaspoon salt
½ teaspoon nutmeg, ground
½ teaspoon allspice, ground
½ cup water

Preheat oven. Combine sugar, oil, and eggs and beat until smooth. Add sweet potatoes and mix well. Sift together remaining ingredients and alternate with water. Bake in greased 9x5x3-inch loaf pan. Temperature: 350 degrees. Baking Time: 1 hour 15 minutes. Yield: 1 loaf.

Tiny Apricot Bread Sandwiches

⅔ cup dried apricots
1⅓ cups milk, scalded
⅔ cup Grape-nuts
1 egg, well beaten
3 tablespoons shortening, melted
    and cooled

2 cups flour, sifted
2½ teaspoons baking powder
1 teaspoon salt
⅔ cup light brown sugar, firmly
    packed
Cream cheese, softened

Preheat oven. Cook apricots half as long as directed on package. Drain, cool, and cut in pieces. Pour scalded milk over cereal in mixing bowl; stir in apricots, cool. Add egg and shortening; mix well. Combine sifted flour, baking powder, salt, and sugar; add to cereal mixture. Stir just until moistened. Pour into greased 9x5x3-inch loaf pan. Bake. Cool. Slice and fill with softened cream cheese. Temperature: 350 degrees. Baking Time: 1 hour. Yield: 1 loaf.

Toasted Coconut Bread

1 cup coconut, toasted
3 cups self-rising flour, sifted
1 cup sugar
1 tablespoon orange rind, grated

1 egg
1⅓ cups milk
1 teaspoon vanilla extract
Almond Butter

Toast coconut in 350 degree oven for 7-12 minutes. Sift flour and sugar mixture together, stir in coconut and orange rind. Beat egg until light; mix with milk and vanilla and add to first mixture. Mix well, but do not beat. Pour into 9x5x3-inch loaf pan. Bake. Cool in pan for 10 minutes. Remove from pan and cool thoroughly. Serve with ALMOND BUTTER. Note: If using plain flour, sift 1 tablespoon baking powder and 1 teaspoon salt with flour and sugar. Temperature: 350 degrees. Baking Time: 55-60 minutes. Yield: 1 loaf.

Almond Butter

1 tablespoon almonds, finely
    chopped
½ teaspoon almond extract

½ cup butter or margarine,
    softened

Blend almonds and almond extract into softened butter. Spread on slices of toasted coconut bread.

Spicy Zucchini Bread

3 cups flour
1 teaspoon baking powder
1 teaspoon baking soda
1 teaspoon cinnamon, ground
1 teaspoon nutmeg, ground
1 cup pecans or walnuts, chopped

¾ cup vegetable oil
3 eggs
2 cups sugar
2 teaspoons vanilla extract
3 cups zucchini, unpeeled and
   shredded

Preheat oven. Combine first 6 ingredients in a mixing bowl, make well in center of mixture. Combine oil, eggs, sugar, and vanilla. Mix well. Stir in zucchini. Add mixture to dry ingredients, stirring just until moistened. Spoon mixture into 2 greased and floured 9x5x3-inch loaf pans. Bake. Cool 10 minutes in pans, remove to wire rack and cool completely. Temperature: 350 degrees. Baking Time: 1 hour. Yield: 2 loaves.

Three "C" Bread

Carrots! Cherries! Coconut! What a treat!

3 eggs, beaten
½ cup vegetable oil
½ cup milk
1 cup sugar
2½ cups flour
1 teaspoon baking powder
1 teaspoon baking soda
1 teaspoon cinnamon, ground

½ teaspoon salt
2 cups carrots, shredded
1⅓ cups coconut, shredded
½ cup maraschino cherries,
   chopped
½ cup raisins
½ cup pecans, chopped

In a large bowl, combine eggs, oil, milk, and sugar. Beat well. Sift together flour, baking powder, baking soda, cinnamon, and salt. Add to egg mixture. Stir until moistened. Add carrots, coconut, cherries, raisins, and nuts, blending thoroughly. Generously grease 9x5x3-inch loaf pan. Pour batter into prepared pan. Bake in preheated oven. Let stand for 10 minutes before turning out to cool thoroughly. Wrap in foil and store in refrigerator or freeze up to 2 months. Temperature: 350 degrees. Baking Time: 55-60 minutes. Yield: 1 large loaf.

Casserole Onion Bread

1 cup milk, scalded
3 tablespoons sugar
1½ tablespoons butter
1 envelope onion soup mix

2 packages yeast
¾ cup warm water
4 cups flour

Blend first 4 ingredients in blender. Soften yeast in water; add to blended mixture when the milk mixture is lukewarm. Blend. Pour into flour and mix well. Cover bowl and let rise in warm place 45 minutes. Stir down batter, beat vigorously, and turn into greased 1½-quart casserole dish. Let rise until doubled and bake in preheated oven. Temperature: 375 degrees. Baking Time: 1 hour. Yield: 1 loaf.

Dilly Casserole Bread

Best served hot.

1 package yeast
¼ cup warm water
1 cup creamed cottage cheese
2 tablespoons sugar
1 tablespoon instant onion,
    minced

1 tablespoon butter
2 teaspoons dill seeds
1 teaspoon salt
¼ teaspoon baking soda
1 egg
2¼-2½ cups flour

Dissolve yeast in water. Heat cottage cheese to lukewarm. Combine sugar, onion, butter, dill seeds, salt, baking soda, and egg in a bowl with cheese and yeast mixture. Add flour to form stiff dough. Cover and let rise until double in bulk. Stir down dough. Turn into well greased 1½-quart casserole or 8-inch round pan. Let rise 30-40 minutes or until light. Bake in preheated oven. Brush with butter and sprinkle with salt. Temperature: 350 degrees. Baking Time: 30-40 minutes. Yield: 1 loaf.

Fluffy Biscuits

¼ cup sugar
1 tablespoon baking powder
1 teaspoon salt
1 teaspoon baking soda
2 cups buttermilk

1 cup shortening
1 package dry yeast
¼ cup warm water
5 cups flour, unsifted

Sift dry ingredients except soda which you will dissolve in buttermilk. Cut in shortening. Dissolve yeast in the ¼ cup warm water. Add to buttermilk and gradually stir into flour. Let rolls rise 1 hour. Temperature: 400 degrees. Baking Time: 10-12 minutes. Yield: 48.

No-Knead Oatmeal Raisin Bread

1 cup rolled oats, uncooked
½ cup molasses
⅓ cup shortening
1 tablespoon salt
1½ cups boiling water

2 packages yeast
½ cup warm water
2 eggs, beaten
1 cup seedless raisins
5½ cups flour, sifted

Put oats, molasses, shortening, and salt in a bowl. Pour in boiling water and stir to blend. While this is cooling to lukewarm, stir yeast into the ½ cup warm water. Add yeast and beaten eggs to oats mixture, stir to blend. Stir in raisins and flour. Cover and allow to rise for 1-2 hours in warm place until double in bulk. Beat dough down and divide into two parts. Turn each half into a well-greased loaf pan. Cover and let rise for 1-2 hours or until double in bulk again. Preheat oven. Bake. Temperature: 350 degrees. Baking Time: 40 minutes. Yield: 2 loaves.

Onion Sesame Bread

May be served as hot bread or split as buns for hamburgers.

⅓ cup very warm water
2 packages yeast
10½ ounces condensed onion
  soup, undiluted

4 cups biscuit mix
¼ cup melted butter or margarine
2 teaspoons sesame seeds
¼ cup Cheddar cheese, grated

Into very warm water, in small bowl, sprinkle yeast and stir until it is dissolved. Add onion soup. Stir into biscuit mix in bowl until well blended. Pour butter or margarine into a 12x8x2-inch baking dish; sprinkle with 1 teaspoon sesame seeds; cool. Spread batter evenly over butter. Sprinkle with cheese and 1 teaspoon sesame seeds. Cover with towel and let rise in warm place about ½ hour or until double. Preheat oven. Bake until done. Temperature: 400 degrees. Baking Time: 25 minutes. Yield: 6 large buns.

Spoon Rolls

1 package dry yeast
2 cups warm water
1 stick margarine

½ cup sugar
1 egg, beaten
4 cups self-rising flour

Dissolve yeast in warm water. Melt margarine. Beat together all ingredients. Refrigerate for 4 hours. Spoon into greased muffin pans and bake in preheated oven. Temperature: 400 degrees. Baking Time: 10 minutes. Yield: 24 rolls.

*"Plant a loving thought
In everything you do.
And the seed will blossom
Into love for you."*

Glazed Cheese Braids

This beautiful bread makes a delicious gift.

2 packages yeast
2 tablespoons sugar
1⅓ cups warm water
¼ cup instant dry milk
½ cup sugar

1¼ teaspoons salt
6 tablespoons salad oil
3 eggs
8 cups flour, sifted

Dissolve 2 packages yeast and 2 tablespoons sugar in warm water. Set aside. Mix together milk, ½ cup sugar, salt, salad oil, and eggs with mixer; add 6 cups flour. Add yeast mixture. Stir into a ball. Add remaining flour. Knead dough on floured surface 3-4 minutes. Place dough in a greased bowl; cover with a wet, warm towel. Let rise in warm place until double in bulk. Divide dough into 8 equal parts. Roll out dough one at a time on lightly floured surface, into a 10x13-inch rectangle. Spread each rectangle with ⅛ of the CREAM CHEESE FILLING. Roll as for jelly roll. Seal edge closed. Place on greased baking sheet edge side down. With scissors, make 2 cuts on a slant all of the way through the roll. Braid the three pieces together. Cover with warm, wet cloth. Let rise in warm place until double in bulk. Preheat oven. Bake. GLAZE while warm. Temperature: 350 degrees. Baking Time: 20 minutes. Yield: 8 loaves.

CREAM CHEESE FILLING

2 (8 ounces) cream cheese
¾ cup sugar
1 egg

⅛ teaspoon salt
2 teaspoons vanilla extract

Cream softened cream cheese and sugar until fluffy. Add remaining ingredients. Mix well.

GLAZE

2 cups powdered sugar, sifted
2 teaspoons vanilla extract

4 tablespoons milk

Combine all ingredients. Mix well.

*"God is your best friend;
The world is the best book;
The heart is the best preacher;
Time is the best teacher."*

Grace Moravian Church

GRACE MORAVIAN CHURCH

The Grace Moravian Church, 1401 North Main Street, Mount Airy, North Carolina, was organized in 1925. The church is best known for the Moravian Love Feast, Candle Service, Putz, Blessing, Moravian Christmas Star, Moravian Sugar Cake, Moravian Cookies, and Brass Band, all of which add special touches to its services.

Andy Griffith found himself in the Moravian Church Brass Band and Choir. He had a stirring voice and was an accomplished soloist. Although he was raised in the Baptist Church, Andy and his family joined Grace Moravian Church. Andy's dream was a slide trombone which the family could not afford. He cleaned the high school for $6.00 a week and saved enough money to buy a slide trombone for $33.00. No one in town knew how to play the instrument. A new Moravian pastor, The Reverend Ed T. Mickey, had just arrived in town and taught the members of the church to play brass instruments in the Moravian Church Band. Andy rode his cousin's bicycle two miles to the Moravian Church. Pastor Mickey did not know how to play a trombone, With the instruction book and Pastor Mickey's help, Andy learned to play the brass instrument. For three years, Pastor Mickey gave Andy free lessons. On Saturdays, Andy and four friends would play their brass instruments at land auction sales. They would earn $5.00 each and bought music supplies for the church. Pastor Mickey was a great influence in Andy's life, so much so, that Andy wanted to become a Moravian Minister. There was no money for Andy's education and with the help of Pastor Mickey, Andy enrolled in the University of North Carolina at Chapel Hill. After one year in college, Andy changed his major to music and drama.

The early Christians met and broke bread together to signify their union, fellowship, and love. In 1727, the Moravian Church revived the "Lovefeast" and has established the custom in celebrating the great church festivals. The Lovefeast is a worship service signifying brotherly love while sharing a simple meal of coffee and a slightly sweetened bun. It is celebrated in the spirit of the agape meal of the early Christians as they gathered to express their love for the Saviour and for one another. It is not a sacrament of the church.

The Candle Service, often celebrated with an accompanying Lovefeast, is a service where each worshipper receives a handmade beeswax candle trimmed with red ribbons which is lighted during the service. The red represents the blood of Jesus. The flame of the candle is the sacrifice of Christ for people and the flame of love which He came to kindle in human hearts. The lighted candle reminds us that Christ said, "I am the light of the world", and "You are the light of the world—let your light so shine before men, that they may see your good works, and glorify your Father which is in heaven", Matthew 5: 14-16.

Moravian Sugar Cake

This is a simple version of the delicious treat.

1 package Pillsbury Hot Roll Mix
¾ cup very warm water (105 to
   115 degrees F.)
⅓ cup sugar
⅓ cup instant nonfat dry milk

⅓ cup instant mashed potato
   flakes
2 eggs
⅓ cup butter, melted

TOPPING
⅔ cup brown sugar, firmly
   packed
1 teaspoon cinnamon, ground

½ cup butter, melted
½ cup nuts, chopped

Grease 13x9-inch pan. Dissolve yeast from mix in warm water. Stir in half of flour from mix and remaining cake ingredients; beat 2 minutes at medium speed. Stir in remaining flour; beat well. Cover; let rise in warm place until doubled in size, about 45 minutes, and stir down; spread in prepared pan. Cover; let rise until doubled in size, about 45 minutes. Preheat oven. Make small pockets in dough by pressing with a floured fingertip. Sprinkle brown sugar-cinnamon mixture over dough. Drizzle with melted butter; sprinkle with nuts. Bake. Temperature: 375 degrees. Baking Time: 15-20 minutes. Yield: 15 servings.

Grandma's Chocolate Dessert

MICROWAVE. Eat til it ouches you!

2 tablespoons margarine
¾ cup sugar
2 tablespoons cocoa
½ cup milk

1 cup flour, unsifted
1½ teaspoons baking powder
¼ teaspoon salt
½ cup nuts, chopped fine

TOPPING
½ cup sugar
1 tablespoons cocoa

½ cup brown sugar, packed
1 cup water

MICROWAVE, HIGH, 2 tablespoons margarine for 30-45 seconds or until melted in medium bowl. Stir in ¾ cup sugar, 2 tablespoons cocoa, milk, flour, baking powder and salt; beat until smooth. Stir in nuts. Spoon batter into ungreased 2-quart casserole dish. Combine all topping ingredients except water. Sprinkle TOPPING evenly on top of cake batter. Pour water all over. MICROWAVE, MEDIUM, uncovered for 13 minutes rotating dish once. Then MICROWAVE, HIGH, 2-3 minutes or until cake is no longer doughy. (Sauce is in the bottom of dish). Serve warm with or without whipped cream or ice cream. Yield: 6-8 servings.

Oatmeal Cake

Eat til it ouches you!

1¼ cups boiling water
1 cup quick oats
½ cup shortening
1 cup brown sugar, packed
1 cup sugar
2 eggs

1⅓ cups flour
1 teaspoon baking soda
½ teaspoon cinnamon, ground
½ teaspoon nutmeg, ground
1 teaspoon vanilla extract

Preheat oven. Pour boiling water over oats. Set aside. Cream together shortening, brown sugar, and sugar. Add eggs, beating after each addition. Whip up oats and add to creamed mixture. Sift together flour, soda, cinnamon, and nutmeg. Add gradually the dry mixture and vanilla. Mix well. Bake in greased and floured 7½x11½-inch pan. Remove from oven and cover with TOPPING. Temperature: 350 degrees. Baking Time: 45-50 minutes. Yield: 24 squares.

TOPPING
1 stick butter or margarine
1 cup brown sugar, packed
2 egg yolks

1 can coconut
1 cup nuts, chopped

Cream butter and sugar, add egg yolks, and beat well. Stir in coconut and nuts. Spread topping over cake, return to oven, and broil until lightly browned.

Pan Coating

¼ cup plus 2 tablespoons flour
¼ cup vegetable oil

¼ cup shortening

Mix together and store in a jar. Keep it hand to grease cake pans to prevent from sticking. Use this instead of shortening and flour.

Peanut Butter Cake

¾ cup butter
¾ cup creamy peanut butter
2 cups brown sugar, firmly
    packed
1 teaspoon vanilla extract
3 eggs

2 cups flour
1 tablespoon baking powder
½ teaspoon salt
1 cup milk
½ cup peanuts, chopped

Preheat oven. Combine butter and peanut butter in a large mixing bowl; cream well. Add sugar, and beat well. Add vanilla, mix well. Add eggs, one at time, beating well after each addition. Sift together flour, baking powder, and salt, gradually add to creamed mixture alternately with milk, beating well. Spoon into a greased 13x9x2-inch baking pan. Bake until cake tests done. When cool, spread with CHOCOLATE FROSTING, and sprinkle with peanuts. Cut into squares. Temperature: 350 degrees. Baking Time: 45-50 minutes. Yield: 15-20 servings.

CHOCOLATE FROSTING

6 tablespoons butter or margarine
2 squares unsweetened chocolate,
    melted

3 cups confectioner's sugar, sifted
1 teaspoon vanilla extract
¼ cup milk (approximately)

Cream butter or margarine until soft; add chocolate; gradually stir in 1 cup sugar. Add vanilla. Add remaining sugar alternately with milk, beating until smooth after each addition, and add milk, a tablespoon at a time until proper consistency to spread.

Christmas Recipe

"Take the early days of December and add a generous portion of snow over which a sparkling of ice has been sifted. Next, take some brisk winter air and the blush of early morning sunlight; cream these two ingredients until the days tingle with expectation. Add to this the joy of a generous heart, blended with the wonder of a radiant-eyed child. Gently fold in the soft touch of a grandparent's hands. Set this aside for a moment while you catch a bit of laughter from under the mistletoe. Marinate this in love before you add it to the above mixture. Form all ingredients into a warmth of good will and set aside to bubble. Keep this bubbling in a surrounding of happiness for days while you address your cards, wrap gifts, clean the house, and prepare for the day when it is to be served on a platter of lasting memories. Then surrounded by the aroma from the Christmas tree, garnish the above mixture with silver, gold, red, and green trimmings, which have been dipped in the love of mankind. Serve December the 25th, after you have offered a prayer of gratitude."

Perfect White Cake

2¾ cups cake flour, sifted
4 teaspoons baking powder
¾ teaspoon salt
¾ cup butter or margarine
1½ cups sugar

1 teaspoon vanilla extract
1 teaspoon almond extract
1 cup milk
4 egg whites

Have all ingredients at room temperature. Preheat oven. Resift flour with baking powder and salt. Cream butter thoroughly. Add 1 cup sugar gradually. Combine flavorings with milk. Add flour and milk alternately to butter mixture. Beat egg whites until they stand in peaks, add ½ cup sugar slowly and beat until satiny. Fold in egg white mixture. Pour into greased and floured three 8-inch pans. Tap pans sharply on table to remove air bubbles. Place ICING between layers on top and sides. Bake. Temperature: 350 degrees. Baking Time: 25 minutes. Yield: 1 cake.

ICING

⅓ cup margarine or butter
3 cups confectioner's sugar

3 tablespoons cream
1 teaspoon rum flavoring

Mix butter, sugar, and cream until smooth and fluffy. Add flavoring.

RUM-BUTTER CUP CAKES: Using PERFECT WHITE CAKE recipe, fill muffin pans (lined with paper cups) two-thirds full. Bake. When cool, remove paper from cakes. Ice top and sides of cakes and roll in pecans chopped in blender. Temperature: 350 degrees. Baking Time: 20 minutes. Yield: 2 dozen.

Earthquake Cake

1½ cups pecans, chopped
3 ounces coconut
1 German chocolate cake mix

1 stick margarine
8 ounces cream cheese
1 box powdered sugar

Preheat oven. Grease a 9x13-inch pan. Sprinkle pecans in bottom of pan. Sprinkle coconut over pecans. Prepare cake mix according to package directions. Pour over pecans and coconut. Melt margarine and cream cheese together, add powdered sugar; mix well. Pour mixture over cake batter. Bake. Remove from oven and cool. Cut into squares and serve. Temperature: 350 degrees. Baking Time: 45 minutes. Yield: 24 servings.

Chess Cake

1 (2 layer) yellow cake mix
1 egg, beaten
1 stick butter, melted

3 eggs
1 box powdered sugar
8 ounces cream cheese

Preheat oven. Mix cake mix, beaten egg, and butter. Pour into greased and floured 9x13-inch dish. Beat 3 eggs, add powdered sugar and cream cheese. Beat well and pour over cake mix mixture. Bake. Note: You can tell if cake is done by moving oven rack—if cake is not done, it will "shake" in middle. Top will "fall" as it cools. Temperature: 350 degrees. Baking Time: 35-40 minutes. Yield: 1 cake.

Hawaiian Sunset Cake

Yum! Yum! Yum!

1 supreme orange cake mix
4 eggs
3 ounces instant vanilla pudding

3 ounces orange gelatin
½ cup oil
1½ cups milk

Mix all ingredients together. Beat 3 minutes on medium speed. Pour into three 9-inch greased and floured cake pans. Bake. Cool layers. Temperature: 350 degrees. Baking Time: 30 minutes. Yield: 1 cake.

FILLING

15 ounces crushed pineapple,
   drained well
12 ounces frozen coconut

8 ounces sour cream
2 cups sugar

Take spoon and remove as much liquid as possible from pineapple. Mix all ingredients. Take out one cup of this mixture and reserve for topping recipe. Spread FILLING between layers and on top of cake.

TOPPING

1 cup filling mixture

8 ounces cool whip

Mix together. Spread TOPPING on sides and top of cake. FILLING is already on the top of the cake.

"The best diet is pushing yourself away from the table."

Banana Crunch Cake

5 tablespoons butter or margarine
7½ ounces coconut pecan frosting
   mix or 8¼ ounces coconut
   almond frosting mix
1 cup regular rolled oats

1 cup sour cream
4 eggs
2 large bananas, mashed
17 ounces yellow cake mix

Grease and flour a 10-inch tube pan. Preheat oven. Melt butter in saucepan; stir in frosting mix and oats until crumbly. Set aside. Blend sour cream, eggs, and bananas in large bowl until smooth. Blend in cake mix; beat 2 minutes at medium speed with electric mixer (high speed with portable mixer.) Pour ⅓ of batter into prepared pan. Sprinkle with ⅓ of crumb mixture. Repeat twice with batter and crumbs, ending with crumb mixture. Bake until toothpick inserted in center comes out clean. Cool in pan 15 minutes. Turn pan upside down on cake rack; then turn cake so crumb mixture is on top. Temperature: 350 degrees. Baking Time: 50-60 minutes. Yield: 1 (10-inch) cake.

Pineapple-Blueberry Upside-down Cake

¼ cup margarine
½ cup brown sugar, packed
1 pound 14 ounces can sliced
   pineapple with syrup

12 or 13½ ounces blueberry
   muffin mix

Drain pineapple; save syrup. Melt margarine in small electric frypan. Sprinkle in sugar evenly, place 4-6 slices of pineapple on top. Sprinkle berries on top of pineapple. Mix muffin batter as directed on package, using pineapple syrup for liquid. (No berries in batter.) Spread batter over pineapple. Bake with lid on and vent opened. Remove lid and let cool 5 minutes; invert on plate. Serve hot. Temperature: 375 degrees. Baking Time: 30-35 minutes. Yield: 6-8 servings.

Poppy Seed Cake

4 eggs, well beaten
8 ounces sour cream
6 ounces vanilla pudding mix,
   instant

1 yellow cake mix
¾ cup cooking oil
½ cup dry sherry
1 container poppy seeds

Preheat oven. Mix all ingredients well. Pour into well-greased bundt cake pan. Bake. Temperature: 350 degrees. Baking Time: 1 hour. Yield: 1 cake.

Cherry Chocolate Cake

1 Devils food cake mix   1 can cherry pie filling
1 teaspoon almond flavoring

Preheat oven. Prepare cake mix according to package directions. Add flavoring and pie filling. Bake in greased and floured jelly roll pan. Pour ICING over cake while cake is hot. Roll cake. Temperature: 350 degrees. Baking Time: 30 minutes. Yield: 1 rolled cake.

ICING
1 cup sugar   5 tablespoons margarine
⅓ cup milk   6 ounces chocolate chips

Mix together sugar, milk, and margarine; boil 1 minute. Add chocolate chips.

Milky Way Cake

4 Milky Way bars   4 eggs
1 stick margarine   2½ cups flour
1 cup pecans, chopped   1½ teaspoons baking soda
1 cup shortening   1½ cups buttermilk
2 cups sugar   2 teaspoons vanilla extract

Preheat oven. Melt Milky Way bars and margarine in saucepan over low heat. Stir in nuts and keep warm. Cream shortening and sugar thoroughly. Add eggs, one at a time, beating after each addition. Sift together dry ingredients and add alternately with buttermilk and vanilla. Add chocolate mixture to batter and mix until well blended. Bake in three 8-inch greased layer pans. Cool thoroughly. Frost with CARAMEL FROSTING. Temperature: 350 degrees. Baking Time: 30-35 minutes. Yield: 3 layers.

CARAMEL FROSTING
½ cup margarine   ½ cup milk
1½ cups brown sugar, packed   3 cups powdered sugar, sifted

In saucepan, melt margarine and brown sugar. Stir and boil over low heat for 2 minutes, stirring constantly. Add milk and stir until mixture boils. Remove from heat and let cool. Slowly add powdered sugar. Beat well until thick enough to spread. Frost cake and serve.

Mound Cake

⅔ cup margarine
1½ cups sugar
2 eggs
2 cups flour, sifted

½ teaspoon baking soda
1¼ teaspoons baking powder
4 tablespoons cocoa
1 cup buttermilk

Preheat oven. Cream together margarine and sugar. Add eggs, blend well. Sift together flour, soda, baking powder, and cocoa. Alternately add flour mixture and buttermilk. Place in two 9-inch greased and floured cake pans. Bake. Cool, split the two layers to make 4 layers. The COCONUT FILLING goes between each layer. Frost cake with FUDGE FROSTING. Temperature: 350 degrees. Baking Time: 25 minutes. Yield: 1 cake.

COCONUT FILLING
1 cup evaporated milk
2 cups coconut
12 large marshmallows

1 cup sugar
1 cup pecans, chopped

Place all ingredients in a saucepan. Boil together for 5 minutes.

FUDGE FROSTING
⅓ cup milk
¼ cup margarine
6 ounces semisweet chocolate
  morsels

1 teaspoon vanilla extract
2¼ cups confectioner's sugar,
  sifted

Combine milk and margarine. Bring to a boil. Remove from heat and add chocolate, vanilla, and sugar. Blend together well.

Baked Devils' Float

1 cup sugar
1¾ cups water
12 marshmallows, quartered
2 tablespoons shortening
⅓ cup nuts, chopped
1 cup flour

½ teaspoon salt
1 teaspoon baking powder
3 tablespoons cocoa
½ cup milk
1 teaspoon vanilla extract

Preheat oven. Boil water and ½ cup sugar for 5 minutes; pour into 1½-quart baking dish; top with marshmallows. Cream shortening and remaining ½ cup sugar. Sift flour, baking powder, salt, and cocoa; add alternately with milk and vanilla to creamed mixture. Add nuts. Drop by spoon over marshmallow mixture, cover. Bake. Temperature: 350 degrees. Baking Time: 45 minutes. Yield: 1 cake.

Chocolate Cherry Upside-down Cake

21 ounces cherry pie filling
2¼ cups flour
1½ cups sugar
¾ cup cocoa
1½ teaspoons soda

¾ teaspoon salt
1½ cups water
½ cup cooking oil
¼ cup vinegar
1½ teaspoons vanilla extract

Preheat oven. Spread cherry pie filling evenly over bottom of greased 13x9x2-inch baking pan. In large bowl, stir together flour, sugar, cocoa, soda, and salt. In another bowl, combine water, oil, vinegar, and vanilla. Add liquid ingredients to flour mixture all at once, stir to moisten. Pour batter evenly over cherry pie filling. Bake until cake tests done. Cool 10 minutes in pan; invert and cool. Temperature: 350 degrees. Baking Time: 30-35 minutes. Yield: 24 squares.

Scotch Chocolate Cake

King of the chocolate cakes!

2 cups flour, sifted
2 cups sugar
½ teaspoon salt
1 teaspoon cinnamon, ground
1 stick margarine
½ cup shortening

1 cup water
3 tablespoons cocoa
2 eggs, well beaten
1 teaspoon baking soda
½ cup buttermilk
1 teaspoon vanilla extract

Preheat oven. Sift flour with sugar, salt, and cinnamon. In a saucepan, put margarine, shortening, water, and cocoa. Bring to boil. Pour gradually over flour and sugar mixture. In another bowl, put eggs, soda, buttermilk, and vanilla. Add to above mixture and mix well. Bake in greased and floured shallow 15½x10½x2-inch pan. Start icing last 5 minutes of baking time. Temperature: 350 degrees. Baking Time: 20 minutes. Yield: 24 squares.

ICING FOR SCOTCH CHOCOLATE CAKE

1 stick margarine
3 tablespoons cocoa
6 tablespoons milk
1 box confectioner's sugar

½ cup pecans, chopped
½ teaspoon vanilla extract
1 cup coconut

Mix margarine, cocoa, milk in saucepan. Heat over low heat (do not boil). Remove from heat, add sugar, pecans, coconut, and vanilla. Mix well; frost cake as soon as you remove the cake from the oven.

Walnut Chocolate Cake

1 cup water
1½ teaspoons baking soda
½ cup cocoa
1¾ cups sugar
⅔ cup butter
2 eggs

2½ cups flour, sifted
½ teaspoon salt
¾ cup buttermilk
1 teaspoon vanilla extract
1 cup walnuts, chopped

Preheat oven. Mix water, soda, and cocoa and let stand while mixing batter. Cream sugar and butter. Add eggs, one at a time. Add alternately flour, salt, buttermilk, and vanilla. Combine batter with first mixture. Add walnuts. Bake in three 8-inch layer pans. Temperature: 350 degrees. Baking Time: 30-40 minutes. Yield: 20 slices.

FILLING
2 cups sugar
2 squares chocolate

½ cup milk
1 stick butter

Mix all ingredients and bring to boil and cook 2 minutes without stirring. Beat well and spread on cooled cake.

Golden Dream Cake

1 cup butter
2½ cups sugar
3 cups cake flour
1 teaspoon baking soda
1 cup buttermilk

5 tablespoons strong coffee
4 teaspoons cocoa
5 eggs, separated
1 teaspoon vanilla extract
Pinch salt

Preheat oven. Cream butter, add sugar, and cream thoroughly. Sift dry ingredients together. Separate egg yolks and whites; add yolks to sugar and butter. Dissolve soda in buttermilk, add dry ingredients alternately with milk. Stir in coffee and vanilla. Fold in beaten egg whites. Bake in 4 (9-inch) layer pans. Place ICING on cooled cake. Temperature: 375 degrees. Baking Time: 30-35 minutes. Yield: 1 cake.

ICING
½ cup butter
2 teaspoons cocoa
1 pound powdered sugar

1 egg yolk, beaten
3 tablespoons strong coffee
1 teaspoon vanilla extract

Sift dry ingredients. Cream butter and dry ingredients, creaming thoroughly. Add beaten egg yolk, coffee, and vanilla. Beat until soft and fluffy.

Chocolate Fruitcake

Best if allowed to ripen—six weeks.

⅓ pound dried apricots,
  quartered
3 ounces candied orange peel,
  chopped
½ pound candied pineapple,
  cubed
15 ounces golden seedless raisins
4 cups pecans halves

½ cup flour, sifted
19-20 ounces chocolate cake mix
4 eggs
1-3 teaspoons instant coffee
2 teaspoons salt
2 teaspoons vanilla extract
¼ cup water

Leave pecans in halves or broken pieces and do not dice fruits finely as cake will slice prettier if you leave them in large pieces. Combine fruits and nuts and dredge with flour. Empty cake mix into small mixer bowl. Add 1 egg, coffee, salt, vanilla, and water. Beat 2 minutes at medium speed on electric mixer. Blend in remaining 3 eggs, one at a time. Beat 2 more minutes at medium speed. Blend batter into fruit-nut mixture. Spread evenly in well-greased, wax-paper lined, 9-inch tube can pan. Line bottom of pan with 3 thicknesses waxed paper and grease top layer of paper. Batter should be slightly rounded when put in pan to prevent depression in center when cake is baked. Place shallow pan of water on bottom rack of oven during baking. Bake in preheated oven. Cool cake in pan for 10 minutes. Turn out, place in upright position to cool thoroughly. Temperature: 275 degrees. Baking Time: 3-3½ hours. Yield: 1 cake.

Little Fruit Cakes

A real treat for tea time!

5 cups flour, sifted
1 pound soft butter
11 eggs yolks
2½ cups sugar
1 lemon (juice)
1 teaspoon vanilla extract
1 pound white raisins
½ teaspoon salt

11 eggs whites
½ pound candied cherries,
  quartered
½ pound candied pineapple, diced
3 cups nuts, chopped fine
1 pound citron and/or 1 package
  orange peel

Preheat oven. Work flour into butter. Mix egg yolks with sugar and combine with flour-butter mixture. Add vanilla and lemon juice. Blend well. Beat egg whites, fold into batter. Fold in fruit which has been dredged with part of the flour. For small individual cakes, bake in greased and floured 1¾-inch muffin pan. Bake. Temperature: 275 degrees. Baking Time: 30-45 minutes. Note: For tube cake, Temperature: 275 degrees. Baking Time: 2-3 hours.

Orange Fruit Cake

Eat til it ouches you!

½ cup butter or margarine
1 cup sugar
2 eggs
1 teaspoon baking soda
⅔ cup buttermilk
2 cups flour

½ teaspoon salt
1 teaspoon orange rind, grated
1 cup dates, seeded and chopped
   or raisins
½ cup pecans, chopped

Preheat oven. Cream the butter and sugar until fluffy, add eggs, one at a time, and beat thoroughly after each addition. Dissolve soda in buttermilk and add alternately with flour and salt (sifted together). Beat until very smooth. Stir in the rind, dates, and nuts. Place in 7½x11½-inch pan. Bake. While cake is hot spread with GLAZE. Temperature: 350 degrees. Baking Time: 40 minutes. Yield: 1 cake.

GLAZE
1 cup sugar
1 teaspoon orange rind, grated

½ cup orange juice

Mix together until sugar has dissolved and spread on top of hot cake. This mixture forms a tasty sugar coating over the cake.

Victorian Applesauce Cake

2 cups cake flour, sifted
1½ cups sugar
1½ teaspoons baking soda
1½ teaspoons salt
2 tablespoons cocoa
½ teaspoon each cinnamon,
   cloves, nutmeg, allspice,
   ground

½ cup shortening
1½ cups applesauce, unsweetened
2 eggs, unbeaten
¾ cup dates, chopped
¾ cup raisins, chopped
⅓ cup citron, diced (optional)
¾ cup nuts, chopped

TOPPING
¼ cup nuts, chopped

2 tablespoons sugar

Mix topping ingredients together, set aside. Preheat oven. Sift flour, sugar, soda, salt, cocoa, and spices into mixing bowl. Drop in shortening (no creaming needed). Add applesauce, mix well. Scrape bowl and spoon. Add eggs, beat well. Add dates, raisins, citron, and nuts; mix thoroughly. Pour batter into greased and floured tube pan. Sprinkle nut-sugar TOPPING over batter. (Topping may be omitted, if desired.) Bake. Temperature: 350 degrees. Baking Time: 1 hour 25-35 minutes. Yield: 1 cake.

Dark Fruit Cake

Makes a wonderful gift!

1 pound raisins
1 pound pitted dates
1 pound citron
1 pound currants
1½ pounds candied cherries
½ pound candied orange peel
¼ pound candied lemon peel
1½ pounds nuts
1 pound butter
1 pound light brown sugar

12 eggs
4 cups flour, sifted
1 teaspoon baking soda
½ teaspoon nutmeg, ground
½ teaspoon mace, ground
½ teaspoon cloves, ground
1 teaspoon cinnamon, ground
1 teaspoon allspice, ground
1 teaspoon salt
1 cup molasses

Cut fruit into small pieces and chop nuts. Preheat oven. Cream butter and sugar together. Beat eggs and add to creamed mixture. Blend well. Sift dry ingredients together and add to creamed mixture alternately with molasses. Add batter to fruits and nuts. Mix together thoroughly, using hands, if necessary. Pour into two large tube pans which have been greased and lined with greased brown paper, cut to fit. Cover tops with aluminum foil squeezed tightly down around the edge of pans. Bake in preheated oven until done. Test the cakes with a toothpick to determine doneness and pans will make the time vary. Remove the foil the last 30 minutes or so to allow tops of cakes to dry out. Temperature: 275 degrees. Baking Time: 4 hours 20 minutes. Yield: 2 cakes or about 15 pounds.

Tennessee Jam Cake

Frost with favorite frosting.

½ cup margarine
1 cup light brown sugar, packed
3 eggs, separated
2 cups cake flour, sifted
½ teaspoon baking soda
2 teaspoons baking powder

1 teaspoon nutmeg, ground
¼ teaspoon cloves, ground
1 cup seedless blackberry
    preserves
⅓ cup buttermilk

Preheat oven. Cream margarine and add sugar slowly, creaming until light and fluffy. Add egg yolks and mix well. Sift dry ingredients together. Add alternately with the combined preserves and buttermilk. Fold in stiffly beaten egg whites. Pour into two 9-inch waxed paper lined and greased layer pans. Bake. Temperature: 375 degrees. Baking Time: 30-35 minutes. Yield: 1 cake.

Oriental Fruit Cake

2 cups flour, sifted
1 teaspoon baking powder
½ teaspoon cloves, ground
½ teaspoon allspice, ground
½ teaspoon cinnamon, ground
½ cup butter or margarine

1¼ cups sugar
3 eggs, well beaten
⅓ cup milk
½ cup nuts, chopped
½ cup seedless raisins

Preheat oven. Sift flour, baking powder, and spices together. Cream butter and sugar until light and fluffy. Add beaten eggs and mix well. Add flour mixture alternately with milk. Stir in nuts and raisins. Save ¾ cup batter for topping. Spread remaining batter in a 9x9x2-inch pan lined on bottom with waxed paper. Bake. Cool cake, then spread with ORIENTAL FRUIT CAKE TOPPING. Temperature: 375 degrees. Baking Time: 25-30 minutes. Yield: 12 servings.

ORIENTAL FRUIT CAKE TOPPING
1 cup sugar
½ cup water
¾ cup ORIENTAL FRUIT CAKE
    BATTER
3 tablespoons lemon juice
1 teaspoon lemon rind, grated
1½ tablespoons butter or
    margarine, melted

2 tablespoons green candied
    cherries, chopped
2 tablespoons red candied
    cherries, chopped
2 tablespoons candied pineapple,
    chopped
½ cup nuts, chopped
1⅓ cups coconut, flaked

Combine sugar and water; boil until syrupy and mixture forms a thread. Add cake batter, lemon juice, and rind. Cook over medium heat until it thickens, stirring constantly. Then add melted butter, candied fruits, nuts, and coconut. Cool slightly. Spread on cool cake.

Hawaiian Pineapple Nut Cake

¾ cup flour
¼ teaspoon baking soda
1 teaspoon salt
½ cup butter, melted
1 cup sugar

2 eggs, beaten
8 ounces crushed pineapple,
    drained
½ cup nuts, chopped
1 cup cream, sweetened, whipped

Preheat oven. Sift together flour, soda, and salt. Combine butter and sugar. Add eggs and mix well. Sift flour mixture into the batter, stirring till blended. Add pineapple and nuts. Pour into greased 9-inch pan. Bake. Top with whipped cream for serving. Temperature: 325 degrees. Baking Time: 1 hour. Yield: 6-8 servings.

Dr. Bird Cake

3 cups flour
1 teaspoon baking soda
1 teaspoon cinnamon, ground
2 cups sugar
1 teaspoon salt
1½ cups vegetable oil

1 cup pecans, chopped
3 eggs
1½ teaspoons vanilla extract
8 ounces crushed pineapple
2 cups bananas, chopped

Preheat oven. In a large bowl, mix together flour, soda, cinnamon, sugar, and salt. Add, but do not beat: vegetable oil, nuts, eggs, vanilla, pineapple, and bananas. Do not use mixer. Stir only until blended. Bake in greased and floured tube pan. Allow cake to cool completely before FROSTING. Temperature: 325 degrees. Baking Time: 1 hour 20 minutes. Yield: 20 servings.

FROSTING

8 ounces cream cheese
1 stick margarine

1 teaspoon vanilla extract
1 pound powdered sugar

Cream together cream cheese and margarine; add vanilla. Add sugar and beat until smooth.

Mincemeat Cake

Freezes well.

½ cup soft shortening or
    margarine
1 cup light brown sugar, packed
2 cups flour, sifted
1 pound mincemeat
1 cup dates, chopped

1 cup pecans, chopped
1 tablespoon baking soda
1 tablespoon hot water
1 teaspoon vanilla extract
2 egg yolks
2 egg whites

Preheat oven. Cream shortening and sugar until light and fluffy. Mix ½ cup flour with fruits, and nuts. Dissolve soda in hot water. Add all ingredients except egg whites to creamed mixture and blend. Fold in stiffly beaten egg whites and turn batter in greased paper lined 9x5x3-inch loaf pan. Bake. Temperature: 300 degrees. Baking Time: 1½-2 hours. Yield: 1 loaf.

What to do if fruit cake is too dry! Cover completely with sliced apples, moist cloth with wine, or apple juice. Wrap tightly with plastic wrap and aluminium foil to seal in moisture. Repeat as needed until fruit cake reaches desired moisture.

Orange Slice Cake

1 package dates	4 eggs
1 pound orange slices (candy)	½ cup buttermilk
2 cups pecans, chopped	3½ cups flour
1 cup margarine	1 teaspoon baking soda
2 cups sugar	1 can coconut

Preheat oven. Prepare the fruit, candy, and nuts by cutting up finely and rolling in a portion of the flour. Cream margarine with sugar and add eggs, one at a time, blending well. Add buttermilk. Sift together all remaining flour with soda and add to mixture. Fold in nuts, dates, and orange slices; add coconut. Grease and flour 10-inch tube pan; add batter. Bake. Pour GLAZE on cake while cake is still in pan and hot. Leave cake in tube pan until well cooled and all juice is absorbed. Temperature: 250 degrees. Baking Time: 3 hours. Yield: 1 cake.

GLAZE

2 cups confectioner's sugar	1 cup orange juice

Mix sugar and orange juice well and spread on top of hot cake in pan.

White Fruit Cake

2 pounds glazed cherries, halved	1 tablespoon lemon extract
2 pounds glazed pineapple, diced	1 teaspoon baking soda
1 pound white raisins	1 teaspoon salt
1 pound pecans, chopped	1 teaspoon cinnamon, ground
4 cups flour	1 teaspoon nutmeg, ground
1 cup butter	1 teaspoon mace, ground
1½ cups sugar	1 cup buttermilk
5 eggs	3½ ounces coconut, flaked
1 tablespoon vanilla extract	

Preheat oven. Dredge cherries, pineapple, raisins, and pecans in 1 cup flour. Cream softened butter and sugar together until fluffy. Add eggs, one at a time, beating well after each addition. Add vanilla and lemon extracts. Sift soda, salt, cinnamon, nutmeg, and mace with remaining 3 cups flour; add to creamed mixture alternately with buttermilk. Mix in coconut. Fold in fruit and nuts. Bake in 10-inch tube pan lined with waxed paper. Temperature: 250 degrees. Baking Time: 3 hours. Yield: 10 pound fruit cake. NOTE: Batter may be used for 1 pound loaves. Temperature: 250 degrees. Baking Time: 1½ hours.

Pineapple Upside-down Cake

Use the electric mixer and frypan.

NOTE: All ingredients for batter should be ready for mixing before starting to preheat frypan for bottom mixture.

BOTTOM MIXTURE

¼ cup butter or margarine
1 cup light brown sugar, packed
20 ounces pineapple slices,
    drained

Maraschino cherries or pecans
    (optional)

Set dial of electric frypan on 220 degrees. Add butter. When melted, add brown sugar and spread evenly over surface of frypan. Arrange drained pineapple slices over sugar mixture. Maraschino cherries, nuts, or other garnishes may be added. Cover and leave at 220 degrees while mixing batter.

BATTER

1½ cups flour, sifted
¾ cup sugar
2 teaspoons baking powder
½ teaspoon salt
⅓ cup soft shortening

½ cup milk
1 teaspoon vanilla extract or ½
    tablespoon orange or lemon
    rind, grated
1 egg, unbeaten

Sift together flour, sugar, baking powder, and salt in large mixing bowl. Add shortening, milk, and flavoring. Beat on low speed 1½ minutes while scraping bowl. Add egg and beat 1½ minutes longer.

Set dial at 280 degrees if using glass cover, 260 degrees if using metal cover. Spread batter evenly over BOTTOM MIXTURE. Cover and bake 20-30 minutes or until cake is no longer moist or sticky on top. Loosen around edges with a spatula; invert onto a square tray or plate. Let stand a few seconds before lifting frypan. Serve garnished with whipped cream or ice cream. Baking Time: 20-30 minutes. Yield: 8-10 servings.

Banana Spice Cake

Eat til it ouches you!

2½ cups cake flour, sifted
1⅔ cups sugar
1¼ teaspoons baking soda
1¼ teaspoons baking powder
1 teaspoon salt
1½ teaspoons nutmeg, ground
¾ teaspoon cloves, ground
⅔ cup shortening

⅔ cup buttermilk
1¼ cups bananas, mashed
    (3 medium)
2 eggs, unbeaten
1 large banana, sliced
2 squares sweet cooking chocolate
1 tablespoon butter or margarine

Preheat oven. Sift dry ingredients into large mixer bowl. Add shortening, buttermilk, and mashed bananas; mix until flour is dampened. Beat at low speed for 2 minutes. Add eggs; beat 1 minute. Turn batter into three 8-inch or two 9-inch greased and floured layer cake pans. Bake until cake springs back when lightly touched with fingertip. Spread QUICK SEA-FOAM FROST-ING between cooled layers; top with banana slices; put layers together. Frost cake; make swirls. Mix melted chocolate and butter; spoon into swirls. Temperature: 350 degrees. Baking Time: 30-35 minutes. Yield: 1 cake.

QUICK SEA-FOAM FROSTING
2 egg whites
1½ cups brown sugar, firmly
    packed

5 tablespoons water
Dash salt
1 teaspoon vanilla extract

Combine egg whites, brown sugar, water and salt in top of double boiler; beat slightly to mix. Place over rapidly boiling water; beat with electric mixer at high speed until frosting stands in peaks, about 7 minutes. Remove from heat; add vanilla. Beat ½ minute or until thick enough to spread.

Red Earth Cake

½ cup butter
1½ cups sugar
2 eggs
4 tablespoons cocoa
3 tablespoons hot coffee
3 teaspoons red food coloring

1 teaspoon vanilla extract
1 teaspoon baking soda
1 cup buttermilk
2 cups flour
Dash salt

Preheat oven. Cream butter and sugar. Beat in eggs, one at a time. Mix together cocoa, coffee, red coloring, and vanilla. Stir into mixture. Add soda to buttermilk. Add flour, salt, and buttermilk to mixture alternately. Bake in two 9-inch layer pans. Ice with your favorite frosting. Temperature: 350 degrees. Baking Time: 25-30 minutes. Yield: 1 cake.

Italian Creme Cake

Eat til it ouches you!

1 stick margarine
½ cup shortening
2 cups sugar
5 eggs, separated
2 cups flour

1 teaspoon baking soda
1 cup buttermilk
1 teaspoon vanilla extract
1 cup pecans, chopped
1 cup coconut, grated

Preheat oven. Cream margarine, shortening, and sugar. Add egg yolks. Sift flour and soda. Add to mixture alternately with buttermilk and vanilla. Stir in pecans and coconut. Fold in beaten egg whites. Line three 9-inch cake pans with waxed paper and then grease and flour. Pour batter into pans. Bake and cool. Spread ICING between layers and cover sides and top of cake. Temperature: 350 degrees. Baking Time: 20 minutes. Yield: 1 cake.

ICING
8 ounces cream cheese
1 stick margarine

1 pound confectioner's sugar
1 teaspoon vanilla extract

Cheese should be at room temperature. Mix all ingredients. If too thick, add milk.

Black Walnut Cake

Eat til it ouches you!

2 sticks butter
½ cup shortening
1½ cups brown sugar, packed
1½ cups sugar
5 eggs
3 cups flour, sifted

1 teaspoon baking powder
½ teaspoon salt (optional)
1 cup milk
1 teaspoon vanilla extract
½ cup walnuts, chopped

Preheat oven. Cream butter, shortening, brown sugar, and sugar together. Add eggs, one at a time, beating after each. Sift together flour, baking powder, and salt. Add dry ingredients alternately with milk. Add vanilla extract and walnuts. Place in a greased and floured tube cake pan. Bake. Temperature: 325 degrees. Baking Time: 1½ hours. Yield: 1 cake.

ICING
8 ounces cream cheese
½ stick butter
1 pound confectioner's sugar,
     sifted

1 teaspoon vanilla extract
½ cup walnuts, chopped

Cream together cream cheese and butter. Add sugar, mix well. Add vanilla extract and walnuts. Frost BLACK WALNUT CAKE with icing.

Brown Sugar Pound Cake

1 cup shortening
1 stick margarine
1 pound light brown sugar, sifted
5 eggs
3 cups flour, sifted

½ teaspoon baking powder
½ teaspoon salt
1 cup evaporated milk
2 teaspoons maple flavoring

Preheat oven. Cream shortening, margarine, and brown sugar. Add eggs, one at a time, beat well. Sift flour, baking powder, and salt together. Alternate the adding of dry ingredients and milk. Add flavoring. Bake in greased and floured tube pan. Temperature: 300 degrees. Baking Time: 1½ hours. Yield: 1 cake.

FROSTING
1 stick margarine
1 cup brown sugar, packed
3 cups powdered sugar

¼ cup milk
1 teaspoon vanilla extract

Melt margarine on medium heat. Add brown sugar and stir for one minute. Cool; add powdered sugar and milk. Beat to spreading consistency. Add vanilla; mix. Spread on cool BROWN SUGAR POUND CAKE.

Cherry Pound Cake

Eat til it ouches you!

1 cup shortening
½ cup margarine
3 cups sugar
6 eggs
½ teaspoon almond extract

½ teaspoon vanilla extract
½ (10 ounces) jar Maraschino
    cherries, drained and chopped
¾ cup milk
3¾ cups flour, sifted

Cream shortening, margarine, and sugar; add eggs, one at a time. Mix well. Add extracts and cherries. Add milk and flour alternately. Place in cold oven. Bake. Cool in pan 15 minutes. Remove from pan. When cold, spread with FROSTING. Temperature: 300 degrees. Baking Time: 1¾ hours. Yield: 1 cake.

FROSTING
3 ounces cream cheese
2 cups confectioner's sugar
½ stick margarine
1 teaspoon vanilla or almond
    extract

½ (10 ounces) jar Maraschino
    cherries, chopped
½ cup coconut
½ cup nuts, chopped

Cream together cheese, sugar, and margarine. Add remaining ingredients. Mix well.

Coconut Pound Cake

Eat til it ouches you!

6 eggs, separated
1 cup shortening
½ cup margarine
3 cups sugar
½ teaspoon almond extract
½ teaspoon coconut extract

3 cups cake flour, sifted
1 cup milk
2 cups coconut, grated fresh or
    frozen
Confectioner's sugar

Separate eggs, placing whites in a large bowl, yolks in another large bowl. Let egg whites warm to room temperature—about 1 hour. Preheat oven. Grease a 10-inch tube pan. At high speed, beat egg yolks with shortening and margarine until blended. Gradually add sugar, beating until light and fluffy. Add extracts, beat until blended. At low speed, beat in flour (in fourths) alternately with milk (in thirds), beginning and ending with flour. Add coconut, beat until well blended. Beat egg whites just until stiff peaks form. With wire whisk or rubber scraper, gently fold egg whites into batter until well combined. Turn into prepared pan. Bake until cake tester inserted near center comes out clean. Cool in pan on wire rack 15 minutes. Remove cake from pan; cool thoroughly on wire rack. To serve, dust top lightly with confectioner's sugar. Temperature: 300 degrees. Baking Time: 2 hours. Yield: 1 cake.

Cream Cheese Pound Cake

A Blue Ribbon Winner!

3 sticks margarine or butter
    (not whipped)
8 ounces cream cheese, softened
3 cups sugar

6 eggs
1½ teaspoons vanilla extract
3 cups cake flour
⅛ teaspoon salt (optional)

Preheat oven. Cream together margarine, cream cheese, and add sugar gradually, beating 5-7 minutes. Add eggs, one at a time; beat well. Add vanilla. Stir in flour and salt; beat until mixed well. Do not overbeat after flour is added. Pour into greased and floured 10-inch tube pan and bake until a wooden pick inserted in center of cake comes out clean. Temperature: 325 degrees. Baking Time: 1½ hours. Yield: 10-inch cake.

All-purpose flour can be substituted for cake flour. Use one cup all-purpose flour minus two tablespoons for every cup of cake flour.

Five Flavor Pound Cake

Eat til it ouches you! Five great flavors is this luscious cake.

3 cups sugar
½ pound butter
½ cup shortening
5 eggs
3 cups flour
¼ teaspoon salt
½ teaspoon baking powder

1 teaspoon lemon flavoring
1 teaspoon vanilla flavoring
1 teaspoon butter flavoring
1 teaspoon coconut flavoring
1 teaspoon rum flavoring
1 cup milk

Preheat oven. In medium bowl, cream sugar, butter, and shortening. In small bowl, beat eggs until lemon in color. In large bowl, sift flour, salt and baking powder together. Add eggs, sugar mixture, flavorings, and milk; blend well. Bake in greased, floured tube pan. As soon as cake is taken out of oven, spoon GLAZE over top of cake and let cool. Then remove cake from pan. Temperature: 350 degrees. Baking Time: 1½ hours. Yield: 1 cake.

GLAZE
½ cup water
1 cup sugar

1 teaspoon each of lemon, vanilla, butter, coconut, and rum flavorings

In saucepan, mix all ingredients. Heat until sugar is melted.

German Chocolate Pound Cake

For chocolate lovers!

2 cups sugar
1 cup shortening
4 eggs
2 teaspoons vanilla extract
1 cup buttermilk

3 cups flour, sifted
½ teaspoon baking soda
1 teaspoon salt
4 ounces German sweet chocolate

Preheat oven. Cream sugar and shortening; add eggs, vanilla, and buttermilk. Sift together flour, soda, and salt. Add and mix well. Add melted German sweet chocolate. Bake in a 9-inch greased and floured tube pan. Temperature: 300 degrees. Baking Time: 1½ hours. Yield: 1 cake.

Remember to cream the sugar and fat mixtures for about 5 minutes. An undermixed cake is more likely to sink and have a coarse grain.

Pineapple Pound Cake

¼ cup shortening
1 cup margarine
2¾ cups sugar
6 eggs
3 cups flour

1 teaspoon baking powder
¼ cup milk
1 teaspoon vanilla extract
¾ cup crushed pineapple,
    undrained

Combine shortening and margarine, gradually add sugar. Cream until light and fluffy. Add eggs, one at a time, beating well after each addition. Combine flour and baking powder in a small bowl, set aside. Combine milk and vanilla together in a cup. Add to creamed mixture alternately beginning and ending with flour mixture. Gently fold in crushed pineapple. Pour into greased and floured 10-inch tube pan. Place in cold oven. Bake until wooden pick inserted in cake comes out clean. Temperature: 325 degrees. Baking Time: 1¼ hours. Yield: 1 cake.

PINEAPPLE DRIZZLE
1 cup powdered sugar, sifted
1 tablespoon margarine, softened

4 teaspoons pineapple, juice

Pierce top of cake with a toothpick. Combine powdered sugar and margarine. Beat in pineapple juice until mixture becomes thin. Drizzle over top and sides of PINEAPPLE POUND CAKE.

Vanilla Wafer Pound Cake

2 sticks butter or margarine
2 cups sugar
6 eggs
2 tablespoons milk

12 ounces vanilla wafers, crushed
2 cups frozen coconut, grated
2 cups pecans, chopped
1 teaspoon vanilla extract

Preheat oven. Cream butter and sugar in bowl. Beat eggs, one at a time. Add milk and wafer crumbs, mixing well. Stir in coconut, pecans, and vanilla. Pour into greased and floured tube pan. Bake. Temperature: 300 degrees. Baking Time: 1½ hours. Yield: 1 cake.

Whipped Cream Pound Cake

3 cups sugar
2 sticks butter
6 eggs
3 cups flour, sifted twice

½ pint whipping cream
1 teaspoon vanilla extract
1 teaspoon almond extract

Cream together butter and sugar. Add eggs, one at a time. Mix in flour and cream. Add extracts. Pour into greased Bundt pan. Place in cold oven. Bake. Temperature: 325 degrees. Baking Time: 1¼ hours. Yield: 1 cake.

Fresh Apple Cake

Eat til it ouches you!

1½ cups vegetable oil
2 cups sugar
3 eggs
3 cups flour
1 teaspoon baking soda

1 teaspoon salt
1 teaspoon cinnamon, ground
1 teaspoon vanilla extract
1 cup nuts, chopped
3 cups apple, chopped

Preheat oven. Blend oil, sugar, and eggs well. Sift flour, soda, salt and cinnamon together. Add to sugar mixture at intervals. Add vanilla and nuts. Peel and chop apples and add at once to prevent browning. Bake in greased tube pan. Temperature: 350 degrees. Baking Time: 1¼ hours. Yield: 1 cake.

TOPPING

1½ cups brown sugar, packed
½ cup butter

1 cup evaporated milk

Mix ingredients. Cook until fairly thick and pour over FRESH APPLE CAKE.

Lemon Buttermilk Cake

Really great homespun cooking!

1 cup shortening
½ cup butter or margarine
2½ cups sugar
4 eggs
3½ cups flour

½ teaspoon salt
1 cup buttermilk
1 teaspoon lemon extract
½ teaspoon baking soda
1 tablespoon hot water

Preheat oven. Cream shortening, butter, and sugar until fluffy. Add eggs, one at a time; beat. Alternate flour sifted with salt and buttermilk mixed with extract. Add soda dissolved in hot water. Bake in tube pan lined in bottom with waxed paper. Temperature: 325 degrees. Baking Time: 1¼ hours. Yield: 1 cake.

TOPPING

½ cup sugar
½ cup hot water

1 lemon, juice and grated rind

Mix ingredients. Cook topping until sugar is dissolved and the syrup is light. Pour over hot LEMON BUTTERMILK CAKE.

Nan's Prune Cake

Eat til it ouches you!

1 cup salad oil
1½ cups sugar
3 eggs, beaten
2 cups flour, sifted
1 teaspoon baking soda
1 teaspoon cinnamon, ground
1 teaspoon cloves, ground

1 teaspoon nutmeg, ground
1 cup prune juice
1 cup pitted prunes, chopped and
  cooked
1 cup nuts, chopped
1 teaspoon vanilla extract

Preheat oven. Mix oil and sugar, add eggs, and blend. Sift together dry ingredients; add to other mixture alternately with prune juice and mix well. Add prunes, nuts, vanilla and blend. Turn into greased and floured tube pan. Bake. Temperature: 350 degrees. Baking Time: 1½ hours. Yield: 1 cake.

Pumpkin Cake

2 cups sugar
4 eggs
1 cup oil
2 cups flour
2 teaspoons cinnamon, ground

2 teaspoons baking soda
½ teaspoon salt
2 cups pumpkin (not pumpkin pie
  filling)

Preheat oven. Mix sugar and eggs. Pour in oil and mix at medium speed until there is no visible trace of oil. Mix at least 3 minutes. Add dry ingredients which have been sifted together. Then add the pumpkin and mix at a slower speed until the batter is well blended. Pour in a well greased tube pan and bake. Temperature: 350 degrees. Baking Time: 1 hour. Yield: 1 cake.

ICING

8 ounces cream cheese
1 stick margarine or butter,
  softened

1 pound confectioner's sugar
2 teaspoons vanilla extract

Blend cream cheese and butter with electric mixer. Add sugar and vanilla and blend until smooth. Frost PUMPKIN CAKE.

Regal Almond Cake

¾ cup almonds, sliced
1 tablespoon sugar
1 cup butter
2 cups sugar
2 teaspoons vanilla extract
1 teaspoon almond extract
1 teaspoon lemon peel, grated

4 egg yolks
3 cups flour
4 teaspoons baking powder
1 teaspoon salt
1⅓ cups milk
1 cup almonds, ground
4 egg whites

Preheat oven. Very generously butter 10-inch tube pan. Press almonds into butter on both bottom and sides. Sprinkle with 1 tablespoon sugar. Thoroughly cream butter and 2 cups sugar. Add extracts and lemon peel. Add yolks and beat until light and fluffy. Stir together flour, baking powder, and salt. Add to creamed mixture alternately with milk, beating after each addition. Add almonds. Beat egg whites until stiff but not dry. Gently fold into batter. Carefully turn into prepared pan. Bake. Cool in pan 10 minutes. Temperature: 325 degrees. Baking Time: 1 hour 25 minutes. Yield: 1 cake.

Supreme Carrot Cake

Eat til it ouches you!

3 cups flour, sifted
2 teaspoons baking soda
2 teaspoons cinnamon, ground
½ teaspoon salt
2 cups sugar
1½ cups cooking oil

2 teaspoons vanilla extract
2 cups raw carrots, finely grated
1½ cups pecans, chopped
1 cup crushed pineapple
3 eggs

Preheat oven. Mix flour, soda, cinnamon, and salt. Combine sugar, oil, and vanilla, and mix with first ingredients. Add carrots, nuts and pineapple. Mix well and add eggs, one at a time. Pour batter into a well-greased and floured large tube pan. Bake. Temperature: 350 degrees. Baking Time: 70 minutes. Yield: 1 cake.

Angel Bavarian Cake

CUSTARD

1 pint milk
4 egg yolks
1 cup sugar

2 tablespoons flour
Pinch salt

OTHER INGREDIENTS

1 envelope gelatin
¼ cup cold water
1 teaspoon vanilla extract
1 large angel food cake

4 egg whites, beaten
1½ pints cream, whipped
2 packages fruit

Mix custard ingredients and cook custard until thick. While hot, stir in 1 envelope of gelatin dissolved in ¼ cup cold water. Let cool, add vanilla. Break angel food cake into small pieces. Into beaten egg whites, fold 1 pint of whipped cream; fold into custard. Place alternate layers of cake and custard in pan. Let stand in refrigerator overnight. Remove from pan and frost with ½ pint whipping cream flavored with sugar and vanilla to taste. Serve with raspberries, strawberries, or peaches. Yield: 16 servings.

Cranberry Cream Angel Cake

1 Angel Food Cake

CRANBERRY PARFAIT FILLING

1 pound jellied cranberry sauce
2 tablespoons sugar
½ pint heavy cream, whipped

½ teaspoon vanilla or almond
  extract
Red vegetable Color (optional)

Hollow out the center of an angel food cake leaving 1-inch wall. Save crumbs to fold into parfait filling. Beat cranberry sauce and sugar together. Fold in whipped cream, flavoring, and the cake crumbs. Spoon into angel cake. Place filled cake on tray and put in freezer for filling to freeze. This may be made the day before serving. At serving time, frost cake with sweetened whipped cream that has been tinted a pale pink with a few drops of red vegetable coloring.

Jiffy Frosted Angels

1 (10x4x2-inch) loaf angel cake
3 tablespoons butter or margarine
⅓ cup milk
1 pound confectioner's sugar,
    sifted

1 teaspoon vanilla extract
7 ounces flaked coconut, toasted
    or 2 cups walnuts, finely
    chopped

Cut angel cake in ten one-inch slices. Cut each slice lengthwise in thirds to make bars. Heat butter and milk. Stir into confectioner's sugar. Add vanilla (if necessary add more milk to make icing proper consistency for brushing onto cake) and roll in coconut. Place on rack to dry. Note: Silver shot is an attractive addition to "angels" at Christmas. Yield: 30 servings.

Tutti Frutti Angel Cake

12 individual angel food cakes
½ pint whipping cream
½ cup walnuts, chopped
½ cup maraschino cherries,
    chopped
½ teaspoon artificial rum
    flavoring

¼ cup frozen orange juice
    concentrate
¼ cup apricot-applesauce baby
    food, strained
½ cup sugar

Split cakes crosswise. Whip cream, fold in walnuts, cherries, and rum flavoring. Spread between halves of cake. Combine the undiluted orange juice concentrate, and apricot-applesauce with sugar. Stir over low heat until sugar melts. Boil gently for 5 minutes. Brush glaze over top of cake, letting it run over sides. Top with more whipped cream mixture. Yield: 12 servings.

"Come Lord Jesus our Guest to be
And bless these gifts bestowed by Thee.
Bless our loved ones everywhere
And keep them in thy loving care.
Amen."
THE MORAVIAN BLESSING

Cookies and Small Cakes

Old Jail

THE OLD JAIL

The old City Hall and Jail, 215 City Hall Street, are thought to be the model for the court house and Andy's office on the "Andy Griffith Show". The old City Hall was built in the early 1900's. In the earlier days, it housed the city stables and wagon shed. The one-story building retains one of the large round arched openings which accommodated wagons; the second arch has been filled in with a door and window. The building housed the Mayor's office, Police Department, Fire Department, City Water Department, Clerk of Court, District Court, and Jail. The Jail was modified in the fifties to meet state regulations. The Jail was in use until the new Municipal Building was erected in 1978. The spaces in the building have been renovated and are used as offices. The jail remains in its original state and is open for visitors.

Apricot Squares

¾ cup dried apricots
1 cup flour, sifted
¼ cup sugar
1 stick margarine
1 cup light brown sugar, packed
2 eggs, well beaten

⅓ cup flour
½ teaspoon baking powder
¼ teaspoon salt
½ teaspoon vanilla extract
½ cup pecans, chopped
Powdered sugar

Cover apricots with water. Boil 10 minutes. Drain, cool, and chop apricots. LOWER LAYER: Preheat oven. Sift flour and sugar into a bowl. Cut in margarine until mixture is consistency of corn meal. Pack into 9-inch square pan. Bake. TOP LAYER: Add brown sugar to eggs. Stir in flour sifted with baking powder and salt. Add vanilla, nuts, and chopped apricots. Mix well. Spread over the baked layer. Return to oven and bake. (Top layer will be soft.) Cool. Cut into squares. Sprinkle with powdered sugar. Temperature: 325 degrees. Baking Time: 35 minutes. Yield: 16 squares.

Brown Sugar Drops

1 cup soft shortening
2 cups brown sugar, packed
2 eggs
½ cup soured milk, buttermilk or
    water

3½ cups flour
1 teaspoon baking soda
1 teaspoon salt

Mix shortening, sugar, and eggs thoroughly. Stir in liquid. Sift dry ingredients and blend. Chill at least 1 hour. Preheat oven. Drop by rounded teaspoonfuls about 2 inches apart on lightly greased baking sheet. Bake in preheated oven until almost no imprint remains when touched lightly with finger. Temperature: 400 degrees. Baking Time: 8-10 minutes. Yield: 6 dozen.

DO NOT USE ALUMINUM FOIL IN THE BOTTOM OF THE OVEN. It will affect the temperature and can short-out your oven unit.

Cherry Bonbon Cookies

½ cup butter, softened
¾ cup powdered sugar, sifted
1½ cups flour
⅛ teaspoon salt

2 tablespoons half-and-half
1 teaspoon vanilla extract
24 maraschino cherries, drained
Powdered sugar

Beat butter at medium speed with an electric mixer until creamy; gradually add sugar, beating well. Stir in flour and next 3 ingredients. Shape into 24 balls. Press each ball round a cherry, covering completely; place on ungreased baking sheet. Bake in preheated oven. Transfer to wire rack and cool completely. Roll in powdered sugar. Temperature: 350 degrees. Baking Time: 18-20 minutes. Yield: 24 cookies.

Mayberry Delight Cookies

¾ cup butter flavored shortening
1¼ cups light brown sugar, firmly
    packed
2 tablespoons milk
1 tablespoon vanilla extract
1 egg

1¾ cups flour
1 teaspoon salt
¾ teaspoon baking soda
1 cup semi-sweet chocolate chips
1 cup pecans, coarsely chopped
    (optional)

If nuts are omitted, add an additional ½ cup chocolate chips. Preheat oven. Combine shortening, brown sugar, milk, and vanilla extract in large bowl. Beat until well-blended. Beat egg into creamed mixture. Combine flour, salt, and baking soda. Mix into creamed mixture just until blended. Stir in chocolate chips and pecans. Drop rounded tablespoons of dough three inches apart onto ungreased baking sheet. Bake. Cool 2 minutes on baking sheets. Remove cookies and cool completely. Temperature: 375 degrees. Baking Time: 8-10 minutes for chewy cookies, 11-13 minutes for crisp cookies. Yield: 3 dozen.

If you burn your cookies or toast, remove any burnt taste from the foods by scraping them gently with a table knife.

Brownies Deluxe

½ cup shortening
¾ cup sugar
2 eggs
¾ cup flour, sifted
¼ teaspoon baking powder

¼ teaspoon salt
2 tablespoons cocoa
1 teaspoon vanilla extract
½ cup pecans, chopped
12 marshmallows, cut in half

Preheat oven. Cream together shortening and sugar until light and fluffy. Blend in eggs, one at a time, beating well. Add sifted dry ingredients and mix. Blend in vanilla and pecans. Spread in greased and floured 12x8-inch pan. Bake for 25-30 minutes. Cover with soft marshmallows. Return to oven 2-3 minutes to melt marshmallows. Spread over surface. Cool and cover with CHOCOLATE FROSTING. Temperature: 350 degrees. Baking Time: 27-33 minutes. Yield: 48 bars.

CHOCOLATE FROSTING

½ cup brown sugar, packed
¼ cup water
2 squares chocolate

3 tablespoons butter
1 teaspoon vanilla extract
1½ cups powdered sugar, sifted

Combine brown sugar, water, and chocolate. Let come to a boil and cook for 3 minutes. Add butter and vanilla. Cool. Blend in sifted powdered sugar. If necessary, thin with a small amount of cream. Spread over marshmallow topping. Cut into bars.

Calypso Bars

Enjoy heaven on earth.

2½ squares unsweetened
    chocolate
⅔ cup hot water
1⅓ cups sugar
1⅓ cups dates, chopped
1 cup butter
1 teaspoon vanilla extract

1¼ cups light brown sugar,
    packed
1½ cups flour, sifted
½ teaspoon salt
½ teaspoon baking soda
1½ cups quick-cooking rolled oats
1 cup nuts, chopped

Preheat oven. Melt chocolate in hot water, over low heat. Add sugar and stir until dissolved. Add dates and cook over low heat until mixture thickens— about 5 minutes. Add ¼ cup butter; blend in vanilla. Cool. Cream remaining ¾ cup butter and brown sugar together until light and fluffy. Sift flour, salt, and soda together. Add to creamed mixture, blending well. Add oats and nuts and mix until crumbly. Press half the nut mixture into bottom of a greased 13x9x2-inch pan. Spread with date chocolate mixture and top with remaining nut mixture. Bake. Cool and cut into squares or serve warm with ice cream. Temperature: 350 degrees. Baking Time: 30 minutes. Yield: 30.

Candy-Stripe Twists

The unique blend of anise gives these cookies their distinctive flavor.

3¼ cups flour, sifted
4 teaspoons baking powder
1 teaspoon salt
½ cup butter or margarine
1¼ cups sugar

1 egg
½ teaspoon oil of anise
¼ cup milk
Red food coloring

Preheat oven. Sift flour, baking powder, and salt together. Cream butter and sugar until fluffy in large bowl; beat in egg and oil of anise. Add dry ingredients and milk alternately; stir until well-blended. Place half of dough into a medium-size bowl; blend in a few drops red food coloring to tint pink, leave other half plain. Pinch off about a teaspoonful each of pink and white doughs at a time, roll each into a pencil-thin strip about 5 inches long on lightly floured pastry cloth. Place strips side by side, pressing ends together. Twist into about 3-inch long rope. Place 1-inch apart, on ungreased baking sheets. Bake until firm. Remove carefully from baking sheets; cool on wire racks. Store, with waxed paper between layers, in container with tight fitting cover. Temperature: 350 degrees. Baking Time: 10 minutes. Yield: 5 dozen.

Chess Pie Cookies

These cookies freeze well.

½ cup butter
2 cups brown sugar, packed
1½ cups flour, sifted
2 teaspoons baking powder

Pinch salt
2 eggs, unbeaten
1 cup pecans, chopped
1 teaspoon vanilla extract

Melt butter in heavy skillet; add brown sugar, and stir over low heat until the sugar is dissolved and bubbles. Cool to lukewarm. Sift flour with baking powder and salt. Stir eggs, one at a time, into sugar mixture. Mix well; add flour mixture and blend. Add nuts, and vanilla. Pour into greased 8x12-inch pan. Bake in preheated oven. When cool, cut into squares. Temperature: 350 degrees. Baking Time: 35 minutes. Yield: 35 cookies.

Chewy Gooeys

Eat til it ouches you! These may be frozen.

14 ounces caramels
⅔ cup evaporated milk
1 German chocolate cake mix
¾ cup butter, melted

1 cup pecans, coarsely chopped
6 ounces semisweet chocolate
   chips

Preheat oven. Melt caramels with ⅓ cup evaporated milk in a double boiler. Grease and flour a 13x9-inch pan. Blend cake mix, butter, ⅓ cup evaporated milk, and pecans until moistened. Press a little less than half of the cake mixture into the pan and bake for 6 minutes.

Sprinkle the chocolate chips evenly over baked mixture and pour caramel mixture on top of chips. Cover with the remainder of the cake mixture. If you can't spread it, flatten mixture between your hands and place on top patchwork style. Bake. Cool before cutting. Temperature: 350 degrees. Baking Time: 15-18 minutes. Yield: 28 servings.

Chewy Noels

Eat til it ouches you!

2 tablespoons butter or
   margarine, melted
¼ cup flour
⅛ teaspoon baking soda
⅛ teaspoon salt

1 cup brown sugar, packed
1 cup nuts, chopped
2 eggs, beaten
1 teaspoon vanilla extract
Confectioner's sugar

Pour melted butter in 9-inch square pan. Sift together flour, soda, salt, and stir in brown sugar and nuts. Stir in eggs and vanilla. Carefully pour batter over butter in pan. Do not stir! Bake in preheated oven. Sprinkle top with confectioner's sugar. Invert pan into cooling rack covered with waxed paper. Sprinkle again with confectioner's sugar. Cut into bars. Optional: Decorate by writing Noel on each bar. Temperature: 350 degrees. Baking Time: 20-25 minutes. Yield: 16 servings.

Corn Meal Brownies

2 squares unsweetened chocolate
⅓ cup butter
1¼ cups brown sugar, packed
2 eggs, beaten
½ cup self-rising flour

½ cup self-rising corn meal
1 teaspoon vanilla extract
⅛ teaspoon salt
1 cup nuts, chopped

Preheat oven. Melt chocolate and butter together, then cool. Add brown sugar to beaten eggs and add to chocolate and butter. Beat in flour, corn meal, vanilla, and salt. Fold in nuts. Pour into greased 8-inch square cake pan. Bake. Cut into squares. Temperature: 350 degrees. Baking Time: 30 minutes. Yield: 16 servings.

Crème De Menthe Bars

MICROWAVE. Eat til it ouches you! A colorful dessert!

BASE

4 ounces unsweetened chocolate
½ cup margarine
½ cup sugar
½ cup brown sugar, packed

2 eggs
1 teaspoon vanilla extract
⅔ cup flour, unsifted
½ teaspoon baking powder

Line a 9x13-inch baking dish with wax paper. MICROWAVE, HIGH, chocolate and margarine in glass mixing bowl, 1-1½ minutes or until melted. Stir until smooth. Blend in sugar. Beat in eggs, one at a time. Stir in remaining base ingredients. Spread into wax paper lined baking dish. Cover with wax paper or plastic wrap. MICROWAVE, HIGH, 5½-6½ minutes or until surface is no longer doughy, rotating dish once or twice. Cool thoroughly.

FILLING

½ cup margarine
2 cups powdered sugar, unsifted
2 teaspoons crème de menthe

3-4 drops green food coloring
¼ teaspoon peppermint extract

MICROWAVE, HIGH, margarine, 15-30 minutes to soften; do not melt. Add powdered sugar and beat on medium speed, using electric mixer. Gradually add remaining ingredients, beating until smooth and creamy. Spread evenly over cooled BASE. Refrigerate to set filling.

FROSTING

1 cup semisweet chocolate pieces

2 tablespoons cooking oil

Combine frosting ingredients. MICROWAVE, HIGH, uncovered, 1½-2 minutes or until glossy; stir until smooth. Spread evenly over FILLING. Refrigerate to set. Store in refrigerator. Allow to stand at room temperature about 10 minutes before cutting into squares. Yield: 24 squares.

Forgotten Cookies

A delicious recipe to bake after baking other dishes. Saves Energy!

2 egg whites
⅔ cup sugar
Pinch salt
1 teaspoon vanilla extract

1 cup pecans, chopped
6 ounces chocolate chips
Aluminum foil

Preheat oven before mixing cookies. Beat 2 egg whites until stiff. While beating egg whites, gradually add sugar, salt, and vanilla. Mix well. Fold in pecans and chocolate chips. Drop by teaspoon on ungreased aluminum foil on baking sheet. Turn oven OFF and place cookies in oven. Do not open oven. Temperature: 350 degrees. Baking Time: Leave all day or over night. Yield: two dozen.

Holiday Fruit Cookies

The more...the merrier!

1 cup shortening
2 cups brown sugar, packed
2 eggs
½ cup rolled oats
3½ cups flour, sifted
2 teaspoons baking powder
1 teaspoon cinnamon, ground
1 teaspoon nutmeg, ground

½ teaspoon salt
½ cup milk
1 cup nuts, chopped
1 cup dates, chopped
1 cup candied mixed fruits
½ cup candied cherries, chopped
Candied cherries and nuts for
    decoration

Preheat oven. Cream shortening and brown sugar together. Beat in eggs. Add rolled oats. Sift flour, baking powder, cinnamon, nutmeg, and salt together. Add to creamed mixture alternately with milk. Stir in nuts, dates, mixed fruit, and cherries. Drop rounded teaspoonfuls of batter onto an ungreased baking sheet. Top cookies with halved cherries or nuts for decoration. Bake until golden brown. Remove cookies to a cooling rack, using wide spatula. Cool. Store in a closed container. Temperature: 375 degrees. Baking Time: 10-12 minutes. Yield: 10 dozen.

"Tell me, I will forget; Show me, I may remember; Involve me, I will understand."

Date Nut Bars

4 eggs
2½ cups light brown sugar,
   packed
1⅔ cups evaporated milk
2 tablespoons lemon juice
2½ cups flour, sifted

1½ teaspoons baking soda
1 teaspoon cinnamon, ground
½ teaspoon salt
1½ cups walnuts, chopped
1½ cups dates, chopped

Preheat oven. In a large mixing bowl, beat eggs. Beat in brown sugar, evaporated milk, and lemon juice. Sift together flour, soda, cinnamon, and salt. Add all at once to egg mixture; stir just until blended. Fold in walnuts and dates being careful not to overmix. Spread batter in two well-greased 15½x10½x1-inch jelly roll pans. Bake. Set pans on racks to cool. When cold, spread ORANGE FROSTING over cakes in pan; then cut into bars. Temperature: 350 degrees. Baking Time: 20 minutes. Yield: 5 dozen.

ORANGE FROSTING
2 cups confectioner's sugar
2 tablespoons frozen orange juice
   concentrate

Evaporated milk

Combine confectioner's sugar and undiluted orange juice concentrate. Blend in evaporated milk, a few drops at a time, until desired consistency for spreading.

Double-Dip Nut Fingers

This luscious cookie can be frozen.

3¼ cups flour, sifted
½ teaspoon baking powder
¼ teaspoon salt
1¼ cups butter or margarine,
   softened
¾ cup sugar
1 egg

2 teaspoons orange rind, grated
6 ounces semisweet chocolate bits
2 tablespoons milk
Colored sprinkles
Chopped nuts
Coconut

Preheat oven. Sift flour, baking powder, and salt together. Mix butter or margarine with sugar in medium-sized bowl until creamy; beat in egg and orange rind; stir in flour mixture; blend thoroughly. Press dough through cookie press, using star tube, onto ungreased baking sheet. Make each cookie 3 inches long. Bake until set, but not brown. Cool on wire rack. Melt chocolate bits over low heat; stir in milk; beat until smooth. Dip end of cookie into chocolate then into sprinkles, nuts, or coconut. Place on wax paper until set. Temperature: 425 degrees. Baking Time: 5-8 minutes. Yield: 3 dozen.

Fry Pan Balls

A great recipe for an electric skillet!

1 stick margarine
1 cup brown sugar, packed
½ pound dates, chopped fine
1 teaspoon vanilla extract
½ teaspoon salt

1 egg, beaten
2½ cups Rice Krispies
½ cup nuts, chopped
1 cup coconut

In electric frypan on "warm", melt and mix margarine with brown sugar, dates, vanilla, salt, and well beaten egg. Cook over low heat for 10 minutes, stirring often. Turn control to "off"; add Rice Krispies and nuts. Let cool until mixture can be shaped with buttered hands into small balls. Roll in coconut or confectioner's sugar. Place on waxed paper to cool. Yield: 4 dozen.

Orange Spritz

A crispy cookie.

¾ cup butter or margarine
½ cup sugar
1 egg yolk
¼ teaspoon salt

1 teaspoon orange peel, finely grated
½ teaspoon orange extract
2 cups flour, sifted
Colored sugar

Preheat oven. Cream butter and sugar. Add egg yolk and beat well. Add salt, orange peel, orange extract, and flour and mix until combined. Press through pastry tube onto baking sheet. Decorate with colored sugar, if desired. Bake. Temperature: 425 degrees. Baking Time: 12 minutes. Yield: 5 dozen.

Drop Sugar Cookies

1 cup sugar
1 cup shortening
2 eggs
1 teaspoon vanilla extract

2½ cups flour, sifted
½ teaspoon baking soda
½ teaspoon salt

Preheat oven. Cream together sugar and shortening until well mixed. Add eggs and vanilla. Sift together flour, soda, and salt. Stir flour mixture into shortening-sugar mixture until no dry flour shows. Drop by rounded teaspoonfuls about 2 inches apart on greased baking sheet. Sprinkle with colored sugar, if desired. Bake. Temperature: 375 degrees. Baking Time: 8-10 minutes. Yield: 4 dozen.

Lemon Bars

Eat til it ouches you!

2 cups flour
½ cup confectioner's sugar
1 cup butter
4 eggs, beaten
2 cups sugar

⅓ cup lemon juice
¼ cup flour
½ teaspoon baking powder
Confectioner's sugar

Preheat oven. Sift together flour and ½ cup confectioner's sugar. Cut in butter until mixture clings together. Pour in greased 13x9x2-inch pan. Bake for 20-25 minutes or until lightly browned. Beat together eggs, sugar and lemon juice. Add ¼ cup flour and baking powder. Pour over baked crust. Bake. Sprinkle additional confectioner's sugar over top. Cool. Cut into squares. Temperature: 350 degrees. Baking Time: 20-25 minutes. Yield: 24 squares.

Little Twinks

2 cups flour, sifted
½ teaspoon salt
⅔ cup butter or margarine
1 cup sugar
2 eggs, separated

1 teaspoon vanilla extract
½ cup coconut, flaked
⅓ cup red raspberry preserves
Dash salt
½ cup confectioner's sugar

Preheat oven. Sift together flour and salt. Cream butter or margarine with sugar until light and fluffy. Add egg yolks and vanilla extract. Beat well. Blend in flour gradually, stirring to make a smooth dough. Add coconut and mix thoroughly. Drop dough by tablespoonfuls onto ungreased baking sheet. Make a depression in the center of each cookie and fill with preserves. Beat egg whites with salt until frothy. Add sugar gradually and continue beating to form stiff peaks. Top each cookie with teaspoon of meringue to cover preserves. Bake. Temperature: 300 degrees. Baking Time: 30 minutes. Yield: 2-3 dozen cookies.

Peanut Butter Balls

Great for peanut butter lovers!

2 sticks butter
½ cup nuts, chopped
1 cup peanut butter

1½ cups graham cracker crumbs
1 teaspoon vanilla extract
1 pound confectioner's sugar

Melt butter and mix remaining ingredients together. Roll into small balls on wax paper. Dip balls into CHOCOLATE MIXTURE and place on wax paper. Yield: 24-36 cookies.

CHOCOLATE MIXTURE
1 large package chocolate chips   ½ cake paraffin

Mix ingredients and melt together.

Peanut Butter Tassies

A very special recipe that's almost too good to be true.

40 miniature Reece Cup candies
Miniature paper liners

1 refrigerated slice and bake
    peanut butter cookies

Unwrap Reece Cups and set aside. Line miniature muffin pans with paper liners. Preheat oven. Slice cookie roll into 10 equal slices, then into quarters. Place one quarter into each lined muffin cup. Bake until puffy and lightly browned. Remove from oven and immediately put one Reece Cup into each cookie. Cool. Temperature: 350 degrees. Baking Time: 8-10 minutes. Yield: 40 tassies.

Snickerdoodles

Eat til it ouches you!

1 cup soft shortening (part butter)
1½ cups sugar
2 eggs
2¾ cups flour
2 teaspoons cream of tartar

1 teaspoon baking soda
¼ teaspoon salt
2 tablespoons sugar
2 teaspoons cinnamon, ground

Preheat oven. Cream shortening, sugar and eggs thoroughly. Sift flour, cream of tartar, soda, and salt; add to shortening mixture. Form into balls the size of small walnuts. Roll balls in mixture of 2 tablespoons sugar and cinnamon. Place about 2 inches apart on ungreased baking sheet. Bake. Temperature: 400 degrees. Baking Time: 8-10 minutes. Yield: 6 dozen.

Rainbow Walnut Slices

A very pretty cookie for the holiday season.

1 cup shortening (half butter)
1¾ cups sugar
2 eggs
2 teaspoons vanilla extract
3 cups flour, sifted
1¼ teaspoons salt
½ teaspoon baking powder
Red and green food coloring

¼ cup candied red cherries, quartered
1½ cups English walnuts, chopped
¼ cup candied green cherries, quartered
1 ounce unsweetened chocolate, melted

Cream shortening, sugar, eggs, and vanilla. Resift flour with salt and baking powder and blend in creamed mixture. Divide into thirds. Tint one portion pink, mix in red cherries and ½ cup walnuts. Pack in layer in waxed paper lined 9x5x3-inch loaf pan. Tint second portion green, mix in ½ cup walnuts and green cherries. Blend melted chocolate in remaining dough, mix in ½ cup walnuts. Pack chocolate portion over pink layer and top with green tinted dough. Cover pan and freeze. To bake, remove dough from pan, slice thin with sharp knife. Cut slices in halves, place cookies on lightly greased baking sheet about 1 inch apart. Bake in preheated oven until done, not browned. Temperature: 350 degrees. Baking Time: 8-10 minutes. Yield: about 100 cookies.

The World's Best Cookie

The name says it all. They stay moist and keep beautifully.

1 cup butter
1 cup brown sugar, packed
1 cup sugar
1 egg
1 cup salad oil
1 teaspoon vanilla extract
1 cup rolled oats

1 cup Corn Flakes, crushed
1 cup coconut, shredded (optional)
½ cup nuts, chopped
3½ cups flour, sifted
1 teaspoon baking soda
1 teaspoon salt

Preheat oven. Cream butter and sugars until fluffy. Add egg, mix well; add salad oil and vanilla, mixing well. Add oats, Corn Flakes, coconut, and nuts, stirring well. Add flour, soda, and salt. Mix well, drop by teaspoonfuls onto ungreased baking sheet. Flatten with fork dipped in water. Bake. Cool on baking sheet for a few minutes before removing. Temperature: 325 degrees. Baking Time: 12 minutes. Yield: 12 dozen.

Fruit Cake Cookies

½ cup shortening
1 cup brown sugar, packed
1 egg
¼ cup buttermilk
2 cups flour
½ teaspoon baking powder

½ teaspoon baking soda
½ teaspoon salt
1 cup pecans, chopped
1 cup dates, cut up
1 cup candied cherries, cut in
   fourths

Mix well shortening, sugar, and egg. Add buttermilk. Sift together and stir in dry ingredients. Mix in pecans, dates, and cherries. CHILL DOUGH ONE HOUR. Preheat oven. Drop by teaspoons about two inches apart on lightly greased baking sheet. Top each cookie with a pecan half or half a cherry. Bake. Temperature: 400 degrees. Baking Time: 10-12 minutes. Yield: 4 dozen.

Fruit 'N Nut Cookies

¼ pound butter
¾ cup sugar
2 eggs
2 cups flour
½ teaspoon salt
1 teaspoon baking powder
1 teaspoon mace, ground

¼ cup water
½ cup candied pineapple, chopped
½ cup candied cherries, chopped
½ cup white raisins
½ cup pecans, chopped
1 teaspoon vanilla extract

Cream butter and sugar. Add eggs, one at a time, and continue to cream. Sift dry ingredients together and add to creamed mixture. Add water and stir. Dust fruit and nuts with flour and stir into batter, add vanilla. Drop by teaspoon 1-inch apart on a greased baking sheet and bake in preheated oven. Temperature: 350 degrees. Baking Time: 12-15 minutes. Yield: 3½ dozen.

Humdingers

1 stick margarine or butter
1 pound dates, chopped
¾ cup sugar
1 cup nuts

1 teaspoon vanilla extract
1½ cups Rice Krispies
Powdered sugar

Mix butter, dates, and sugar in saucepan. Cook on low 10 minutes. Stir well. Add nuts, vanilla, and Rice Krispies. Shape into balls, roll in powdered sugar. Yield: 2 dozen.

Swiss Treats

1 cup butter or margarine
1¼ cups sugar
1 egg, beaten
1 teaspoon vanilla extract
2½ cups flour, sifted
1½ teaspoons baking powder
½ teaspoon salt
½ cup pecans, chopped
½ cup maraschino cherries, cut in
   pieces
½ cup coconut, flaked
6 ounces chocolate pieces

Preheat oven. Cream butter; add sugar gradually. Blend in egg and vanilla. Combine flour, baking powder, and salt; stir into creamed mixture. Add nuts, cherries, coconut, and chocolate pieces. Spread dough in greased 15x10-inch jelly roll pan. Bake. Cool slightly, cut into bars. Temperature: 375 degrees. Baking Time: 20 minutes. Yield: 7 dozen.

Peach Refrigerator Cookies

This makes a chewy cookie.

¾ cup butter
1½ cups dark brown sugar,
   packed
1 egg
2½ cups flour
1 tablespoon baking powder
1 teaspoon salt
1 teaspoon cinnamon, ground
¼ cup milk
1 cup nuts, chopped
1 cup dried peaches, chopped

Cream butter, sugar, and egg. Sift dry ingredients, add to first mixture alternating with milk. Add nuts and peaches; mix well. Shape into rolls, wrap in waxed paper and place in refrigerator until ready to bake. Preheat oven. Slice thin and bake. Temperature: 400 degrees. Baking Time: 10-12 minutes. Yield: 5 dozen.

Pink Clouds

3 egg whites
¼ teaspoon cream of tartar
2 cups confectioner's sugar
¼ teaspoon almond extract
2 drops red vegetable coloring
¾ cup coconut, finely grated

Preheat oven. Beat egg whites until foamy. Add cream of tartar and continue beating until they stand in peaks. Gradually add sugar, beating thoroughly until meringue stands in stiff peaks. Fold in the extract, coloring, and coconut. Drop from spoon on a greased baking sheet. Bake. Do not allow cookies to brown. Remove from sheet at once. Temperature: 275 degrees. Baking Time: 20-25 minutes. Yield: 5½ dozen.

Thimble Cookies

¾ cup butter
½ cup light brown sugar, packed
½ cup peanut butter
½ teaspoon salt
1 egg

½ teaspoon orange extract
1¾ cups flour, sifted
Red-currant jelly
Nuts
Crystallized fruits

Preheat oven. Cream butter and sugar. Blend in peanut butter, salt, egg, orange extract, and flour. Shape into 1-inch balls, place on baking sheet, flatten just a little, and make thimble-size dent in top. Bake; remove from oven. Fill hole with red-currant jelly. Note: If the cookies are to be frozen, do not add jelly until just before serving. Nuts, crystallized fruits may be added before freezing, if desired. Temperature: 350 degrees. Baking Time: 12-15 minutes. Yield: 4 dozen.

Thumbprint Cookies

COOKIE DOUGH
1½ cups flour, sifted
½ teaspoon salt
½ cup butter or margarine
½ cup brown sugar, packed

1 teaspoon vanilla extract
2 tablespoons milk
¼ cup semisweet chocolate pieces
Confectioner's sugar

CHOCOLATE FILLING
¾ cup semisweet chocolate pieces
1 tablespoon shortening
2 tablespoons light corn syrup

1 tablespoon water
1 teaspoon vanilla extract

Preheat oven. Sift flour and salt together. Cream butter or margarine until soft, add brown sugar gradually to make a smooth mixture. Stir in vanilla and flour mixture. Mix thoroughly. Add milk and ¼ cup chocolate pieces. Shape dough in balls about the size of a walnut and place 2 inches apart on an ungreased baking sheet. Press your thumb down firmly on the top of each cookie to make a depression. Bake, remove from oven, and sprinkle with a little confectioner's sugar while still warm. While cookies cool, make the filling; melt ¾ cup chocolate pieces and shortening over hot water, stirring frequently. Remove from heat and stir in corn syrup, water, and vanilla until smooth. Fill each cookie depression with the CHOCOLATE FILLING. Temperature: 375 degrees. Baking Time: 10-12 minutes. Yield: 3 dozen.

"Bless us, O Lord, this food, and give us thankful hearts. Amen."

Pinwheel Cookies

FILLING

½ pound dates, chopped
¼ cup sugar
⅓ cup water

¼ cup nuts, chopped
⅛ teaspoon salt

Cook together dates, sugar, and water about five minutes. Remove from heat and add nuts and salt. Cool mixture while preparing dough.

DOUGH

2 cups flour
¼ teaspoon salt
½ teaspoon baking soda
½ cup shortening

½ cup brown sugar, packed
½ cup sugar
1 egg, well beaten

Sift flour, salt, and soda. Cream shortening and sugars. Add egg and dry ingredients. Chill dough. Then roll about ⅛-inch thin and spread with FILLING. Roll up, wrap in wax paper, chill. Preheat oven. Slice and bake. Temperature: 375 degrees. Baking Time: 8-10 minutes. Yield: 5 dozen.

Two For Tea Cookies

3 cups flour, sifted
2 teaspoons baking powder
1 teaspoon salt
1 cup butter or margarine
2 cups brown sugar, packed
2 eggs
1 cup whole bran

½ cup milk
1 teaspoon vanilla extract
½ cup each—nuts, candied
   cherries, dates, chopped
2 squares unsweetened chocolate,
   melted

Preheat oven. Sift together flour, baking powder, and salt. Cream butter, gradually beat in brown sugar, blend well. Add eggs, one at a time, beating well after each addition. Add whole bran, milk, and vanilla. Fold in sifted dry ingredients. Divide dough equally. Fold into half the dough; nuts, cherries, and dates. To remaining dough add melted chocolate. Drop by teaspoonfuls onto greased baking sheets, decorate with candied cherry halves and pecan or walnut halves. Bake until done. Temperature: 375 degrees. Baking Time: 10-12 minutes. Yield: 6-7 dozen.

Toffee Bars

Eat til it ouches you!

1 cup butter
1 cup brown sugar, packed
1 egg yolk
2 cups flour, sifted

1 teaspoon vanilla extract
6 ounces milk chocolate
1 cup nuts, chopped

Preheat oven. Cream butter and sugar until light and fluffy. Mix in egg yolk. Add flour gradually, stirring only to blend; add vanilla. Spread about ¼-inch thick in lightly buttered 10x15-inch jelly roll pan. Bake until golden brown. Remove from oven and while hot distribute chocolate on top. When soft, spread smoothly over surface, sprinkle with nuts. While still warm, cut into bars. Temperature: 350 degrees. Baking Time: 20-25 minutes. Yield: 5 dozen bars.

Surprise Cupcakes

BATTER

⅔ cup semisweet chocolate chips
1 stick margarine
1¼ teaspoons vanilla extract

4 large eggs
1 cup flour
1½ cups sugar

Preheat oven. Line thirty small or fourteen large cupcake pans with paper cupcake liners. Melt chocolate chips and margarine in MICROWAVE oven. Stir until smooth. Add vanilla. Beat eggs until fluffy. Gradually beat in flour and sugar. Fold in chocolate mixture. Fill cupcake liners one-half full.

FILLING

8 ounces cream cheese, softened
¼ cup sugar

1 large egg, beaten
½ cup semisweet chocolate chips

Cream together cream cheese and sugar. Add egg and mix well. Fold in chocolate chips. Drop filling on top of BATTER in liners by teaspoonfuls. Bake. Cool completely before storing in covered container. Temperature: 350 degrees. Baking Time: 25-30 minutes. Yield: 26-30 small cupcakes; 14-16 large cupcakes.

Raspberry Squares

2½ cups flour, sifted
1½ cups sugar
1 cup butter, softened
2 egg yolks
¾ cup raspberry preserves

4 egg whites
½ cup sugar
1½ cups blanched almonds, finely
 chopped

Preheat oven. In large bowl, combine flour, sugar, butter, and egg yolks. Press dough into well buttered 10x15-inch jelly roll pan. Prick with fork. Bake for 15-20 minutes or until golden. Spread raspberry preserves over layer after baking. Beat egg whites until they hold soft peaks. Add ½ cup sugar gradually, continuing to beat until meringue is very stiff. Fold in almonds and spread mixture over the preserves. Bake for 25 minutes more. Cool and cut into squares. Temperature: 350 degrees. Baking Time: 40-45 minutes. Yield: about 5 dozen.

World Renowned Chewy Cookies

1½ cups flour
Pinch salt
1⅓ sticks butter, lightly salted
2 cups light brown sugar, packed

2 medium eggs
2 teaspoons almond extract
1½ cups almonds, sliced

Preheat oven. Sift flour and salt together. Cream butter and sugar; stir in eggs, creaming again until fluffy. Stir in almond extract and 1 cup almonds, reserving ½ cup for garnish. Gradually add flour mixture. Mix well. Spread evenly into greased and floured 9x13-inch dish. Sprinkle remaining almonds over top. Bake until mixture rises and falls again, completely. Cool several hours and cut into squares. Temperature: 325 degrees. Baking Time: 15-25 minutes. Yield: 52 squares.

Historic Downtown
Mount Airy

HISTORIC DOWNTOWN MOUNT AIRY

The early settlers called this 1,100 foot high valley ringed by mountains, "The Hollows". In 1801 Martin Armstrong, Revolutionary War captain and high sheriff of Surry County, sold his plantation to Thomas Perkins, a large land owner, who called it Mount Airy. It was from this plantation that the town of Mount Airy got its name. In February 1832, a post office was established, which replaced the post riders of the earlier days. Mount Airy was incorporated in 1885. Located at the foothills of the Blue Ridge Mountains, Mount Airy was a resort town. From the late 1900's through the 1920's, the nearby White Sulphur Springs Hotel served as a fashionable summer resort. Because of their supposed curative powers and the opportunities for a variety of social activities, the mineral springs gained wide popularity.

How long has it been since you've been in a Drug Store with a Coke and Pepsi dispenser, or a player piano, or cherry smashes? Remember the episode when Andy tells Barney that they could take the girls down to the drugstore and "weigh on the big scales". The old scales and player piano are in the former Lamm Drug, 175 North Main Street.

Experience historic downtown on a cold winter day and walk to the back of Holcomb Hardware, 226 North Main Street, and warm up around the black pot-bellied stove which was there when the store was bought. See the four-faced copper, brass, and colored glass clock suspended on the old First National Bank, now the home of the Mount Airy Chamber of Commerce, circa 1893, located on the corner of North Main Street and Moore Avenue. The upper façade of the former Workman's Federal Savings and Loan Building, circa 1891, 218 North Main Street, features abstractly designed owls and squirrels, symbols of wisdom and thrift, which are most appropriate for a savings and loan institution. The three-story Classical granite Bank of Mount Airy, circa 1923, 201 North Main Street, emphasizes the enframed monumental Tuscan columns. The 1906 Banner building with cast-iron entrance columns, 153-155 North Main Street, was once the post office, an emergency hospital during the flu epidemic of 1918, and the second floor housed a Commercial Club with ballroom and card room.

Downtown Mount Airy hosts the annual Autumn Leaves Festival the second Friday of October and is the largest event in Surry County. It celebrates the pageantry of the magnificent fall colors and the old-time mountain ways through bandstand entertainment with ole-time bluegrass music and street dancing, a wagon-train, homemade crafts, historic open homes, native demonstrations, church suppers, and food, such as homemade apple pies. It's another opportunity to experience the "real" Mayberry in Mount Airy, North Carolina.

Candy Strawberries

Lovely for a special party.

14 ounces sweetened condensed
    milk
1 pound coconut, grated fine
2 tablespoons sugar
1 (3 ounce) package plus 3
    tablespoons strawberry
    gelatin

½ teaspoon almond extract
3 tablespoons strawberry gelatin
Almonds, slivered
Green food coloring

Mix first five ingredients together. Chill in refrigerator for 4 hours. Roll into balls and shape in berries. Roll in 3 tablespoon gelatin. Top with leaves made from almonds dyed green or green tinted powdered sugar icing.

Caramel Pecan Log

5 ounces marshmallow cream
1½-2 cups confectioner's sugar
⅛ teaspoon almond extract
1 package caramels

¼ cup butter
1 tablespoon cream
3 cups pecan halves

Mix together thoroughly marshmallow cream and sugar, using hand to form stiff dough. Add almond extract. Divide into 4 parts. Make each in roll about 5 inches in length. Wrap and freeze while making sauce. In top of double boiler, add caramels, butter, and cream. Blend until smooth. Place log in caramel sauce (working quickly) until coated with sauce. Then roll in pecan halves to cover log. Place on rack until set. Wrap and store in covered container.

Chocolate Covered Balls

2 cups powdered sugar
2½ cups graham cracker crumbs
2 sticks butter or margarine,
    melted
7 ounces coconut, flaked

12 ounces crunchy peanut butter
1 cup nuts, chopped
½ pound semisweet chocolate,
    melted

Add sugar to crumbs. Blend in melted butter. Add coconut, peanut butter, and nuts. Blend well with hands or spoon. Shape into tightly packed small balls. Dip in chocolate which has been melted over hot water. Yield: 6 dozen.

Coffee Dot Fudge

Eat til it ouches you!

3 cups sugar
1 cup milk
½ cup light cream
2 tablespoons instant coffee
1 tablespoon corn syrup

Dash salt
3 tablespoons butter or margarine
1 teaspoon vanilla extract
½ cup semisweet chocolate bits
½ cup pecans, broken

Butter sides of heavy 3-quart saucepan. Combine sugar, milk, light cream, instant coffee, corn syrup, and salt. Cook on medium, stirring constantly until sugar dissolves. Cook to soft-ball (234 degrees). Remove from heat; add butter; cool to lukewarm without stirring. Add vanilla and beat until creamy. Stir in chocolate bits and pecans. Spread in buttered 9x9-inch pan. Cut into squares. Yield: 16 squares.

Cream Mints

Delicious and beautiful to use for special occasions.

2 tablespoons margarine
2 tablespoons shortening
2 tablespoons warm water
1 teaspoon butter flavoring

3-10 drops oil of peppermint
About 1½ pounds confectioner's
sugar, sifted

Mix all ingredients together until easy to handle and shape. Press mixture into a rubber mint mold and carefully unmold. Repeat until all mixture is shaped. Store in cool place.

Fantasy Fudge

Eat til it ouches you!

3 cups sugar
1 cup evaporated milk
1 cup butter or margarine
1 pint marshmallow creme

1 teaspoon vanilla extract
1½ cups nuts, chopped
12 ounces chocolate morsels

Combine sugar, milk, and butter in large saucepan. Cook over medium heat to soft-ball (234 degrees), stirring frequently. Remove from heat; add remaining ingredients. Beat until chocolate is melted and blended. Pour into a buttered 13x9x2-inch pan. Score in squares while warm. Cut, when firm. Yield: 4½ dozen—1½-inch pieces.

Graham Cracker Log

4 cups graham cracker crumbs
½ pound miniature marshmallows
1 pound dates, chopped
1 small bottle Maraschino
   cherries, drained
2 cups nuts, chopped
1 cup heavy cream

Combine crumbs with other ingredients. Add cream, NOT WHIPPED. Shape into roll and roll in extra crumbs. Chill overnight. Slice and serve with ice cream or whipped cream.

No-Bake Orange Balls

An excellent recipe for children to make.

7¼ ounces vanilla wafers, crushed
¾ cup coconut, grated
¾ cup confectioner's sugar
½ cup frozen orange juice
   concentrate, thawed

Mix all ingredients. Form into 1-inch balls. Roll balls in additional confectioner's sugar. Store in covered container. Yield: 3 dozen.

Nut Clusters

Eat til it ouches you!

7 ounces marshmallow creme
1½ pounds chocolate kisses
5 cups sugar
12 ounces evaporated milk
½ cup margarine
6 cups nuts

Place marshmallow creme and kisses in large bowl; set aside. Combine sugar, milk, and butter in saucepan. Bring mixture to a boil; cook for 8 minutes. Pour over marshmallow cream and kisses, stirring until well blended. Stir in nuts. Drop by teaspoonfuls onto waxed paper. Yield: 12 dozen.

"Life is short. Eat dessert first."

Peanut Brittle

MICROWAVE. Eat til it ouches you!

1 cup raw peanuts	⅛ teaspoon salt
1 cup sugar	2 tablespoons butter
¼ cup white corn syrup	1 teaspoon vanilla extract
¼ cup dark corn syrup	2 teaspoons baking soda

Stir peanuts, sugar, syrups, and salt together in deep bowl. MICROWAVE, HIGH, 4 minutes. If roasted salted peanuts are used, omit salt and add peanuts after first 4 minutes of cooking. Stir candy so all sugar is mixed and MICROWAVE, HIGH, 1-3 more minutes. Add butter and vanilla to syrup, blending well. MICROWAVE, HIGH, 1-3 minutes. Add soda and stir until light and foamy. Pour immediately onto lightly buttered surface spreading it out. Cool and break into pieces. Store in airtight container.

Peanut Butter Pinwheels

For peanut butter lovers!

½ cup potatoes, cold mashed	½ teaspoon vanilla extract
Dash salt	1 cup peanut butter
4 cups confectioner's sugar, sifted	

In a large bowl with spoon, combine potatoes, salt, and enough confectioner's sugar to make easily handled fondant. Add vanilla and mix well. Turn half of mixture onto board lightly dusted with confectioner's sugar. Roll into rectangle ¼-inch thick. Spread with ½ peanut butter. Roll up from short side in jelly roll fashion. Repeat with rest of fondant. Slice.

White Christmas Crunches

1 stick margarine	15 ounces raisins
¾ cup peanut butter	24 ounces peanuts or pecans,
8 ounces semisweet chocolate	roasted
morsels	1 pound powdered sugar
12.3 ounces Crispix cereal	

Melt margarine, peanut butter, and chocolate morsels. Set aside. Combine cereal, raisins, and nuts in large container. Pour chocolate mixture over it. Mix well. Sift a box of powdered sugar into a large brown bag. Pour the mixture in; shake until coated. Serve in a large lined bowl. Yield: 60 servings.

Cranberry Sherbet

2 cups cranberries
1½ cups water
1 teaspoon gelatin
1¼ cups sugar

1 cup orange juice
5 teaspoons dried egg whites
2 ounces water

Cook cranberries in water until they are soft and rub them through a fine sieve. Soften gelatin in 2 tablespoons cold water and dissolve it over hot water. Combine the gelatin with the cranberries, sugar, and orange juice. Freeze the sherbet in trays as quickly as possible for 1 hour—or until it is mushy but not solid. Turn the sherbet into a chilled bowl and beat it rapidly with electric mixer until it is smooth. Work quickly to minimize melting. Beat dried egg whites and 2 ounces of water until stiffly beaten. Fold in stiffly beaten egg whites and return the sherbet to the freezer. When it is almost solid, beat it until it is smooth. Return the tray to the freezer, covering it to prevent ice crystals from forming, and freeze until it is solid. Yield: 6-8 servings.

Lemon Snow Freeze

1 cup graham cracker crumbs
6 tablespoons sugar
3 tablespoons butter or
    margarine, melted
2 egg yolks
1 tablespoon lemon rind, grated

½ cup lemon juice
14 ounces sweetened condensed
    milk
1 cup coconut, grated
5 teaspoons dried egg whites
2 ounces water

Combine crumbs with 2 tablespoons sugar and butter. Press mixture on bottom and sides of lightly buttered refrigerator tray; chill. Beat egg yolks until thick and combine with milk. Add lemon rind and juice gradually, stirring until thickened. Stir in ¾ cup coconut. Whip dried egg whites and 2 ounces water until foamy and gradually beat in rest of sugar until stiff. Fold into lemon mixture. Pour into refrigerator tray. Sprinkle top with remaining coconut. Chill in freezer until firm, about 4-6 hours. Yield: 10 servings.

SPECIAL NOTE: Uncooked egg yolks and/or egg whites should not be used in recipes due to bacterial problems in foods. Substitute dried egg yolks and/or egg whites in recipes calling for uncooked egg yolks and/or egg whites.

Gingerbread Peach Dessert

⅓ cup cold water
⅓ cup powdered milk
1 package unflavored gelatin
6 tablespoons sugar
1¼ cups boiling water

2½ cups peach purée
6 tablespoons lemon juice
1 tablespoon crystallized ginger,
   finely chopped

To make peach purée, blend frozen or fresh peaches. Combine iced water and powdered milk in small bowl that has been chilled. Beat with electric mixer until stiff, about 6 minutes. Place in refrigerator. Mix gelatin and sugar together in saucepan. Add boiling water; stir until gelatin is dissolved. Blend in peach purée and lemon juice. Place in bowl of ice water. Chill gelatin mixture, stirring constantly until it almost reaches the consistency of un-beaten egg white. Fold in whipped powdered milk; pour into two small refrigerator trays. Freeze until almost firm. Put mixture into chilled bowl, add ginger, beat with electric mixer until smooth and fluffy. Pour into refrigerator trays. Freeze until firm.

Applesauce

North Carolina apples hit the spot. Use the blender.

4 apples
1 teaspoon salt
¼ cup apple juice or water

¼ cup sugar
½ teaspoon cinnamon, ground

Wash and cut apples into eighths. Remove core. Put pieces into a bowl of water to which the salt has been added. Put ¼ cup apple juice and 4-5 pieces of apple into blender container. Cover and turn to medium speed. With blender running, add remaining apples, a few at a time, through the center of the lid. Blend in sugar and cinnamon. Cook slightly if desired. Yield: 2 cups.

Strawberry Cloud

12 ounces frozen strawberries,
   drained
2½ teaspoons dried egg white

1 ounce water
½ cup sugar

In large mixing bowl, beat dried egg whites and water until foamy. Gradually add sugar and berries. Continue beating until mixture has more than doubled in bulk. Serve Strawberry Cloud as is, with pound cake, or as a frozen dessert. Yield: 2 quarts.

Heavenly Hash

Wonderful at Christmas Time!

3 eggs, well beaten
¼ cup white vinegar
¾ cup sugar
1 pound large marshmallows, cut
    in four pieces

1 large can sliced pineapple, cut
1 cup blanched almonds, chopped
½ pint whipping cream, whipped

Cook eggs, vinegar, and sugar in top of double boiler until thick and cool. Combine all ingredients and sauce, then fold in cream. Refrigerate until ready to use.

Sweet Potato—Apple Sauce Pie

Yummy is the word for this autumn treat!

1¼ cups sweet potatoes, mashed
1¼ cups apple sauce
½ cup brown sugar, packed
1 teaspoon cinnamon, ground
½ teaspoon nutmeg, ground

½ teaspoon salt
¼ cup butter, melted
3 eggs
Unbaked 9-inch pastry shell

Combine sweet potatoes, apple sauce, brown sugar, cinnamon, nutmeg, salt, and butter. Beat eggs and add to mixture. Pour into unbaked pastry shell and bake in preheated oven until firm. Temperature: 425 degrees. Baking Time: 45 minutes. Yield: 6-8 servings.

Carrot Pie

1 pound carrots, peeled and sliced
1½ cups water
1 teaspoon salt
4 eggs
6 ounces evaporated milk
1 cup sugar

1 tablespoon flour
1 teaspoon ginger, ground
1 teaspoon cinnamon, ground
½ teaspoon nutmeg, ground
⅛ teaspoon cloves, ground
Unbaked 9-inch pastry shell

Place carrots, water, and ½ teaspoon salt in saucepan and bring to boil; cook until tender. Drain. Place carrots, eggs, milk, and all dry ingredients in blender and blend until smooth. Pour into pastry shell. Bake in preheated oven. Serve warm or cold topped with whipped cream. When pie is done, insert a knife in center and it will come out clean. Temperature: 400 degrees. Baking Time: 45-50 minutes. Yield: 1 pie.

Banana Breeze Pie

Use the electric mixer.

8 ounces cream cheese, softened
14 ounces SWEETENED
   CONDENSED MILK
⅓ cup lemon juice

1 teaspoon vanilla extract
4 medium bananas, sliced
Lemon juice
Graham cracker pastry shell

Beat cream cheese until fluffy. Gradually beat in SWEETENED CON-DENSED MILK until smooth. Stir in lemon juice and vanilla. Dip bananas in additional lemon juice and drain. Fold in sliced bananas by hand. Pour filling into pastry shell. Cover. Chill for 3 hours or until set. Yield: 6-8 servings.

Sweetened Condensed Milk

Use the blender and in any recipe. $ Saver.

1 cup instant dry milk
½ cup boiling water
3 tablespoons margarine, melted

⅔ cup sugar
¼ teaspoon salt

Combine all ingredients in blender. Chill. It becomes thicker when chilled. Yield: equals a 14-ounce can.

Chocolate Angel Pie

Eat til it ouches you!

2 egg whites
⅛ teaspoon salt
⅛ teaspoon cream of tartar
½ cup sugar
½ cup nuts, chopped

½ teaspoon vanilla extract
4 ounces German sweet chocolate
3 tablespoons water
1 teaspoon vanilla extract
1 cup whipping cream

Preheat oven. Beat egg whites, salt, and cream of tartar with mixer until soft peaks form. Add sugar gradually and continue beating until mixture is very stiff. Fold in nuts and ½ teaspoon vanilla. Turn into lightly greased 8-9-inch pie pan and make a nestlike shell, building sides up ½-inch above edge of pan. Bake. Cool. To make FILLING, place chocolate and water in saucepan over low heat. Stir until chocolate is melted. Cool until thickened, then add 1 teaspoon vanilla. Whip cream. Fold chocolate mixture into whipped cream. Spoon into meringue shell. Chill about 2 hours before serving. Temperature: 300 degrees. Baking Time: 50-55 minutes. Yield: 1 pie.

My Favorite Chocolate Pie

Roy's Restaurant, Elkin, N.C., famous Chocolate Pie is similar.

1 cup sugar
3 tablespoons flour
1 tablespoon corn starch
3 tablespoons cocoa
¼ teaspoon salt
2 cups milk

3 egg yolks
1 teaspoon vanilla extract
"Hunk" (about 2 tablespoons)
 butter
Baked 9-inch pastry shell

Mix well all dry ingredients and stir in milk in top of double boiler. When mixture begins to thicken, dip out a small amount and beat with egg yolks, then add back to filling in double boiler, stirring until mixed well. Add butter, put lid on, and cook 10 minutes, stirring occasionally. Cool, add vanilla and beat until smooth. Pour filling into baked pastry shell and top with whipped cream or meringue. Yield: 6-8 servings.

Lemon Corn Meal Chess Pie

Eat til it ouches you!

2 cups sugar
2 tablespoons corn meal
1 tablespoon flour
4 eggs, unbeaten
¼ cup butter, melted

¼ cup milk
¼ cup lemon juice
4 teaspoons lemon rind, grated
Unbaked 9-inch pastry shell

Mix sugar, corn meal, and flour. Add eggs, one at a time, beat well after each. Stir in butter, milk, lemon juice, and rind; mix well. Pour mixture into unbaked pastry shell. Bake on lower shelf of oven in preheated oven. Allow to cool before cutting. Temperature: 350 degrees. Baking Time: 45 minutes. Yield: 1 pie.

Peanut Butter Pie

A frozen summer delight!

8 ounces cream cheese, softened
1 cup crunchy peanut butter
½ cup cream
2 cups confectioner's sugar

16 ounces non-dairy whipped
 topping
2 (9-inch) graham cracker crusts

Combine the first four ingredients and mix until smooth. Fold in whipped topping. Pour into graham cracker crusts and freeze. Serve while frozen. Yield: 2 pies.

Coconut Pie

Easy! It's out of this world; serve warm.

2 eggs, beaten
½ cup milk
1 cup sugar
1 teaspoon vanilla extract

½ stick butter, melted
1 cup coconut, grated
Unbaked 8-inch pastry shell

Mix together and pour into an unbaked pastry shell and bake in preheated oven. Temperature: 325 degrees. Baking Time: 25-35 minutes. Yield: 6 servings.

Frozen Limeade Pie

1¾ cups chocolate wafer crumbs, finely crushed
5 tablespoons butter or margarine, melted
½ tablespoon unflavored gelatin

6 ounces cold water
6 ounces frozen limeade
½ pound (32) marshmallows
½ pint heavy cream, whipped
Green food coloring

Combine crumbs and melted butter. Set aside ¼ cup crumb mixture for garnish. Pat remaining crumbs into 9-inch pie plate, pressing firmly against sides and bottom. Chill. Soak gelatin in water. Combine with limeade in saucepan. Add marshmallows and heat until dissolved. Chill mixture until cool and syrupy. Whip with electric mixer on highest speed. Fold in whipped cream. Pile filling in chilled crust; garnish. Freeze. When solid, wrap in freezer paper. Remove from freezer about 30 minutes before serving. Yield: 8 servings.

Impossible Piña Colada Pie

Eat til it ouches you!

4 eggs
¼ cup milk
¼ cup rum or 2 teaspoons rum extract plus 2 tablespoons milk
2 tablespoons margarine

15 ounces cream of coconut
8 ounces crushed pineapple, well drained
2 cups coconut, flaked
½ cup biscuit mix

Preheat oven. Grease 10x1½-inch pie plate. Beat all ingredients, except 1 cup coconut, together until well-blended. Pour mixture into pie plate. Sprinkle with remaining 1 cup coconut. Bake until knife inserted in center comes out clean. Temperature: 350 degrees. Baking Time: 35-40 minutes. Yield: 6-8 servings.

Hot Cherry Pudding

1 cup Bisquick
1¼ cups sugar
1 can sour cherries, drained
⅓ cup milk

1¼ cups cherry juice and water
    mixed
2 tablespoons butter or margarine
½ teaspoon almond extract
Red food coloring

Preheat oven. To Bisquick, add ¼ cup sugar and the drained cherries. Stir in milk to make a stiff dough. Spread in greased 8x8x2-inch pan. Add water to cherry juice to make 1¼ cups; add remaining 1 cup sugar and heat. Add almond extract and a few drops of red coloring. Add butter and bring to a boil. Pour over the dough and bake. Serve hot with milk or ice cream. Temperature: 375 degrees. Baking Time: 30 minutes. Yield: 1 pudding.

Cherry Rum Balls

A pretty dessert that freezes nicely.

12 ounces maraschino cherries
    with stems
2 cups vanilla wafer crumbs,
    finely crushed
2 tablespoons cocoa, unsweetened
1 cup nuts, finely chopped
½ cup light corn syrup

3-4 tablespoons light or dark
    (80 proof) rum
Coatings: flaked coconut, finely
    chopped walnuts, grated
    semisweet chocolate squares
    or confectioner's sugar

Drain cherries. Syrup may be used in cold fruit beverages. In mixing bowl, stir together the wafer crumbs and cocoa; stir in nuts, then corn syrup. Stir in just enough rum to hold mixture together, mixing well. Form mixture into a long roll about 1½ inches in diameter, cut into slices (40-48) to equal the number of cherries. Press each slice around a cherry, leaving stem exposed. Roll each ball in one of the coatings. If using confectioner's sugar, apply just before serving. Store in a covered container, put wax paper between layers, and place in refrigerator. Keeps for weeks. In serving, flatten bottoms so the stems can stand straight up. Yield: 4 dozen.

Double or triple recipes that freeze well. Wrap them in serving portions ready to use so they can be taken out of the freezer and reheated.

Date Nut Cake Roll

Eat til it ouches you!

1 cup pitted whole dates, snipped
1 cup water
¼ cup sugar
⅛ teaspoon salt
3 eggs
½ cup sugar

1 cup flour
1 teaspoon baking powder
½ teaspoon salt
½ teaspoon allspice, ground
¾ cup walnuts, chopped

In small saucepan, combine dates, 1 cup water, ¼ cup sugar, and ⅛ teaspoon salt. Bring to boiling. Cook and stir over low heat till thick, about 4 minutes. Remove from heat; cool to room temperature. In mixer bowl, beat eggs at high speed of electric mixer for 5 minutes. Gradually beat in ½ cup sugar. Stir flour, baking powder, ½ teaspoon salt, and allspice. Fold into egg mixture. Fold in date mixture. Spread in greased and floured 10x15-inch jelly roll pan. Top with walnuts. Bake in preheated oven. Turn out onto towel, sprinkle with a little powdered sugar. Starting at narrow end, roll up cake and towel together; cool. Unroll and spread with CREAM CHEESE FILLING. Reroll. Chill. Temperature: 375 degrees. Baking Time: 12-15 minutes. Yield: 16 servings.

CREAM CHEESE FILLING
6 ounces cream cheese
4 tablespoons butter or margarine

½ teaspoon vanilla extract
1 cup powdered sugar, sifted

Soften cheese and butter, beat until fluffy. Add vanilla and powdered sugar.

Lemon Charlotte Russe

1 envelope unflavored gelatin
½ cup fresh lemon juice
4 egg yolks
1½ cups sugar
⅛ teaspoon salt
3 tablespoons butter or margarine
2 teaspoons lemon peel, grated

1 teaspoon vanilla extract
2 packages lady fingers
10 teaspoons dried egg whites
4 ounces water
1 cup heavy cream, whipped
Whipped cream to garnish top

Soften gelatin in lemon juice. Beat egg yolks, 1 cup sugar and salt. Add gelatin and butter. Cook over medium heat, stirring until thick, about 10 minutes. Stir in lemon peel and vanilla. Remove from heat and cool. Line bottom and sides of 9-inch spring form pan with lady fingers. Beat dried egg whites and 4 ounces water until peaks form. Gradually add ½ cup sugar and beat until stiff. Fold egg whites and whipped cream into lemon mixture. Place into pan and refrigerate until firm. About 2 hours. Garnish with whipped cream. Yield: 8 servings.

Japanese Orange Fluff

Eat til it ouches you!

1 egg, well beaten
3 tablespoons lemon juice
3 tablespoons sugar
½ cup heavy cream, whipped
11 ounces mandarin oranges,
    drained

1 cup miniature marshmallows
1 cup bananas, sliced
½ cup toasted almonds, slivered
Angel food cake

Combine egg, lemon juice, and sugar in top of double boiler. Cook over hot water, stirring until thickened. Cool. Fold in whipped cream, mandarin oranges, marshmallows, and bananas. Refrigerate until chilled. Fold in almonds. Spoon over slices of cake. Yield: 10 servings.

Nut Log

Easy to make!

1 box vanilla wafers
⅔ (15 ounces) box raisins
2 cups nuts, chopped

14 ounces sweetened condensed
    milk
Powdered sugar

Crush vanilla wafers. Add raisins, nuts, and milk. Roll into log. Roll in powdered sugar. Chill. Slice and serve.

Snowballs

Eat til it ouches you!

1 stick margarine or butter
1 cup sugar
1 large can crushed pineapple
½ cup dates, chopped
½ cup white seedless raisins

1 cup pecans, chopped
1 tablespoon rum extract
1 box butter cookies
2 packages dessert topping
8 ounces coconut, flaked

Melt butter and add sugar, fruit, nuts, and extract. Stack 3 cookies with filling between and on top. Chill for at least 3 hours or overnight. Whip dessert topping. Ice top and side of cookies. Cover with coconut and chill. Yield: 15 servings.

Tea-Time Tassies

Lovely for a party!

CHEESE PASTRY

3 ounces cream cheese
½ cup butter or margarine

1 cup flour, sifted

Let cream cheese and ½ cup butter soften at room temperature; blend. Stir in flour. Chill slightly, about 1 hour. Shape in 2 dozen 1-inch balls; place in tiny ungreased 1¾-inch muffin cups. Press dough on bottom and sides of cups.

PECAN FILLING

2 eggs
1½ cups brown sugar, packed
2 tablespoons soft butter or
    margarine

2 teaspoons vanilla extract
Dash salt
1⅓ cups pecans, coarsely broken

Preheat oven. Beat together eggs, sugar, butter, vanilla, and salt until smooth. Divide half the pecans among CHEESE PASTRY-lined cups; add FILLING and top with remaining pecans. Bake until filling is set. Cool; remove from pans. Freezes well. Temperature: 325 degrees. Baking Time: 25 minutes. Yield: 24.

Date And Nut Tarts

¼ pound butter
3 ounces cream cheese

1 cup flour

Cream butter and cheese. Add flour. Roll out and cut with cutter; place in greased muffin pans.

FILLING

¼ cup butter
1 cup sugar
2 eggs, separated

2 teaspoons vanilla extract
1 cup nuts, ground
1 cup dates, ground

Preheat oven. Cream butter and sugar; add beaten egg yolks and vanilla. Add nuts, dates, and fold in egg whites. Place FILLING in PASTRY CUPS. Bake. For party tarts, use small muffin pans. Temperature: 350 degrees. Baking Time: 10-15 minutes.

*"Almighty God, Extend your hand from your holy dwelling place
and bless the food and drink that we are about to receive."*
GREEK BLESSING

The Cinema
(Old Earle) Theater

THE CINEMA (OLD EARLE) THEATER

The "Old Earle" Theater was across the street from the Grand Theater which was mentioned frequently on the "Andy Griffith Show". Late night shows were frequent on Saturday nights. Remember the marquee, which the locals called the "Owl Shows". Even the Weenie Burger stayed open after the "Owls". There were no Sunday movies at that time. In 1938, the "Old Earle" Theater had one of the southern premiers of "Gone With the Wind". In 1958, the premier of "A Face in the Crowd" was held at the "Old Earle". When Andy Griffith was a boy his mother would give him twenty-five cents to come to town. Andy would go to the movie priced ten cents. After the movie, he would walk across the street to Snappy Lunch and buy a hot dog and drink for fifteen cents. In 1991, the theater was donated to the Surry Arts Council by Carmike Theater of Columbus, Georgia. In 1994, the Arts Council began showing $1.00 subrun movies in the theater and Bluegrass band concerts are frequent.

Mayberry Days, an annual event that began in 1990 by the Surry Arts Council, is held the last weekend in September. This is homecoming weekend for thousands of fans of "The Andy Griffith Show". They come from all corners of the U.S. and other countries, hoping to find the "real" Mayberry. We all know that Mayberry was created by talented writers and actors. Smiling faces; interesting people with names, like Taylor, Emmett, Pike, Virginia Beasley, Earle Gilley, Andy; places, like Pilot Mountain, Blu-Vue, Snappy Lunch, Floyd's Barber Shop; and streets, such as Haymore and Rockford, and the genuine friendliness of the Mount Airy people, help to create a state of mind, a condition of the heart, and soul to give the hometown feeling of the "real" Mayberry. It's "FAN" tastic!

Brunch Casserole

This one-dish meal can be mixed together the day before serving, refrigerated, and baked the following day. Recipe may be doubled.

6 ounces Betty Crocker hash
  brown potatoes with sweet
  onions
1½ cups cheddar cheese, shredded
1 cup Swiss cheese, shredded
½ cup Parmesan cheese
1 teaspoon salt
1 cup ham or bacon, cooked and
  finely chopped

1 teaspoon dry mustard
Dash pepper
½ cup onion, chopped
6 eggs, well beaten
1½ cups water
1 cup milk
Paprika

Mix all ingredients together, except paprika, until potatoes began to get a little soft. Pour into a greased 12x7x2-inch baking pan. Sprinkle paprika on top. Bake. Let set 3-4 minutes before serving. Temperature: 350 degrees. Baking Time: 40-45 minutes. Yield: 8 servings.

Marzetta

Freeze in individual servings and heat in microwave.

4 medium onions, chopped
1 stalk celery, chopped
2 large green peppers, chopped
3 tablespoons butter
2 pounds ground beef
1 pound ground veal
1 pound ground pork

1 pound sharp cheese, grated
2 boxes flat narrow noodles
3 cans tomato soup
2 cans mushroom soup
Almonds
Season to taste

Sauté celery, onion, and pepper in butter until tender; add meat, cook until done. Add ½ cheese. Cook noodles separately, add tomato soup, and noodles to meat mixture. Season to taste. Put in casserole dish. Put mushroom soup on top. Sprinkle cheese and almonds on top. Bake in oven until cheese browns. Temperature: 350 degrees. Baking Time: until heated and cheese browns. Yield: three 2-quart casseroles.

Eating parsley after onions helps to kill the onion odor. It freshens your breath.

All Time Favorite Roast/Gravy

Quick! Easy! Want to do something special for a friend? This is it.

3 pounds chuck roast
1 can mushroom soup

1 envelope dry onion soup mix

In baking pan, place roast on large piece of heavy duty aluminum foil. Add soups to top of roast. For more gravy add an extra can and/or package of soup. Use drug-store wrap to seal foil and keep in moisture. Bake. Temperature: 325 degrees. Baking Time: 3 hours. Yield: 1 roast.

Bar-B-Que Meat Balls

Perk up your winter meals with the colorful entrée.

1 cup soft bread crumbs
½ cup milk
1 pound ground beef

1 teaspoon salt
1 teaspoon pepper

SAUCE
¼ cup vinegar
1 tablespoon sugar
½ cup catsup
½ cup water

½ green pepper, chopped
½ cup onion, chopped
1½ tablespoons Worcestershire sauce

Cover crumbs in milk and add ground beef, salt, and pepper. Shape meat into balls. Place in casserole dish. Mix all ingredients for sauce and pour SAUCE over BAR-B-QUE MEAT BALLS. Bake. Temperature: 375 degrees. Baking Time: 45 minutes. Yield: 6-8 servings.

Marinated Flank Steak

¾ cup maple syrup
½ cup soy sauce
¼ cup vinegar
2 teaspoons dry mustard

1 teaspoon salt
½ teaspoon pepper
1 clove garlic, crushed
1½-2 pounds flank steak

Combine the marinade ingredients and pour over flank steak in shallow baking dish. Marinate in refrigerator for 24 hours. Remove steak from marinade and place on broiler pan. Broil 5 inches from source of heat about 7 minutes on each side. Starting at the narrow end, thinly slice steak diagonally across the grain of the meat. Yield: 6 servings.

All—Day Stew

Great for using the slow cooker.

2 pounds beef, 1 inch cubes
2 tablespoons shortening
3½ cups water
1 medium onion, sliced
1 tablespoon salt
1 teaspoon Worcestershire sauce
¼ teaspoon pepper

6 medium potatoes, cubed
4 medium carrots, sliced
2 medium onions, sliced
1 cup catsup
10 ounces frozen lima beans or
   peas

Brown meat in shortening. Add water, 1 sliced onion, salt, Worcestershire sauce, and pepper. Cover and simmer about 1 hour until tender, stirring occasionally. Add potatoes, carrots, 2 onions. Cover. Cook 30 minutes-1 hour until vegetables are tender. Stir in catsup, lima beans, or peas. Cover and simmer until done. Yield: 10-12 servings.

Beef and Peach Paprika

1 pound and 13 ounces cling
   peach slices
1½ pounds bottom round steak,
   1 inch thick
¼ cup flour
2 teaspoons paprika

1½ teaspoons salt
½ teaspoon pepper
2 tablespoons salad oil
1 pound tomatoes, canned
1 teaspoon caraway seeds
Hot buttered noodles

Drain peaches saving ½ cup syrup. Cut steak into 2x1x½-inch strips. Combine flour, 1 teaspoon paprika, ½ teaspoon salt and pepper. Heat oil in skillet. Dust meat with flour mixture and brown in oil. (Save remaining flour mixture). Add peach syrup, remaining paprika and salt, tomatoes, and caraway seeds. Cover and simmer 1½ hours. Mix remaining flour mixture with a little cold water and stir into mixture. Cook, stirring until thickened. Add peach slices and heat through. Serve with hot buttered noodles. Yield: 6-8 servings.

DO NOT COVER THE REFLECTOR PANS UNDER THE SURFACE UNIT WITH ALUMINIUM FOIL. It can trap the heat and ruin your surface unit or get in the electrical connection and short-out the unit.

Beef Spanish Rice

Use electric frypan.

¼ cup shortening
¾ cup white rice, cooked
1 pound ground beef
¼ cup celery, chopped
1 teaspoon onion, chopped
¼ cup green pepper, chopped
2 beef bouillon cubes

2 cups boiling water
2 cups tomatoes, cooked
⅔ cup tomato paste
½ bay leaf
½ teaspoon chili powder
1½ teaspoons salt
1 teaspoon sugar

Melt shortening in electric frypan using medium heat. Add rice and stir. When browned, remove rice. Add meat and stir until meat is lightly browned. To meat, add rice, celery, onion, and green pepper. Dissolve bouillon cubes in water and add to remaining ingredients. Pour over meat mixture and stir thoroughly. Cover and reduce heat to low. Simmer 30-45 minutes. Yield: 4 servings.

Chinese Meatballs In Mushroom Sauce

1 pound ground beef
¼ teaspoon pepper
1 tablespoon soy sauce
2 teaspoons brown gravy sauce
¾ cup Fancy Chow Mein Noodles
1 egg, beaten
¼ teaspoon monosodium
    glutamate

2 tablespoons butter
1 small onion, chopped
1 can cream of mushroom soup
2 tablespoons flour
¼ teaspoon salt
1 cup milk
1 teaspoon soy sauce

Mix lightly together beef, pepper, soy sauce, brown gravy sauce, noodles, egg, and monosodium glutamate. Shape into 10 balls; brown in butter in electric frypan at 250 degrees. Remove balls from frypan. Cook onion in drippings for 5 minutes. Blend in mushroom soup, flour, and salt. Gradually stir in milk and soy sauce. Cook over moderate heat until thickened, stirring constantly. Arrange meatballs in sauce. Cover. Simmer for 20 minutes. Yield: 4-6 servings.

Cantonese Beef

⅓ cup dark corn syrup
¼ cup soy sauce
¼ cup cooking sherry
¼ cup teaspoon ginger, ground
2 pounds beef chuck,
    cut in ½-inch cubes

1¼ cups water
2 tablespoons corn starch
2 tablespoons water
Hot cooked rice

Combine syrup, soy sauce, sherry, and ginger in shallow dish. Add meat; marinate 1 hour in refrigerator; stir occasionally. Mix meat and marinade with 1¼ cups water in saucepan. Cover; simmer 1 hour or until meat is tender. Blend corn starch with 2 tablespoons water; stir into meat mixture. Simmer 2 minutes, stirring constantly. Serve on hot cooked rice. Yield: 6-8 servings.

Chinese Stir Fry

Fast and easy in wok or electric frypan.

1 pound beef top round steak,
    1-inch thick
3 tablespoons soy sauce
1 tablespoon corn starch
4 tablespoons vegetable oil
½ teaspoon ginger, ground
1 clove garlic, minced (optional)

2 small onions, sliced
1 red or green pepper, cut into
    strips
3 cups broccoli flowerets
2 medium carrots, diagonally
    sliced
½ cup beef broth or consommé

Steak should be partially frozen. Cut steak diagonally across the grain into ⅛-inch thick slices. Mix together soy sauce and corn starch until smooth. Set aside. Since cooking time is short, prepare all remaining ingredients. In wok or electric frypan over high heat, add 2 tablespoons oil, ginger, and garlic. Cook 1 minute to flavor oil. Add meat, cook about 3 minutes or until meat browns and loses pink color. Spoon meat into bowl. Add 2 more tablespoons oil. Add onions and green pepper. Stir fry 2 minutes. Add broccoli and carrots. Stir fry 2 minutes or until tender crisp. Return meat to wok. Warm beef broth by pouring it around edges of wok. Cold liquids will make meat tough. Add soy sauce mixture. Bring to boil, stirring frequently until sauce thickens. Serve with rice. Yield: 5 servings.

Hamburger Stroganoff

This budget version of Beef Stroganoff has all the fine flavor of the original.

½ cup onion, finely minced
1 clove garlic, minced
¼ cup butter
1 pound ground beef
2 tablespoons flour
1 teaspoon salt
¼ teaspoon pepper

8 ounces mushrooms, sliced
½ can cream of chicken soup,
  undiluted
1½ cups sour cream
2 tablespoons parsley, snipped
Noodles, cooked

Cook onion and garlic in butter until transparent. Add meat cook and stir until it has lost red color. Add flour, salt, pepper, and mushrooms; cook 5 minutes. Add soup; simmer 10 minutes. Add sour cream and heat. Top with parsley; serve on noodles. Yield: 4-6 servings.

Hamburger Quiche

Pastry for 9 inch Quiche pan
¾ pound ground beef
2 teaspoons Worcestershire sauce
¾ teaspoon salt
⅛ teaspoon pepper
⅛ teaspoon garlic powder
⅓ cup onion, chopped
⅓ cup green pepper, chopped

1 tablespoon salad oil
½ cup mayonnaise
½ cup milk
2 eggs, beaten
1 tablespoon corn starch
1½ cups Cheddar or Swiss cheese,
  shredded, divided

Line a 9 inch quiche pan with pastry, and trim off excess around edge of pan. Cover with foil. Bake at 400 degrees for 10 minutes; remove foil. Prick shell and bake 3-5 additional minutes or until lightly browned. Cool. Brown ground beef in skillet; drain well. Add seasoning and set aside. Sauté onion and green pepper in salad oil; add to meat mixture. Combine mayonnaise, milk, eggs, and corn starch; mix thoroughly. Add custard to meat mixture. Stir in half of cheese. Pour into quiche shell and sprinkle with remaining cheese. Bake at 375 degrees for 35-45 minutes or until firm in center. Baking Time: 48-60 minutes. Yield: one 9-inch quiche.

Coca Cola Roast

Salt to taste
Pepper to taste
3 pounds beef roast

4 tablespoons flour
4 tablespoons fat
8 ounces Coca Cola drink

Salt and pepper roast. Flour on all sides and brown in hot fat. When brown on both sides, drain fat off. Place in container. Pour cola drink over roast. Cover. Bake. Temperature: 325 degrees. Baking Time: 2½-3 hours. Yields: 8-10 servings.

Hot Diggety Dogs

Use the food processor and frypan.

3 tablespoons shortening
1 onion, thinly sliced
1 pound beef franks, sliced
1 pound can baked beans

¼ cup catsup
1 tablespoon brown sugar, packed
1 teaspoon prepared mustard

Heat shortening in skillet at 350 degrees until indicator light goes out. Add onion and franks. Brown lightly. Turn temperature control to 225 degrees. Add beans, catsup, brown sugar, and mustard. Cover and simmer 10 minutes. Yield: 6-8 servings.

Husband's Delight

1½ pounds ground beef
1 teaspoon salt
1 teaspoon sugar
1 teaspoon pepper
2 small cans tomato sauce
1 small onion, chopped

3 ounces cream cheese
½ pint sour cream
8 ounces thin egg noodles, cooked
4 ounces cheddar cheese,
     shredded

Brown and drain ground beef. Add salt, sugar, pepper, and tomato sauce. Simmer 15 minutes. Cream together onion, cream cheese, and sour cream. Using 9x12-inch baking dish layer noodles, meat mixture, and sour cream mixture. Repeat. Top with cheddar cheese. Bake. Temperature: 350 degrees. Baking Time: 20-25 minutes. Yield: 8 servings.

Lasagna

This is an excellent recipe to freeze.

3 pounds ground beef
1 pound ground lean pork
4 cups onions, sliced
1½ cups green pepper, chopped
4 cloves garlic, mashed
1 teaspoon sage
1 tablespoon oregano
1 tablespoon basil
1 tablespoon celery salt
2 teaspoons paprika
4 teaspoons salt
¼ cup parsley, snipped
1 tablespoon Worcestershire
   sauce

1 beef bouillon cube
1 chicken bouillon cube
4 teaspoons monosodium
   glutamate
2 teaspoons sugar
4 (4 ounces) tomato paste
2 (1 pound) tomatoes
8 ounces mushrooms
2 (10 ounces) lasagna noodles
2 pounds dry cottage cheese
2 pounds mozzarella cheese
½ cup Parmesan cheese

Brown meat; add onions and pepper and sauté. Drain fat. Add seasonings, tomato paste, tomatoes, and mushrooms. Cover and simmer for 1-2 hours. Cook noodles. In a 2-quart greased casserole dish, layer noodles, sauce, cottage cheese, mozzarella cheese, and Parmesan cheese. Repeat layers and top with sauce. Bake uncovered. Temperature: 350 degrees. Baking Time: 25-30 minutes. Yield: 25 servings or four 2-quart casseroles.

Microwave Swiss Steak

2 pounds beef round or chuck
¼-⅓ cup flour
1 envelope onion soup mix

8 ounces tomato sauce
2 teaspoons parsley flakes
¼ cup water

Cut beef in serving size pieces. Pound meat with meat mallet to tenderize and flatten it to ¼-½ inch thickness. Coat meat with flour. Place in 2-quart baking dish. Sprinkle with soup mix. Combine remaining ingredients in a 2-cup measure. Pour over meat. Cover with plastic wrap, vented. MICROWAVE, MEDIUM, 25 minutes. Rearrange meat. Cover. MICROWAVE 25 minutes longer. Meat should be fork tender. Let stand covered 10 minutes. Yield: 8-10 servings.

Microwave Lasagna

Quick! Easy! The uncooked noodles make this a lazy day delight.

1 pound ground beef
14½ ounces tomatoes, undrained
6 ounces tomato paste
1¼ teaspoons salt
1½ teaspoons basil
½ teaspoon oregano
⅛ teaspoon garlic powder
½ cup water

2 cups cottage cheese
¼ cup Parmesan cheese
1 egg
1 tablespoon parsley flakes
8 lasagna noodles, uncooked
8 ounces Mozzarella cheese,
    shredded

Crumble ground beef into 1½-quart glass casserole. MICROWAVE, HIGH, uncovered, 5-6 minutes or until no longer pink. Stir once to break meat into small pieces. Drain. Stir in tomatoes, tomato paste, salt, basil, oregano, garlic powder, and water. Cover. MICROWAVE, HIGH, 4-5 minutes or until mixture boils. Combine cottage cheese, Parmesan cheese, egg, and parsley; mix well. Pour 1½ cups tomato sauce mixture into 12x8-inch glass baking dish. Spread evenly in dish. Place 4 uncooked noodles evenly over sauce. (Overlap, if necessary.) Top with half the cottage cheese mixture, spreading evenly. Sprinkle with half the Mozzarella cheese. Spoon 1 cup sauce evenly over cheese. Place 4 more noodles on sauce. Top with even layers of remaining cottage cheese mixture, Mozzarella cheese, and tomato sauce. Cover with plastic wrap. MICROWAVE, HIGH, 15 minutes. Rotate dish. MICROWAVE, MEDIUM, 15-20 minutes or until noodles are tender. Remove plastic wrap. Sprinkle lasagna with an additional 2 tablespoons Parmesan cheese. MICROWAVE, HIGH, uncovered, 1½-2 minutes or until cheese is melted. Let stand about 10 minutes before cutting into squares to serve. This recipe may be prepared in advance and refrigerated, but increase last cooking time to 20-25 minutes before adding cheese to melt. Yield: 6 servings.

New England Meat Loaf

16 ounces whole cranberry sauce
1½ pounds lean ground beef
1 cup bread crumbs
1 egg, well beaten
3 tablespoons onion, chopped

3 tablespoons green pepper,
    chopped
½ cup carrot, chopped
Salt and pepper to taste

Spread cranberry sauce in bottom of baking dish. Mix remaining ingredients and place on top of cranberry sauce mixture. Bake. Slice and serve with sauce in pan. Temperature: 350 degrees. Baking Time: 1 hour. Yield: 1 meat loaf.

Tasty Meat Loaf

The luscious tomato sauce creates a gourmet dish.

1½ pounds ground beef
1 onion, chopped
½ small can tomato sauce or paste
1 egg, beaten

1½ teaspoons salt
¼ teaspoon pepper
1 cup bread crumbs or oats

SAUCE
½ small can tomato sauce or paste
2 tablespoons prepared mustard
1 cup water

2 tablespoons vinegar
2 tablespoons sugar

Mix ground beef, onion, ½ can tomato sauce or paste, egg, salt, pepper, and bread crumbs or oats together and put in 9x5x3-inch loaf pan. Mix sauce ingredients and pour SAUCE over MEAT LOAF. Bake until done. Temperature: 350 degrees. Baking Time: 1 hour. Yield: 6-8 servings.

Impossible Taco Pie

Use the food processor, electric frypan, blender and oven.

1 pound ground beef
½ cup onion, chopped
1¼ ounce taco seasoning mix
4 ounces green chilies, drained
    and chopped
1¼ cups milk

¾ cup Bisquick
3 eggs
2 tomatoes, sliced
1 cup Monterey Jack or cheddar
    cheese, shredded

Preheat oven. Grease 10-inch quiche dish or pie plate. Cook and stir beef and onion over medium heat until beef is brown; drain. Stir in seasoning mix. Spread in plate; sprinkle with chilies. Beat milk, Bisquick, and eggs until smooth, 15 seconds in blender on high or 1 minute with hand beater. Pour into plate. Bake in preheated oven for 25 minutes. Top with tomatoes; sprinkle with cheese. Bake until knife inserted in center comes out clean, 8-10 minutes longer. Cool 5 minutes. Serve with sour cream, chopped tomatoes, and shredded lettuce, if desired. Temperature: 400 degrees. Baking Time: 33-35 minutes. Yield: 6-8 servings.

The secret of making light meat loaf and hamburgers is to handle the meat as little as possible.

Meat Shell Potato Pie

Southern mainstays...meat and potatoes!

10¾ ounces condensed cream of
   mushroom soup
1 pound ground beef
¼ cup onion, finely chopped
1 egg, slightly beaten
¼ cup bread crumbs, fine dry

2 tablespoons parsley, snipped
¼ teaspoon salt
Dash pepper
2 cups potatoes, mashed
¼ cup mild cheese, shredded
Cooked bacon, crumbled

Mix thoroughly ½ cup soup, beef, onion, egg, bread crumbs, parsley, and seasonings. Press firmly into 9-inch pie plate. Bake, 25 minutes; drain fat. Frost with potatoes; top with remaining soup, cheese, and bacon. Bake 10 minutes more or until done. Temperature: 350 degrees. Baking Time: 35 minutes. Yield: one 9-inch meat pie.

Strips-Of-Beef Casserole

1 pound round steak
¼ cup shortening
1½ cups onion, chopped
2 tablespoons flour
1 cup tomatoes, canned
1 cup water
6 ounces tomato paste

1 tablespoon sugar
1½ teaspoons salt
¼ teaspoon black pepper
½ teaspoon Worcestershire sauce
½-¾ cup mushrooms, sliced
¾ cup sour cream

Cut steak in ½-inch strips. Brown meat in shortening in skillet; stir occasionally. Add onion and 2 tablespoon flour. Cook until onion is tender; stir occasionally. Add tomatoes, water, tomato paste, sugar, salt, pepper, and Worcestershire sauce. Cover. Simmer 1½ hours. Stir occasionally. Add mushrooms and sour cream; cook 5 minutes. Place in 2-quart casserole. Top with SOUR CREAM PUFFS. Brush with cream; sprinkle with sesame seed. Bake. Temperature: 425 degrees. Baking Time: 20-25 minutes. Yield: 6-8 servings.

SOUR CREAM PUFFS

1¼ cups flour, sifted
2 teaspoons baking powder
½ teaspoon salt

¼ cup shortening
¾ cup sour cream
Sesame seeds

Sift flour with baking powder and salt. Cut in shortening until particles are fine. Add sour cream; stir until dough clings together. Pat out on well-floured surface to ½ inch thickness. Cut six to eight 2½-inch biscuits and top each with 1-inch biscuits. Bake on top STRIPS-OF-BEEF CASSEROLE.

Skillet Beef Macaroni Casserole

2 tablespoons margarine
1½ cups uncooked macaroni
1 pound ground beef
1 cup onion, chopped
½ cup green pepper, chopped
1 teaspoon oregano
1 teaspoon salt

¼ teaspoon pepper
1 beef bouillon cube
1½ cups boiling water
1 tablespoon flour
12 ounces evaporated milk
¼ pound Cheddar cheese, grated
2 tablespoons pimento, chopped

Melt margarine in electric skillet at 350 degrees. Add first seven ingredients. Cook and stir until meat browns. Dissolve bouillon cube in boiling water and add to meat mixture. Bring mixture to boil; cover and simmer at 200 degrees for 20 minutes. Sprinkle flour over top. Stir in last 3 ingredients and cook for 5 minutes. Yield: 6 servings.

Taco Bells

MICROWAVE.

3 medium green peppers
1 pound ground beef
1 small onion, chopped
8 ounces tomato sauce
2 tablespoons green chiles, chopped
½ teaspoon onion salt
¼ teaspoon coriander, ground

¼ teaspoon cumin
⅛ teaspoon cayenne pepper
5 drops Tabasco sauce
1 tomato, chopped
¼ cup cheddar cheese, shredded
6 tablespoons taco sauce
½ cup taco chips, crushed
1 cup lettuce, shredded

Halve green pepper, core, and rinse. Place peppers cut-side up in 12x8-inch glass baking dish. Cover with waxed paper. MICROWAVE, HIGH, 4-5 minutes or until heated through, rotating dish once. Let stand covered. Crumble ground beef in 1½-quart casserole; add onion. MICROWAVE, HIGH, uncovered, 5-6 minutes or until meat is no longer pink, stir. Stir in tomato sauce, chiles, onion salt, coriander, cumin, cayenne pepper, and Tabasco sauce. Stir in tomato. Spoon filling into drained peppers. Sprinkle with cheese. MICROWAVE, HIGH, uncovered, 3-4 minutes until meat is heated, rotating dish once. Top each pepper with a tablespoon of taco sauce. Sprinkle with taco chips and lettuce. Yield: 6 servings.

The Mountain

MICROWAVE.

1 pound lean ground beef
8 ounces hot salsa or jalapeño
   relish, divided
¼ teaspoon salt
¼ teaspoon garlic powder
¼ teaspoon pepper
16 ounces refried beans
1½ cups Cheddar cheese,
   shredded

1½ cups Monterey Jack cheese,
   shredded
Chopped tomatoes
Green onion slices
Black olive slices
Sour cream
Guacamole
Tortilla or corn chips

Crumble beef into 2-quart casserole. Stir in ½ cup salsa, salt, garlic powder, and pepper. Cover. MICROWAVE, HIGH, 4-6 minutes or until beef is no longer pink, stirring once or twice to break apart. Drain. Stir in remaining ½ cup salsa and beans. On 12-inch platter, mound mixture into rounded shape, about 9 inches. Mix cheeses together. Sprinkle over meat and bean mixture, covering completely. MICROWAVE, MEDIUM, 7-10 minutes, or until cheese melts, rotating platter every 2 minutes. Sprinkle tomatoes, onions, and olives in center of cheese. Alternate scoops of sour cream and guacamole around edge of platter. Serve with tortilla chips. Yield: 4 servings.

Thirty Minute Chili

Wonderful on a cold winter night!

1 tablespoon shortening
1 small onion, finely chopped
½ pound ground beef
1 cup tomatoes, canned
1 cup kidney beans, canned
⅓ cup water

1½ teaspoons chili powder
1 teaspoon vinegar
1 teaspoon salt
Pepper to taste
Crackers

Heat fat. Add onion and beef and brown. Add all other ingredients. Cover. Cook slowly 20-30 minutes. Serve hot with crackers. Yield: 3-4 servings.

Wild Rice Casserole

2 medium onions, chopped
2 tablespoons butter
1 pound ground chuck
1 can cream of mushroom soup

1 can cream of chicken soup
½ cup wild rice, cooked
½ cup almonds, slivered
1½ cups herb seasoned stuffing

Cook onions in butter until tender, not brown. Add meat, stir and cook until it loses redness. Add soups, rice, and almonds. Mix and place in casserole. Top with stuffing, mixed according to package directions. Bake. Temperature: 375 degrees. Baking Time: 30 minutes. Yield: 6 servings.

Western Bologna Barbecue

Great for outdoor entertaining! $ Saver.

5-6 pounds bologna roll, unsliced
Whole cloves
½ cup brown sugar, packed
¼ cup water

¼ cup light corn syrup
2 tablespoons prepared mustard
2 tablespoons water
Spiced crab apples

Remove outer casing from bologna roll. Score entire bologna roll in a diamond-shaped pattern cutting into bologna about ¼ inch deep. Insert a whole clove at each point of the diamond pattern. Mix brown sugar, water, and corn syrup and heat on medium heat; stir until sugar is dissolved. Combine mustard with 2 tablespoons water and stir into hot sugar mixture. Spoon this mixture over bologna during the last 15-30 minutes of cooking. Bake. Serve bologna hot on platter garnished with spiced crab apples. Carve and serve with sliced pumpernickel or dark rye bread. Temperature: 300 degrees. Baking Time: 15-20 minutes per pound. Yield: 20-24 servings.

Quiche Tarts

3 (9 inch) deep dish frozen pastry
  shells
8 slices bacon
3 eggs

1 cup sour cream
½ teaspoon Worcestershire sauce
½ teaspoon salt
1 cup Swiss cheese, shredded

Defrost pie shells. Cut to fit mini-biscuit pans. Fry bacon until crisp and crumble. Line tart shells with cheese and bacon. Combine remaining ingredients and spoon into tarts. Bake. Temperature: 375 degrees. Baking Time: 20-25 minutes. Yield: 36 tarts.

Western Skillet Scramble

¼ cup butter
¾ cup onion, sliced
1½ pounds ground beef chuck
2 teaspoons salt
½ teaspoon pepper
¼ cup flour

12 ounces evaporated milk
¾ cup catsup
2 tablespoons parsley flakes
8 hamburger rolls, split and
    toasted

Preheat electric frypan to 300 degrees. Melt butter in frypan, add onion and cook until tender, about 5 minutes. Add ground beef, salt, and pepper, breaking up meat with a fork. Increase temperature to 340 degrees and cook mixture until meat is browned, about 8-10 minutes, stirring occasionally. Reduce heat to 220 degrees, gradually blend in flour. Gradually stir in evaporated milk. Continue cooking until mixture is thickened, stirring occasionally, about 3-4 minutes. Stir in catsup and parsley, heat to serving temperature about 2-3 minutes longer. Serve over toasted rolls. Garnish with green pepper rings, if desired. Yield: 8 servings.

Cheese Stuffed Manicotti

MICROWAVE.

10 manicotti noodles
Cooking oil
1½ cups mozzarella cheese,
    shredded
2 cups ricotta cheese
½ cup Romano cheese

7¾ ounces can spinach, drained
½ teaspoon garlic powder
½ teaspoon salt
¼ teaspoon pepper
15 ounces tomato sauce
Marjoram

Brush manicotti with oil. Cook in casserole dish filled with water. Cook 20 minutes. Turn noodles every 5 minutes. Cover noodles in dish with plastic wrap. Reserve about ⅓ cup mozzarella cheese for topping. Combine rest of mozzarella with ricotta, Romano, spinach, garlic, salt, and pepper. Stuff cooked noodles with cheese filling. Arrange in 12x8x2-inch dish. Pour tomato sauce over top, covering all manicotti. Sprinkle with cheese and marjoram. Cover with wax paper. MICROWAVE, HIGH, 15-18 minutes, rotating dish ½ turn after 8 minutes. MICROWAVE until hot. Yield: 10 stuffed noodles.

Macaroni And Cheese

Use the crock pot.

8 ounces elbow macaroni
1 stick butter or margarine
2½ cups sharp cheddar cheese,
    grated

1½ cups milk
2 eggs, beaten
12 ounces evaporated milk
Salt and pepper to taste

Cook and drain macaroni. Put in crock pot. Add butter and 2 cups cheese and stir. Add milk, beaten eggs, evaporated milk, salt, and pepper. Pour in crock pot and stir. Top with ½ cup of cheese and cover. Cook 3 hours on low heat. Yield: 8-10 servings.

Cheese Pastry Casserole

For cheese lovers!

1 package crescent rolls
¼ pound medium cheddar cheese
¼ pound Swiss cheese
¼ pound Muenster cheese
¼ pound sharp cheddar cheese

8 ounces cream cheese, softened
1 egg, beaten slightly
¼-½ bunch parsley, snipped
Butter, melted
½ cup sesame seeds, toasted

Pat ½ rolls in the bottom of an 8-inch square pan. Cover completely. Grate all hard cheeses and mix well with cream cheese. Mix egg with parsley and add to cheese. Mix well. Spread on top of roll layer. Roll out rest of roll sections to fit pan and cover cheese mixture. Brush with melted butter and sprinkle with sesame seeds. Bake until golden brown on top. Cut into squares. Temperature: 350 degrees. Baking Time: 30 minutes. Yield: 4-6 servings.

South Of The Border Crustless Quiche

Recipe may be halved. May be mixed ahead and baked the following day.

8 eggs, beaten
1 cup flour
1 teaspoon baking powder
2 cups cottage cheese
½ pound cheddar cheese, grated

½ pound Monterey Jack cheese,
    grated
¼ cup butter, melted
7 ounce can green chiles, diced
1 can water chestnuts, sliced
½ small onion, chopped

Stir all ingredients together. Pour into greased 2-quart flat baking dish. Bake until set. Temperature: 375 degrees. Baking Time: 30-40 minutes. Yield: 6-8 servings.

Vegetable Lasagna

MICROWAVE. The colorful vegetarian entrée makes a nutritious meal.

10 ounces frozen spinach, chopped
16 ounces low-fat cottage cheese
¼ cup Parmesan cheese
2 tablespoons margarine
2 tablespoons flour
1 cup skim milk

16 ounces frozen broccoli, carrot, and cauliflower combination
1 teaspoon instant chicken bouillon
⅛ teaspoon basil
6 lasagna noodles, cooked
2 ounces Mozzarella cheese, shredded

Remove any foil from spinach, MICROWAVE, HIGH, 5-6 minutes or until thawed. Drain spinach. Combine spinach with cottage and Parmesan cheeses. Set aside. Combine margarine and flour in 2-quart glass mixing bowl. To melt margarine, MICROWAVE, HIGH, uncovered, 30-40 seconds. Gradually stir in milk. MICROWAVE, HIGH, uncovered, 3-3½ minutes or until mixture boils and thickens slightly; stir once. Add vegetables, bouillon, and basil. MICROWAVE, HIGH, uncovered, 7-8 minutes or until vegetables are tender; stir once. Place 3 cooked lasagna noodles in single layer in 12x8-inch microwave-safe baking dish. Spoon half of vegetable mixture over noodles; spread evenly. Top with half of spinach mixture, spreading evenly. Repeat with remaining noodles, vegetable, and spinach mixtures. Cover with waxed paper. MICROWAVE, HIGH, 7-8 minutes or until mixture is heated through, rotating dish once. Sprinkle with Mozzarella cheese. Let stand about 10 minutes before cutting into squares. Yield: 9 servings.

Blackened Seasoning

Use on beef, chicken, fish, vegetables, and potatoes.

⅔ cup paprika
¼ cup onion powder
¼ cup cayenne pepper
⅛ cup black pepper
⅛ cup oregano

¼ cup salt
¼ cup granulated garlic
⅛ cup white pepper
⅛ cup thyme
1 tablespoon butter

Combine all dry ingredients. Dust meats or vegetables in seasoning. Heat butter in pan and sauté meat on both sides. Finish cooking either in the oven or on the grill. Store leftover seasoning in a sealed container. For a milder spice, reduce cayenne pepper to ⅛ cup. Yield: 2 cups.

Lamb And Cranberries

2 pounds lamb steaks
Flour
2 tablespoons oil
1½ teaspoons salt
⅛ teaspoon pepper
¾ cup onion, chopped

1 garlic clove, sliced
15 ounces tomato sauce
1 cup grape juice
¾ cup whole cranberry sauce
¼ teaspoon ginger, ground
¼ teaspoon oregano

Dredge steaks in flour; brown in oil. Add salt, pepper, onion, garlic and tomato sauce. Add water as needed. Simmer gently 45 minutes. Add rest of ingredients and simmer 45 minutes longer. Yield: 6 servings.

Lamb With Vegetables

2 pounds lamb shoulder
1 can tomatoes
1 cup celery, 1-inch pieces
6 small carrots
Salt and pepper to taste
1 bay leaf

½ teaspoon cloves, ground
1 can small onions
1 green pepper, sliced
1 small head cauliflower, broken up
1 cup lima beans, cooked

Cut lamb in chunks. Sauté lamb. Cut celery in 1-inch pieces. Add tomatoes, celery, carrots, salt, pepper, bay leaf, and cloves. Cover and simmer about one hour until meat is tender. Add onions, green pepper, cauliflower, and lima beans; cook about 30 minutes more. Yield: 6 servings.

Sausage Wild Rice Casserole

½ cup wild rice
1 pound bulk pork sausage
½ cup onion, chopped
3 ounces mushrooms, drained and sliced
½ cup celery with tops, chopped

⅓ cup minute rice
1 cup beef broth
¼ teaspoon thyme, crushed
Dash pepper
½ cup light cream or milk

Cook wild rice according to package directions. Drain. In large skillet, cook sausage and onion, till meat is browned and onion is tender. (Break meat apart as it cooks.) Drain excess fat. Stir in mushrooms, celery tops, minute rice, beef broth, thyme, and pepper. Cover; simmer 25-30 minutes. Stir in wild rice and cream. Turn into 1½-quart casserole. Cover and bake. If making ahead, be sure to cool before putting in refrigerator or freezer. Temperature: 375 degrees. Baking Time: 25 minutes. Yield: 6 servings.

Orange Country - Style Ribs

6 pounds country style ribs
1 tablespoon salt
6-7 cups water
1 teaspoon basil
6 ounces frozen orange juice
    thawed, undiluted

⅛ teaspoon garlic salt
1 tablespoon Worcestershire
    sauce
1 tablespoon brown sugar, packed
1 teaspoon corn starch
1 tablespoon water

Cut ribs in eight pieces. Place ribs in large saucepan; sprinkle with salt; add water to cover. Bring to boiling. Cover; simmer over low heat 1 hour. Preheat oven. Using slotted spoon, remove ribs from saucepan to 14x10x2-inch baking pan. Reserve ¼ cup cooking liquid. Sprinkle ribs with basil. Bake 15 minutes. Combine orange juice, garlic salt, Worcestershire sauce, and reserved liquid. Pour over ribs. Bake 15 minutes more, basting frequently. Transfer ribs to serving platter. Keep warm in hot oven. Pour orange sauce from baking pan into small saucepan. Add brown sugar; heat to boiling. Mix corn starch and 1 tablespoon water. Add to boiling orange mixture. Cook, stirring constantly until thickened. Temperature: 350 degrees. Baking Time: 30 minutes. Yield: 6-8 servings.

Hawaiian Supper

15 ounces pineapple chunks
2½ cups ham strips, cooked
½ cup green pepper, chopped
2 tablespoons butter
2-4 tablespoons vinegar
2 tablespoons brown sugar,
    packed

½ teaspoon dry mustard
Salt and pepper to taste
2 tablespoons corn starch
1⅓ cups water
2 tablespoons green onion,
    chopped
1⅓ cups instant rice

Drain pineapple, reserving juice; add enough water to juice to make 1½ cups liquid. Sauté ham and green pepper in butter. Combine pineapple liquid, vinegar, brown sugar, mustard, salt, pepper, and corn starch; mix well. Add to ham; cook over medium heat, stirring constantly until sauce is thickened and transparent. Stir in pineapple. Combine water, salt, pepper, and green onions in a medium saucepan; bring to a boil. Stir in rice; cover and remove from heat. Let stand 5 minutes. Yield: 6 servings.

Golden Glaze For Baked Ham

1 cup light molasses   ½ cup prepared mustard

Mix ingredients. Brush on ham for final hour of baking. Yield: enough glaze for 10-15 pound ham.

Smoked Ham Slices

2 smoked ham slices, 1½-inch thick
12 whole cloves
10-12 peach halves, drained
¾ cup brown sugar, packed
½ teaspoon cinnamon, ground
¼ teaspoon nutmeg, ground
¾ cup crushed pineapple, drained
2 tablespoons butter
½ cup peach syrup

Slash fat on edge of ham. Place ham slices on rack of large roasting pan. Insert cloves around edge of ham slices. Add enough water to cover bottom of the pan. Combine peach syrup with ½ cup sugar, cinnamon, and nutmeg. Glaze ham with mixture. Bake, uncovered for 1½ hours. Brush occasionally with glaze. Remove ham from oven. Place peach halves cut side up on rack. Spoon 1 tablespoon pineapple, 1 teaspoon brown sugar, and ½ teaspoon butter on each peach half. Return to oven until peaches are heated through and glazed. Serve peaches and SWEET POTATO NUT LOGS around ham. Temperature: 325 degrees. Baking Time: 1 hour 40 minutes. Yield: 8-10 servings.

Sweet Potato Nut Logs

1 pound can sweet potatoes, drained
¼ cup butter, melted
1 teaspoon salt
½ cup nuts

Mash sweet potatoes in large mixing bowl. Blend in butter and salt. Form into 6-8 small logs. Roll in nuts. Place in greased shallow pan. Bake. Temperature: 325 degrees. Baking Time: 30-45 minutes. Yield: 6-8 servings.

Dieter's Delight Bar-B-Que

A surprise treat!

1 large can tuna, drained
¼ teaspoon chili powder
1 tablespoon Worcestershire
   sauce
1 tablespoon vinegar
Sprinkle celery salt or seeds

1 tablespoon brown sugar, packed
   or artificial sweetener
1 tablespoon onion flakes or
   powder
1 tablespoon mustard
½ cup ketchup

Simmer all ingredients together over low heat until ready to serve. Yield: 4-6 servings.

Italian-Style Seafood Creole

½ cup eggplant, peeled and cubed
½ cup zucchini, thinly sliced
½ cup fresh mushrooms, sliced
½ cup onion, chopped
½ medium green pepper, sliced
¼ cup celery, chopped
2 tablespoons cooking oil
16 ounces can tomatoes, cut up
½ cup dry red wine
1 tablespoon soy sauce

1 teaspoon Italian seasoning
1 teaspoon oregano, crushed
¼ teaspoon sage, ground
¼ teaspoon garlic powder
⅛ teaspoon pepper
½ cup shrimp, peeled and
   deveined
6 ounces can tuna, drained
Cooked rice

Cook eggplant, zucchini, mushrooms, onion, pepper, and celery in hot oil until tender. Add undrained tomatoes, wine, soy sauce, and seasonings. Simmer uncovered 30 minutes. Add shrimp. Simmer 8 minutes. Stir in tuna, heat through. Serve in bowls with hot cooked rice. Yield: 4 servings.

Scalloped Oysters

Eat til it ouches you!

½ cup butter, melted
2 cups coarse cracker crumbs
1 pint oysters

Salt, pepper, and nutmeg to taste
½ cup heavy cream

Butter a baking dish, cover with a layer of cracker crumbs. Add alternate layers of crackers, oysters, seasonings, cream, and butter. Top with buttered cracker crumbs and remaining cream. Bake. Temperature: 425 degrees. Baking Time: 20-25 minutes. Yield: 4-6 servings.

Tuna Biscuit Casserole

3 tablespoons margarine
2 tablespoons onion, chopped
¼ cup celery, diced
3 tablespoons flour
½ teaspoon salt
¼ teaspoon pepper

1¼ cups milk
1½ cups cheddar cheese, shredded
6 ounces can tuna
1 cup peas and carrots
1 can refrigerator biscuits

Melt margarine in saucepan. Add onion and celery; cook until lightly browned. Blend in flour, salt, and pepper to form a smooth paste. Gradually add milk and cook over medium heat, stirring constantly until mixture thickens. Add cheese, tuna, and vegetables. Pour into 1½ quart casserole. Top with biscuits and bake. Temperature: 350 degrees. Baking Time: 20-25 minutes. Yield: 4-6 servings.

California Casserole

2 pounds veal round steak
⅓ cup flour
1 teaspoon paprika
¼ cup salad oil or shortening
½ teaspoon salt
⅛ teaspoon pepper

2¾ cups water
2 cans condensed cream of
    chicken soup
1¾ cups small onions, cooked and
    drained
1 cup sour cream

Cut veal in 2-inch pieces. Coat veal with mixture of flour and paprika, brown in oil; add salt, pepper, and 1 cup of water. Cover. Simmer 30 minutes. Transfer to baking dish. Heat 1 can of soup in skillet used for browning meat. Blend in remaining 1¾ cups of water, gradually. Bring to boil, stirring constantly. Combine with meat and gravy. Add onions. Top with BUTTER CRUMB DUMPLINGS. Bake uncovered. Serve with sauce made by heating 1 can of soup and sour cream just to boiling. Temperature: 425 degrees. Baking Time: 20-25 minutes. Yield: 8-10 servings.

BUTTER CRUMB DUMPLINGS
2 cups flour
1 teaspoon baking powder
½ teaspoon salt
1 teaspoon poultry seasoning
1 teaspoon celery seeds
1 tablespoon poppy seeds
    (optional)

1 teaspoon dry onion flakes
¼ cup salad oil
1 cup milk
¼ cup butter, melted
1 cup bread crumbs

Sift flour with baking powder, salt, and poultry seasoning. Add seeds and onion flakes. Stir in oil and milk until dry particles are moistened. Drop by tablespoons into mixture of butter and bread crumbs. Roll to coat with crumbs.

Christmas Time Menu

Grace
Love   Kindness   Good Cheer
Conscience Clear
Charity Served with Discretion
Tender Memories
Long Life Stuffed with Usefulness
Peace   Happiness
Sweet Thoughts
Rich Desserts   Best Wishes

Joveal

1 large veal cutlet
2 tablespoons oil
1½ teaspoons seasoned salt
1 can cream of mushroom soup

1 soup can water
2 medium onions, chopped
½ cup green pepper, diced
2 ounces mushrooms, sliced

Cut veal cutlet into 2-inch squares. Brown in oil in electric skillet. Sprinkle both sides with the seasoned salt. Turn heat down to 200 degrees, add rest of ingredients. Simmer about 1½ hours or until tender. Yield: 4 servings.

Veal Madeleine

2 pounds boneless veal, cubed
2 tablespoons flour
1 teaspoon salt
¼ teaspoon pepper

4 tablespoons butter, melted
2 (1-inch) wide strips lemon peel
1 cup boiling water
1 cup heavy cream

Coat veal with seasoned flour. Brown in melted butter. Add lemon peel and water. Cover and simmer until tender, about 1½ hours. Remove peel; stir in cream. Yield: 6 servings.

Recipe For Making A Home

Take one-half cup of
FRIENDSHIP;
add one cup of
THOUGHTFULNESS;
cream together with a pinch of powdered
TENDERNESS;
very lightly heat in a bowl of
LOYALTY
With one cup of
FAITH,
one of
HOPE,
and one of
LOVE.
Be sure to add a spoonful each of gaiety that sings, and the ability to laugh
at little things, moisten with sudden tears of heartfelt sympathy and bake in
a good nurtured pan.
Serve repeatedly.

Pasta
and Rice

Rufus L. Haymore
House

RUFUS L. HAYMORE HOUSE

The Rufus L. Haymore House, 615 North Main Street, Mount Airy, circa 1905-1910, was home to R. L. Haymore, son of the founders of National Furniture Company, and his sister, Martha.

Today, this home and its gardens are a memorial to Dr. Robert Smith and occupied by The Gilmer Smith Foundation and formerly the Mount Airy Visitors Center. It houses the exhibits of Donna Fargo, Tommy Jarrell, "the Siamese Twins", and some visitor information.

The Mount Airy Chamber of Commerce, 202 N. Main Street downtown Mount Airy, is presently serving as the Mount Airy Visitors Center, a place to find southern hospitality and friendly down-home folks. Mount Airy, 1994 All-America City, is listed as one of the top 50 best small towns to live in America and in 1996, voted best small town in North Carolina by "The State" Magazine. Famous people who call Mount Airy home are Andy Griffith, Donna Fargo, Tommy Jarrell, and Eng and Chang Bunker, the "Siamese Twins".

Andy Griffith and Emmett Forrest attended Rockford Street school and are still friends. Emmett has amassed one of the country's largest and most impressive collections of Andy Griffith memorabilia, including movie posters, records, an actual TV "Matlock" suit, photographs and samples of the products his friend, Andy has endorsed over the years. The twelve-minute film will give you an introduction to Mount Airy. The rare collection of Andy Griffith memorabilia on Andy's impressive life and career is now located on the third floor of the Main Oak Emporium, 245 City Hall Street, or at the back of The Good Life Café, 248 N. Main Street, downtown Mount Airy.

Fiddler Tommy Jarrell (1901-1985), famed folk musician, enjoyed sharing his love of music with people. His favorite song was "Brunken Hiccups" or "Jack of Diamonds". The Smithsonian Institution is now the home for Tommy Jarrell's famous fiddle.

"Siamese Twins", Eng and Chang Bunker, came to Surry County in the mid-nineteenth century following worldwide tours in traveling shows. They established two homes along Stewarts Creek. Eng reared a family of ten and Chang's family had a home on the opposite side of the Creek. They would alternate their time between the two houses. Chang Bunker's home has undergone some alterations, but the two-story frame house retains many original features which reflect the influence of the Greek Revival style. In 1865, the White Plains Baptist Church was organized. Traditions claim that the original church was built with their manual and financial support. They were originally buried on Chang's property. In the 1920's their remains were moved to the churchyard, located in the White Plains community.

Donna Fargo was born Yvonne Vaughn. She made a name for herself as a teacher in Mount Airy. Donna became known as a country music singer in 1972, with a song she wrote, called "The Happiest Girl in the Whole U. S. A." The song was followed by the equally popular "Funny Face."

Tommy Jarrell's Chicken And Dumplings

Famed folk musician Tommy Jarrell's favorite recipe!

1 chicken	½ cup milk
1 stick butter	Salt and pepper to taste

Wash and cut up chicken. Cover with water; add butter, milk, salt, and pepper. Simmer until chicken is done. Cool. Remove skin and bones. Cut chicken into bite-sized pieces.

DUMPLINGS

1½ cups self-rising flour	Buttermilk
½ cup shortening	

Cut shortening into flour. Add enough buttermilk to make dough. On floured board, roll dough thin. Cut into 1x2-inch strips. Heat chicken and broth until very hot. Slowly drop a few strips of dough into chicken and broth; cook as you go. Continue adding dough strips until all are added. Cook until all dough is done.

Donna Fargo's Date-Nut Goodies

The favorite recipe of Donna Fargo, country music singer.

½ cup dates, chopped	1 cup chunky peanut butter
½ cup raisins, chopped	1 to 2 tablespoons orange juice
1 cup walnuts, coarsely	(unsweetened)
chopped	½ cup coconut, shredded
¼ cup molasses	

Using a wet knife or scissors, cut the dates and raisins into small pieces. Combine the walnuts, dates, and raisins in a medium-sized bowl.

Stir in the molasses. Add the peanut butter, stirring until the fruit and nuts are evenly distributed. Stir in enough orange juice to moisten the mixture. Roll a teaspoonful of batter into a small ball, then roll the ball in the coconut. Form all the batter into balls. Store in an airtight container. The flavor of these cookies is enhanced after a day of storage. Yield: 3 dozen.

Baked Ziti

Team this sensational entrée with a loaf of crunchy French bread!

1 cup onion, finely chopped
1-2 garlic cloves
1½ tablespoons olive oil
8 ounces tomato sauce
6 ounces tomato paste
6 ounces water
½ teaspoon basil
¼ teaspoon black pepper

⅛ teaspoon red pepper
1 teaspoon salt
1 bay leaf
½ teaspoon oregano
8 ounces penne or ziti pasta
¼ cup Parmesan cheese
4 ounces mozzarella cheese
1 tablespoon Parmesan cheese

Sauté onion and garlic in olive oil until transparent. Add next eight ingredients and simmer 30 minutes, stirring occasionally. Remove bay leaf and add oregano. Simmer additional 15 minutes. Cook pasta according to package directions. Remove sauce from heat and stir in Parmesan cheese and pasta. Place in 9x9-inch baking dish. Sprinkle top with mozzarella and additional Parmesan cheese. Bake until cheese melts. Temperature: 350 degrees. Baking Time: 15 minutes. Yield: 8 servings.

Pasta Parmesan

MICROWAVE.

2 cups elbow macaroni, uncooked
3 cups hot water
½ teaspoon salt
½ teaspoon oil
2 (3 ounces) cream cheese
¼ cup margarine

⅔ cup water
2 tablespoons parsley, snipped
½-¾ teaspoon basil
¼ teaspoon salt
Dash pepper
½ cup Parmesan cheese

Combine macaroni, 3 cups hot water, salt, and oil in 1½-quart casserole dish. MICROWAVE, HIGH, uncovered 8-10 minutes or until pasta is tender, stirring once or twice. Drain, rinse, and return to casserole. Add cream cheese and margarine to macaroni. MICROWAVE, HIGH, uncovered, 2-3 minutes or until cheese and margarine are softened. Stir lightly to mix with macaroni. Add water, parsley, basil, salt, pepper, and Parmesan cheese; mix lightly. MICROWAVE, HIGH, uncovered 3-4 minutes or until heated. Yield: 6 servings.

"A house is not a home, unless it provides food and warmth for the soul as well as for the body."

Poppy Seed Noodles

8 ounces noodles
3 quarts water
1 tablespoon salt

3 tablespoons margarine or
    butter, melted
2 teaspoons poppy seeds

Cook noodles in boiling, salted water until tender—about 10 minutes. Drain. Stir in butter and seeds. Season with salt to taste. Yield: 6 servings.

Baked Rice, Tomatoes, & Cheese

Eat til it ouches you!

3 tablespoons butter
⅓ cup onion, finely chopped
1 clove garlic, minced
1 cup rice, uncooked
½ cup tomatoes, diced
¼ teaspoon thyme
½ bay leaf

1¼ cups chicken broth
3-4 tablespoons Parmesan cheese,
    grated
3-4 tablespoons Gruyère cheese,
    grated
1 tablespoon fresh parsley,
    snipped

Preheat oven. Melt the butter in an ovenproof serving dish. Add onion and garlic and cook, stirring until onion is translucent. Add rice, tomatoes, thyme, bay leaf, and broth. Stir until well mixed. Cover and bring to a boil. Remove from heat and remove bay leaf. Stir in cheeses and parsley. Bake. Assemble this ahead of time to the point of bringing the mixture to a boil. Refrigerate. Then continue preparation just before meal time. Temperature: 400 degrees. Baking Time: 20 minutes. Yield: 4 servings.

Green Rice

3 ounces Parmesan cheese, grated
1 cup rice, cooked
1 egg, beaten
⅓ cup cooking oil
1 cup milk

1½ medium onions, chopped
½ cup parsley, snipped
1 medium green pepper, chopped
1 teaspoon salt

Combine all ingredients in 1-quart casserole dish. Bake uncovered. Temperature: 300 degrees. Baking Time: 40 minutes. Yield: 6 servings.

Fried Rice

A tasters choice!

1 bunch green onions with some
  green tops, chopped
1 cup celery, chopped
2 tablespoons salad oil
2 cups rice, cooked

¼ teaspoon salt
2 tablespoons soy sauce
¼ cup blanched almonds, chopped
2 tablespoons butter, melted

Sauté onions and celery in oil, do not brown. Add rice, salt, and soy sauce. Mix and place in casserole. Bake until heated. Brown almonds in butter and toss on top before serving. The casserole can be a main dish by adding cooked shrimp, chicken, ham, or turkey. Temperature: 350 degrees. Baking Time: 30 minutes. Yield: 6 servings.

Baked Rice And Peas

3 tablespoons butter or margarine
1 cup raw rice
1 beef bouillon cube
2 cups boiling water

10 ounces frozen green peas,
  partially thawed
1 teaspoon salt
1 pimento, cut in strips

Melt 2 tablespoons of the butter in casserole. Add rice and bake 10 minutes. Remove from oven. Dissolve bouillon cube in boiling water; add to rice with peas and salt. Cover tightly with aluminum foil and bake.

Dot top with remaining tablespoon butter and garnish with pimento. Temperature: 375 degrees. Baking Time: 35-40 minutes. Yield: 4-6 servings.

Bell Pepper - Rice Casserole

1½ cups rice
¾ cup bell pepper, chopped
3 cups water
2 pimentos, cut in strips

6 hard-cooked eggs
1 can mushroom soup
1 can cream of chicken soup
½ cup sharp cheese, grated

Cook rice and bell pepper in water until done. Place layer of rice (one-half) in buttered 8x10x2-inch casserole dish. Add 1 pimento, cut into strips, and three hard-cooked eggs (sliced in rounds). Mix together the 2 cans of soup and pour one-half over the rice. Add another layer of rice, three more hard-cooked eggs, and 1 more pimento in strips, followed by remaining soups. Garnish with pimento and sprinkle grated sharp cheese over top. Bake. Temperature: 350 degrees. Baking Time: 20 minutes. Yield: 6-8 servings.

Broccoli Rice Casserole

Eat til it ouches you!

10 ounces frozen broccoli,
    chopped and thawed
2 cups cooked rice
8 ounces processed cheese spread

1 can cream of mushroom soup
½ cup celery, chopped
½ cup onion, chopped

Mix all ingredients. Bake. Temperature: 350 degrees. Baking Time: 30-35 minutes. Yield: 6 servings.

Herbed Vegetable Rice

Use the food processor and frypan or wok.

2 tablespoons butter
1 clove garlic
½ cup green onions, sliced
½ cup celery, sliced
2 cups chicken broth
1 cup rice, uncooked

4 ounces mushrooms, drained and
  sliced
½ teaspoon salt
¼ teaspoon basil
¼ teaspoon marjoram, ground
¼ teaspoon thyme
Dash black pepper

Melt butter in electric cooker at 350 degrees. Sauté garlic, green onions, and celery until crisp-tender. Stir in chicken broth, rice, and mushrooms. Add spices. Bring to a boil. Reduce heat to simmer. Simmer for 20 minutes or until rice is tender. Yield: 6 servings.

Rice O'Brien

1 cup rice, uncooked
2 cups water
3 chicken bouillon cubes
1 teaspoon salt
¼ cup butter

½ cup green onions, sliced
½ cup green pepper, diced
3 tablespoons pimento, diced
½ cup pitted ripe olives, sliced
  (optional)

Cook rice in water, flavored with bouillon cubes and salt until done. Melt butter in electric frypan; add green onions and green pepper. Sauté until vegetables are tender crisp. Add to cooked rice. Toss with pimento and ripe olives. Yield: 6 servings.

Rice Pilaf

2 tablespoons margarine
½ cup onion, chopped
½ cup mushrooms, sliced
½ cup green or red bell pepper,
  chopped

2 cups water
½ teaspoon salt
½ teaspoon lemon pepper
1 cup long grain rice, uncooked

Melt margarine in 2-quart saucepan, add vegetables, and sauté one minute. Stir in water, spices, and rice. After water boils, cook covered 20 minutes. Let stand 5 minutes before servings. Yield: 6 servings.

*Mount Airy Museum
of Regional History*

MOUNT AIRY MUSEUM OF
REGIONAL HISTORY

History comes alive in "The Hollows" with the dedication of the Mount Airy Museum of Regional History in October 1994. The Museum is located in the Merritt Building at 301 North Main Street in historic downtown Mount Airy.

The Merritt Building, circa 1905, was built by William Edward Merritt and originally, was a hardware and furniture store. The handmade brick building has a pilastered facade, curved corner, granite window sills and lintels, and classical cornices. The building in itself is a historic gem.

In December 1995, a $2 million fund-raising program began. It was successfully completed in late 1997. After an extensive renovation program, the Museum reopened in June 1999 with an additional 10,000 square feet of exhibit space. Presently, more than 20,000 square feet of exhibits has been completed and the third floor will house another 10,000 square feet, once that area is remodeled. The additions of an enclosed courtyard, stair tower with an illuminated 8-foot clock, a copper roof observatory, and parking facilities have enhanced the charm of the entire facility. On a clear day, the view from the Woltz Clock Tower, four stories high, depicts the panorama of mountains that no doubt lead to the designation of Mount Airy as "The Hollows."

The Museum is a step back in time. It is laid out in a chronological method and each exhibit can be viewed independently. It's an American story that takes place in "The Hollows," the back country of northwestern North Carolina, at the foot of the Blue Ridge Mountains. It was the "promised land" for adventurous people searching for freedom, owning land, and a desire for independence.

Your tour begins with a 100-foot mural of the surrounding mountains. Have a stop at the natural history exhibit. The story of granite is told with a model of the granite quarry and a replica of the carved buffalo head that is on the Arlington Bridge in Washington, D.C.

The Grand Philadelphia Wagon Train exhibits how the early settlers traveled from Pennsylvania to Georgia. A Yadkin River display tells of one of the world's oldest rivers and evidences of inhabitants of more than 1,000 years ago.

The 1888 Cape Fear and Yadkin Valley Railroad, a 70-foot scale model recreated by the local Railroad Club, takes you from Sanford to Kibler Valley in Virginia. It carried granite and brought tourists to Mount Airy.

The James Robert Hall family cabin, 1786-1864, shows how early settlers lived. The general store, household items, clothing, and toys show life at the turn-of-the-century. An 1874 coverlet, a real jewel, was made out of thread by sixteen-year-old Virginia Elizabeth Stone Taylor, who grew, spun, and wove the flax. The Victorian toy exhibit is a must-see at Christmas time.

Exhibits on the surrounding communities document the people, the industries, and their history. Wagons were made in White Plains and Winston-Salem.

The unique story is told of Orlena Puckett Hawks, a midwife, reputed to have safely delivered 1,000 babies but who lost all of her own 24 children at birth and in their infancy.

Highlights of the museum are numerous with programs and exhibits changing from time to time.

Barbecue Chicken

Yes, cook this one in a large well greased paper grocery bag.

2 teaspoons tomato catsup
2 teaspoons vinegar
2 teaspoons butter, melted
2 teaspoons Worcestershire sauce
4 teaspoons water
2 teaspoons lemon juice

1 teaspoon prepared mustard
1 teaspoon paprika
1 teaspoon chili powder
½ teaspoon cayenne pepper
Salt and pepper to taste
1 frying-size chicken

In a bowl large enough to dip the chicken, mix thoroughly the catsup, vinegar, melted butter, Worcestershire sauce, water, lemon juice, mustard, paprika, chili powder, and cayenne pepper. Salt and pepper the chicken and dip in sauce. Place in large well greased paper grocery bag and tie tightly with a string. Place in a baking pan and bake. Temperature: 350 degrees. Baking Time: 1 hour. Yield: 4-6 servings.

Cashew Chicken

A quick and easy stir-fry!

3 tablespoons butter or cooking
   oil
½ cup cashews, coarsely chopped
2 cups chicken or turkey,
   uncooked
1 cup cauliflower or broccoli,
   thinly sliced

4 green onions, sliced
1 cup chicken bouillon
1 tablespoon corn starch
2 tablespoons soy sauce
Cooked rice
1 orange, peeled and sliced

Cut chicken in thin slivers. In large skillet, heat butter or oil; add cashews, cook over medium-high heat, stirring until nuts are lightly toasted. Remove nuts from pan, leaving butter or oil. Stir in chicken and cauliflower or broccoli; cook about 5 minutes, stirring constantly. Add onions and bouillon. Cover and cook several minutes. Dissolve corn starch in soy sauce; stir into chicken mixture. Cook, stirring until thickened. Add toasted cashews. Serve over rice. Garnish with orange slices. Yield: 4-6 servings.

The poorest man is not a man without a cent, but a man without a dream.

Chicken Bundles

1 cup All-Bran or Bran Buds
  cereal
¼ cup nuts, chopped
5 tablespoons margarine or
  butter, melted
⅛ teaspoon pepper
⅛ teaspoon sage, ground

⅛ teaspoon thyme, ground
½ teaspoon lemon juice
2 tablespoons onion, chopped
1 tablespoon pimento, chopped
1 cup chicken, cooked and cubed
8 ounces can crescent dinner rolls

Combine ¼ cup of cereal, 2 tablespoons nuts, 3 tablespoons margarine, and the remaining ingredients except rolls. Crush remaining cereal to coarse crumbs and mix with remaining nuts. Separate rolls into 4 squares, pressing perforations together. Place chicken mixture in center of each. Gather corners together pinching to seal; brush with remaining margarine. Roll in nut mixture. Place on baking sheet and bake. Serve with white sauce, if desired. Garnish with chives. Temperature: 350 degrees. Baking Time: 25 minutes. Yield: 4 servings.

Chicken Croquettes

Eat til it ouches you! This is super to freeze.

¼ cup butter
2 tablespoons onion, minced
5 tablespoons flour
½ cup milk
½ cup chicken stock or broth
½ teaspoon salt
⅛ teaspoon pepper
1 egg, beaten

2 cups chicken, finely diced and
  cooked
1 tablespoon lemon juice
½ cup pecans, chopped
1 tablespoon parsley, snipped
1 egg
1 tablespoon water
Fine dried bread crumbs

Melt butter in heavy saucepan, add onion, and sauté until transparent. Add flour and blend. Add milk, stock, and seasonings. Cook over low heat, stirring until very thick. Add small amount of sauce mixture to beaten egg; then return this to rest of sauce in pan. Cook two minutes. Add chicken, lemon juice, nuts, and parsley. Chill thoroughly. Shape into balls. Dip each croquette in slightly beaten egg to which water has been added, then in dried bread crumbs. Place in container and freeze or bake on baking sheet. Temperature: 375 degrees. Baking Time: 20-25 minutes. Yield: 4-6 servings.

Chicken Casserole Supreme

Eat til it ouches you!

4 ounces package dried beef
3 slices bacon
6 halves chicken breast, boned

Pepper to taste
1 can cream of mushroom soup
1 cup sour cream

Shred dried beef into bottom of shallow casserole. Wrap half slice of bacon around each piece of chicken, place on top of beef and sprinkle with pepper. Blend soup with sour cream, pour over chicken, cover. Bake. Temperature: 275 degrees. Baking Time: 3 hours. Yield: 6 servings.

Chicken Strata

2 cups chicken, diced
½ cup onion, chopped
½ cup celery, chopped
½ cup green pepper, chopped
½ cup mayonnaise
Salt and pepper to taste
6 slices bread (broken in pieces)

2 eggs
1 cup milk
1 cup mushroom soup
½ cup croutons, buttered
¼ cup butter, melted (for croutons)
½ cup cheese, grated

Combine chicken, onion, celery, peppers, mayonnaise, salt, and pepper. In casserole dish alternate layers of chicken mixture and bread pieces. Beat eggs and mix with milk. Pour over casserole. Refrigerate. Before baking, spread mushroom soup over top and sprinkle with buttered croutons and cheese. Bake. Temperature: 350 degrees. Baking Time: 1 hour. Yield: 4 servings.

Crunchy Snack Chicken

Eat til it ouches you!

1 cup buttermilk farm style dressing
20 chicken drumettes

8 ounces corn bread stuffing mix, crumbled
¼ teaspoon pepper

Prepare buttermilk dressing according to package directions. Wash and dry chicken with paper towel. Dip each piece of chicken in prepared buttermilk dressing, coating all sides thoroughly. In shallow dish, place dry stuffing mix; roll chicken in mix to coat well. On greased baking sheet, arrange chicken pieces and sprinkle with pepper. Bake until fork can be inserted in chicken with ease. Temperature: 350 degrees. Baking Time: 35 minutes. Yield: 4-5 servings.

Chicken Tetrazzini

*Eat til it ouches you! A wonderful way to use
leftover turkey or chicken. It freezes well.*

1 large hen, boiled and cooled in
   broth
1 cup celery, chopped
1 cup onion, chopped
2-3 tablespoons butter
2 cups chicken broth
1 can cream of mushroom soup

½ pound thin spaghetti, cooked
   and drained
1 small bottle stuffed olives, sliced
½ pound sharp cheese, grated
Salt and pepper to taste
½ cup almonds, slivered (optional)
½ cup bread crumbs, buttered

Remove chicken from bones and cut in bite-size pieces. Sauté celery and onions in butter until transparent, but not brown. Stir in chicken broth, mushroom soup, spaghetti, chicken, olives, and cheese. Season to taste and spread in buttered shallow baking dish. Sprinkle top with nuts and buttered crumbs and heat in oven until lightly brown. Temperature: 350 degrees. Baking Time: 20-30 minutes. Yield: 8-10 servings.

Little Red Chick

Eat til it ouches you!

½ cup onion, sliced
½ cup green pepper, sliced
½ clove garlic, minced
1 bay leaf
2 sprigs parsley
½ teaspoon oregano
¼ teaspoon cayenne pepper
1 pound tomato purée
2 tablespoons brown sugar,
   packed

2 tablespoons prepared mustard
1 teaspoon salt
¼ teaspoon pepper
¼ cup vinegar
1 tablespoon Worcestershire
   sauce
2½ pounds chicken, cut in 8 pieces
1 chicken bouillon cube
6 ounces mushroom pieces and
   liquid

Mix all ingredients, except the last three ingredients in blender. Pour over chicken in baking pan. Bake, uncovered for 1½ hours. Dissolve bouillon cube in boiling mushroom liquid. Add liquid and mushrooms and pour over chicken. Return to oven for 30 minutes. Temperature: 350 degrees. Baking Time: 2 hours. Yield: 4 servings.

Easy Chicken Casserole

⅔ stick margarine
8 ounces herb stuffing mix
1 cup chicken broth

1 chicken, cooked and cubed
1 can cream of chicken soup
8 ounces sour cream

Melt margarine and combine with stuffing mix and broth. Place half this mixture in a 9-inch square pan and save the other half for the top. Place chicken over stuffing. Mix soup and sour cream and pour over chicken. Top with remaining stuffing mixture. Bake. Temperature: 350 degrees. Baking Time: 20 minutes. Yield: 6 servings.

Italian Chicken Casserole

The king of the chicken dishes!

4 eggs
5 chicken breasts, halved
½ cup Italian bread crumbs
6 tablespoons butter

10¾ ounces condensed chicken
    broth
2.5 ounces can mushrooms
8 ounces Monterey Jack cheese,
    grated

Beat eggs. Cube chicken and put in egg mixture. Cover and REFRIGERATE OVERNIGHT. Roll cubed chicken in bread crumbs; brown in butter, place in 9x13-inch Pyrex dish. Pour chicken broth over chicken. Add mushrooms, sprinkle with cheese. Cover and bake. Temperature: 350 degrees. Baking Time: 50 minutes. Yield: 4 servings.

Oven Barbecued Chicken

1 can small tomato paste
3 cans water
2 tablespoons prepared mustard
2 tablespoons salt
¼ cup vinegar
2 large whole garlic buds

3 tablespoons Worcestershire
    sauce
1 tablespoon Tabasco sauce
2½ tablespoon sugar
¼ cup salad oil
1 chicken, cut up

Preheat oven. Combine all ingredients, except chicken; bring to boil. Let simmer for about 15 minutes. Place uncooked pieces of chicken (unsalted) in baking pan and pour sauce over it. Bake uncovered for 45 minutes. Turn chicken and bake 45 minutes more or until tender. Temperature: 400 degrees. Baking Time: 1½ hours. Yield: 4 servings.

Russian Chicken

A unique combination of Russian dressing and apricot preserves.

4 ounces Russian dressing
5 ounces apricot preserves
½ package dry onion soup mix
⅛ teaspoon garlic powder

⅛ teaspoon salt
4 chicken breasts
Butter

Mix together dressing, preserves, and soup mix. Sprinkle garlic powder and salt on chicken; lay in pan. Dot each piece with butter. Pour dressing mixture over top. Cover casserole with foil. Bake for 30 minutes. Turn chicken and bake for 30 minutes more. Temperature: 325 degrees. Baking Time: 1 hour. Yield: 4 servings.

Savory Crust Chicken Pie

Nothing beats a homemade chicken pie!

FILLING
¼ cup onion, chopped
2 tablespoons margarine
2 cups chicken or turkey, cooked
   cubed

2 cups leftover vegetables
1 can cream of chicken soup

Mix together and pour in crust.

CRUST
1 stick margarine
1 cup sour cream
1 egg
1 cup flour

1 teaspoon salt
1 teaspoon baking powder
½ teaspoon thyme or sage, ground
½-1 cup cheese, shredded

Combine margarine, sour cream, and egg. Beat at medium speed until smooth. Add flour, salt, baking powder, and thyme or sage. Blend at a low speed until thoroughly combined. In ungreased 9-inch pie pan (1½-inch deep) or shallow 2-quart baking dish, spread batter evenly over bottom and up sides to within 1-inch of rim. Spoon FILLING into CRUST, sprinkle with cheese. Bake. Let cool 10 minutes before cutting. Temperature: 400 degrees. Baking Time: 25-30 minutes. Yield: 6 servings.

"A Diamond is made from coal, put under pressure."

Sweet-Sour Chicken

Use the food processor and wok.

2 whole chicken breasts, boned,
  cut into slivers
2 tablespoons cooking oil
1 carrot, thinly sliced
1 cup mushrooms, sliced
1 green pepper, slivered
4 green onions, sliced
1 cup chicken broth or bouillon
1 tablespoon vinegar
1 tablespoon brown sugar, packed
½ teaspoon salt
2 tablespoons corn starch
2 tablespoons soy sauce
1 tomato, chopped
12 warm cooked crêpes or 6 cups
  cooked rice
2 tablespoons sesame seeds,
  toasted

Use the food processor to cut chicken and slice vegetables. In wok, heat oil; add chicken and carrot. Stir-fry for several minutes. Add mushrooms, green pepper, and green onions. Cook for 1 minute. Pour in broth, vinegar, brown sugar, and salt. Dissolve corn starch in soy sauce. Add to mixture. Stir in tomato. Cover pan; cook on low heat several minutes or until crisp-tender. Fill warm crêpes with mixture or serve over rice. Top with sesame seeds. Serve immediately. Yield: 6-8 servings.

Sweet And Spicy Chicken

*For bar-b-que lovers! Substitute pork or turkey
for the chicken and cooked noodles or crêpes for rice.*

15 ounces prepared spaghetti
  sauce
½ cup purple grape jam
1 tablespoon lemon juice
2 teaspoons Worcestershire sauce
2 teaspoons prepared mustard
¼ teaspoon salt
2½ cups chicken, cooked, cut into
  pieces
1 small onion, peeled and
  quartered
4 cups cooked rice

Add spaghetti sauce, jam, lemon juice, Worcestershire sauce, mustard, and salt to food processor container. With steel blades, process until smooth. Add chicken and onion. Process for 2-3 seconds to blend. DO NOT OVERPROCESS. Pour all ingredients into frypan. Simmer, stirring occasionally for 10 minutes. Serve over rice. Yield: 4-5 servings.

"The more we share, the more we have."

Sour Cream Marinated Chicken Breasts

8 ounces sour cream
¼ cup lemon juice
2 teaspoons Worcestershire sauce
2 teaspoons celery salt
1 teaspoon paprika
2 cloves garlic, minced

2 teaspoons pepper
5 whole chicken breasts, split
Salt to taste
Bread crumbs
½ cup margarine, melted
¼ cup shortening, melted

Combine first seven ingredients in large mixing bowl. Sprinkle chicken with salt and coat with sour cream mixture. Cover and refrigerate at least 24 hours. Remove chicken and coat with bread crumbs. Place in lightly greased pan. Combine margarine and shortening. Pour ½ of mixture over chicken. Bake for 45 minutes. Pour remainder of margarine over chicken and continue to bake for 15 minutes. Temperature: 350 degrees. Baking Time: 1 hour. Yield: 5 servings.

Lady Di's Chicken Cacciatore

MICROWAVE.

3 tablespoons flour
1 tablespoon sugar
¼ teaspoon ginger, ground
1 teaspoon oregano
1 teaspoon parsley
½ teaspoon basil, crushed
½ teaspoon garlic powder
1 teaspoon onion powder

¼ teaspoon black pepper
½ teaspoon salt
8 ounces tomato sauce
14½ ounces stewed tomatoes
4 chicken breasts, boneless and
  skinless
Rice or pasta

Mix flour and seasonings together. Add tomato sauce and stewed tomatoes. Pour into an 8x8-inch glass dish. Cut chicken breasts into bite-size pieces and place on top of tomato mixture. Cover with plastic wrap, venting one corner. MICROWAVE, MEDIUM, 6 minutes. Stir. Rotate dish and stir. Continue cooking (MEDIUM) 6 more minutes. Stir. MICROWAVE, HIGH, 4 minutes. Rotate dish and stir. Continue cooking 3 more minutes. Let stand covered 5 minutes. Serve over rice or pasta. Yield: 4-6 servings.

Piercing the skin of chicken allows marinade to penetrate the skin and prevents shrinkage.

Cornish Game Hens With Pineapple-Wild Rice Stuffing

8 Rock Cornish game hens
1½ teaspoons salt
¾ cup butter or margarine
1⅓ cups mushroom pieces, drained
½ cup onion, chopped

¼ cup green pepper, chopped
3 cups cooked wild rice
3 cups cooked rice
1 cup crushed pineapple, drained
¼ teaspoon pepper

Lightly sprinkle cavity of hens with 1 teaspoon salt. Melt ¼ cup butter. Sauté mushrooms, onion, and green pepper in butter. Add both kinds of rice, pineapple, ½ teaspoon salt, and pepper. Toss lightly. Stuff hens. Fasten with skewers or picks. Place breast side up on rack of roasting pan. Brush hens in remaining melted butter. Bake for 1 hour. Cover and bake for 1 hour longer until tender. Temperature: 325 degrees. Baking Time: 2 hours. Yield: 8 servings.

Topnotch Turkey Loaf

4 cups turkey, coarsely ground cooked
1½ cups soft bread crumbs
6 ounces evaporated milk
⅓ cup chicken broth
⅔ cup celery, finely chopped

2 eggs, slightly beaten
¾ teaspoon salt
Dash of each pepper, ground nutmeg, dried rosemary, and dried marjoram, crushed

Lightly combine all ingredients. Line bottom of greased 9x5x3-inch loaf dish with foil; grease foil. Pour in turkey mixture. Bake. Invert onto serving platter; remove foil. Serve with heated PIMENTO SAUCE. Temperature: 350 degrees. Baking Time: 45 minutes. Yield: 6 servings.

PIMENTO SAUCE

1 can condensed cream of chicken soup

⅓ cup milk
2 tablespoons pimento, chopped

Mix all ingredients and heat. Serve over TOPNOTCH TURKEY LOAF.

Turkey Crunch Casserole

3½ cups herb-seasoned croutons
2 cups turkey or chicken, cooked
   cubed
1 can condensed cream of
   mushroom soup
⅔ cup water

½ cup celery, finely chopped
½ cup onion, finely chopped
2 eggs, slightly beaten
8 ounces water chestnuts, drained
   and sliced
1 cup cheddar cheese, shredded

Combine all ingredients except cheese. Spread in greased 2-quart casserole dish. Bake, uncovered, 30 minutes. Remove from oven. Sprinkle with cheese. Continue baking for 10 minutes until cheese melts. Temperature: 350 degrees. Baking Time: 40 minutes. Yield: 6-8 servings.

15 Minute Turkey Shortcake

Quick and easy!

1 can cream of mushroom soup
⅓ cup milk
1 cup turkey, cooked cubed

½ cup peas, cooked
1 tablespoon pimento, chopped
4 biscuits, split

In saucepan, blend soup and milk. Add turkey, peas, and pimento. Heat; stir occasionally. Serve over split biscuits. Yield: 4 servings.

Turkey Hash Supreme

¼ cup onion, chopped
2 tablespoons butter or margarine
1 cup turkey, cooked cut-up
1 can cream of mushroom soup
½ cup peas, cooked

1 cup potatoes, diced and cooked
1 tablespoon pickle relish
¼ cup sharp cheese, grated
Paprika

Cook onions in butter until transparent but not brown. Add turkey, soup, peas, potatoes, and pickle relish. Heat slowly. Turn into 1-quart casserole, cover with cheese, add paprika. Bake. NOTE: This hash is very good baked in 3 green pepper cups, boiled 5 minutes in water and drained. Temperature: 350 degrees. Baking Time: 30 minutes. Yield: 3 servings.

Turkey Timbales

4 tablespoons butter or margarine
6 tablespoons flour
1½ cups milk
2 eggs, slightly beaten
1½ cups turkey, cooked and finely
    minced

2 tablespoons pimento, chopped
2 teaspoons onion, minced
1 teaspoon lemon juice
½ teaspoon sage, ground
½ teaspoon salt
Dash pepper

Melt butter or margarine in saucepan; blend in flour. Gradually, add milk and cook over medium heat, stirring constantly, until mixture thickens and comes to a boil. Stir in beaten eggs, blend well. Add remaining ingredients and pour into 6 greased custard cups or 1-quart mold. Bake in pan of hot water until knife inserted in center comes out clean. Serve hot. Temperature: 350 degrees. Baking Time: 35-40 minutes. Yield: 6 servings.

Easy Turkey Broccoli Bake

Eat til it ouches you!

20 ounces frozen broccoli,
    chopped, thawed, and drained
1 package dry onion soup mix
1 cup sour cream
2 cups cooked turkey, diced

1 cup whipping cream, softly
    whipped
1 tablespoon Parmesan cheese,
    grated
Bread crumbs, buttered

CONVENTIONAL: Prepare ingredients as directed; layer into casserole. Bake covered. Temperature: 350 degrees. Baking Time: 25-30 minutes. Yield: 6 servings.

MICROWAVE: Spread broccoli in 2-quart oblong baking dish. Cover with water; cook in MICROWAVE, HIGH, 8 minutes; drain. Stir soup mix into sour cream; spread ½ mixture over broccoli. Top with diced turkey. Fold whipped cream into remaining soup-sour cream mixture; spoon over turkey. Cover, MICROWAVE, HIGH, 10-12 minutes, turning dish halfway through cooking time. Mix cheese and crumbs. Sprinkle over casserole. MICROWAVE, MEDIUM, 1 minute longer. Yield: 6 servings.

Crouton-topped Turkey Bake

½ pound medium noodles
2 tablespoons butter or margarine
1½ cups sharp cheese, grated
1 medium onion, minced
1 garlic clove (optional)
4 ounces pimento, drained and
    diced

4 cups turkey or chicken, cooked
    cubed
2 cups turkey or chicken broth
3 tablespoons margarine
1½ cups bread crumbs, toasted

Cook noodles as package directs, drain, and toss with butter, grated cheese, onion, garlic, and pimento. In 3-quart casserole, place layer of noodles, then 2 cups turkey or chicken. Repeat layers ending with noodles. Pour in broth. In saucepan, melt margarine and stir in toasted crumbs to coat. Sprinkle buttered crumbs over noodles. Bake until hot and bubbling. Temperature: 350 degrees. Baking Time: about 30 minutes. Yield: 8 servings.

Turkey In A Bag

MICROWAVE. A great treat for Thanksgiving dinner!

1 frozen turkey breast
1 stick margarine, melted
1 package dry Italian dressing
    mix

1 package dry onion soup mix
1 cooking bag

Thaw frozen turkey breast in original wrapper in refrigerator. Allow 1 day for 4 pound breast. Mix together margarine and dry mixes. Place turkey in cooking bag and pour butter mixture over turkey in bag. Fasten with closure that comes with cooking bag. Make slits in bag. Bake according to directions with bag. MICROWAVE. Using temperature probe, MICROWAVE, HIGH, to 190 degrees.

Holiday Problem Solvers

1. **Only have one oven to cook all foods?**
   - *Plan menu to reserve oven space for turkey. Include stove top, microwave, and refrigerator recipes.*
   - *Allow 30 minutes for turkey standing time and for carving. Bake extra stuffing and reheat side dishes during that time.*
   - *To avoid food safety problems, do not partially cook the turkey ahead of time.*

2. **Turkey is still frozen the day before serving?**
   - *Speed defrosting by placing turkey in original wrapping in cold water and allow 30 minutes defrosting time per pound.*
   - *Do not leave a turkey on the counter overnight to defrost. Room temperatures allow bacteria to grow.*

3. **Getting a large turkey done without having to start in the middle of the night?**
   - *Using the Foil Wrapped or Oven Bag Methods you can roast a 24 pound turkey in about 3½ hours.*
   - *Do not cook turkey all night at a low temperature.*
   - *Cooking at low temperatures risks food poisoning.*

4. **Cooking a turkey and transporting it for a special dinner?**
   - *Turkey roasting should be done by the host/hostess.*
   - *Assign guests traveling from a distance pies, cakes, bread, or side dishes that can be kept chilled in a cooler.*

5. **Stuffing the turkey the day before?**
   - *Cook giblets and sauté vegetables for stuffing. Cover with plastic wrap and refrigerate. Mix dry ingredients for stuffing, cover, and set aside.*
   - *When ready to stuff the turkey, reheat the vegetables and giblets in the microwave and combine with dry ingredients.*
   - *For food safety, do not stuff a turkey until it's ready to be cooked.*

6. **Roasting the turkey the day before and reheating it whole?**
   - *Reheating risks loss of moisture and fresh taste.*
   - *If you must prepare the turkey ahead of time, slice the roasted turkey and place it in an aluminum foil-lined pan. Spoon broth over the turkey to prevent drying. Cover with foil and refrigerate. Reheat covered in 350 degree oven until hot.*

(Continued on next page)

Holiday Problem Solvers, *continued*

7. **Saving time by purchasing a roasted turkey to reheat?**
   - *Compare roasting times. Reheating a purchased roasted turkey usually will not save time or oven space.*
   - *Generally, a roasted 12-14 pound turkey will take 2¼ to 2¾ hours to reheat at 325 degrees.*

8. **Leaving cooked turkey and leftovers out for afternoon snacking?**
   - *Refrigerate all leftovers.*
   - *Keep in mind the two hour rule for food safety. Two hours is the maximum amount of time roasted turkey, stuffing, and gravy can be left at room temperature.*

9. **Spending hours cleaning up?**
   - *Line pans for casseroles and extra stuffing with aluminum foil.*
   - *When finished, rinse, and recycle the aluminum foil. Pans stay clean.*

Salads and Salad Dressings

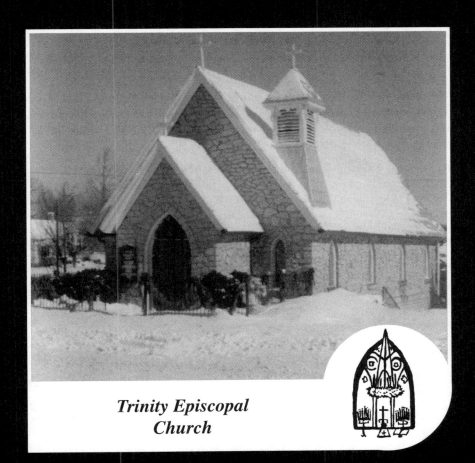

Trinity Episcopal Church

TRINITY EPISCOPAL CHURCH

Episcopal services were begun in Mount Airy in 1852 when Bishop Silliman Ives confirmed the sister of Civil War General J. E. B. Stuart. Construction of Trinity Church began in the spring of 1896, and the first service was held in July, 1896. The building is an identical copy of a chapel in Oxford, England, and the ivy on the walls was rooted from cuttings brought directly from Oxford. Trinity was consecrated on October 13, 1900 and was dedicated to "...the Worship and Service of Almighty God, the administration of His Holy Sacraments, the Reading and Preaching of His Holy Word, and for the performance of All Holy Offices."

Trinity Episcopal Church was not the first church to be built in Mount Airy, but it is the oldest religious structure remaining in the town today. It was the first local structure to be built of Mount Airy granite, a distinguishing feature of Mount Airy architecture. The small Gothic Revival Structure features a lancer-arched entrance and windows, a projecting front narthex and a steeple gable roof with a belfry on the south slope. Crosses top the belfry, the main roof and the narthex roof. The magnificent interior features wooden wainscot beneath sand-plaster finished walls, and three handsome arches divide the nave from the chancel.

The Episcopal Church, like most area churches, has an Advent Wreath celebrating Advent. Advent is a four week preparatory period in the church year before Christmas Day. It focuses on the doctrine of the incarnation of Christ — God becomes a man in Jesus Christ, His Son. This is emphasized in the Advent Liturgy.

The Advent Wreath is a circular wreath of greenery which speaks of God's never ending love and care for His own and of the life He brings to all. The wreath is topped with five candles, one lighted for each of the four Sundays in Advent, with the fifth candle or center candle, symbolizing the Christ of Christmas, which is lighted at Christmas and celebrates the Birth of Christ.

"AK" Salad Dressing

3 hard-cooked eggs, chopped
¾ cup sweet pickle, chopped
¾ cup tomato catsup
½ cup mayonnaise
1 small onion, diced
½ teaspoon salt

Combine all ingredients. Chill and serve over lettuce. Yield: 2½ cups.

French Dressing

1 can tomato soup
½ cup sugar
2 tablespoons Worcestershire
    sauce
2 tablespoons mustard
½ teaspoon salt
½ teaspoon pepper
½ cup vinegar
½ teaspoon garlic salt
1 cup cooking oil

Place all ingredients except oil in blender. Blend well; add oil and blend until mixed. Yield: 2½ cups.

Poppy Seed Dressing

Excellent served on fresh fruit salad and chopped cabbage.

⅓ cup vinegar
1½ teaspoons onion juice
¾ cup sugar
1 teaspoon mustard
1 teaspoon salt
1 cup salad oil
1½ teaspoons poppy seeds

To blender jar, add vinegar, onion juice, sugar, mustard, and salt, and blend on medium speed. Add oil slowly and blend until thick. Add poppy seeds. Store in refrigerator. Yield: 1¾ cups.

Roquefort Cheese Dressing

Add a zesty accent! Substitute blue cheese, if you wish.

8 ounces sour cream
1 small package Roquefort cheese,
    crumbled
1 cup mayonnaise
1 tablespoon lemon juice
1 small onion, grated extra fine
Salt to taste
Paprika (if color desired)

Mix all ingredients well. Yield: 2½ cups.

Bacon Pecan Dressing

4 slices bacon, chopped
2 tablespoons chili sauce
½ teaspoon prepared mustard
¼ teaspoon salt

Dash pepper
¼ cup pecans, broken
½ cup sour cream or yogurt

In an electric frypan, brown bacon until crisp; drain. Sauté pecans in bacon drippings; drain. Blend together chili sauce, mustard, salt, pepper, crumbled bacon, and pecans; fold in sour cream. Yield: 1 cup.

Boiled Salad Dressing

Good in turkey or chicken salad, or used with vegetable or potato salad.

½ teaspoon dry mustard
1 tablespoon sugar
½ teaspoon salt
2 tablespoons flour
¼ teaspoon paprika

½ cup cold water
1 whole egg or 2 yolks
¼ cup vinegar
2 tablespoons butter

Dissolve mustard, sugar, salt, flour, and paprika in cold water. In saucepan, beat egg and add vinegar. To this add first mixture and cook over low heat until thick and smooth. Add butter and stir. Chill. This may be thinned with cream. Yield: 1 cup.

Fluffy Blue Cheese Dressing

Dressing has a strong flavor.

1 cup cottage cheese
1 tablespoon lemon juice
¼ teaspoon onion salt

¼ cup water
¼ cup instant nonfat dry milk
¼ cup blue cheese, crumbled

In blender, beat cottage cheese, lemon juice, and onion salt until smooth. Add water and nonfat dry milk and beat until fluffy; blend in blue cheese. Yield: 1¼ cups.

House Special Dressing

Serve with your favorite vegetable salad or as a dip for fresh vegetables.

2 tablespoons onion, minced
2 tablespoons cucumber, minced
2 tablespoons green pepper,
    minced
½ package ranch-style bacon
    flavor dressing mix

½ pint sour cream
¼ cup mayonnaise
2 tablespoons milk
¼ teaspoon pepper

Combine all ingredients in blender or food processor and blend until smooth. Yield: 1¼ cups.

Maple Lemon Dressing

This dressing may be frozen until ready to serve. Excellent with fruit.

½ cup maple syrup
3 tablespoons flour
1 egg yolk, slightly beaten
3 tablespoons lemon juice

1 teaspoon lemon peel, grated
¼ teaspoon salt
1 cup cream, whipped

Stir syrup into flour; mix well and add egg yolk. Cook over low heat or hot water until thick, stirring constantly, 5-10 minutes. Add lemon juice, grated peel, and salt. Fold this mixture into whipped cream. Yield: 1½ cups.

Mayonnaise

A great recipe for the blender or food processor.

1 egg
¾ teaspoon salt
½ teaspoon dry mustard
¼ teaspoon paprika (optional)

1 tablespoon vinegar
1 tablespoon lemon juice
1 cup salad oil, divided

In container with steel blade: Add egg, salt, dry mustard, paprika, vinegar, lemon juice, and ¼ cup oil. Process, while slowly adding remaining oil in a slow, steady stream through feed tube. Continue to process until all of the oil has been added and the mayonnaise has thickened. Refrigerate mayonnaise before serving. Yield: 1¼ cups.

Nippy Nectar Dressing

A quick and easy tart dressing that blends well with fruit salads.

3 ounces cream cheese
2 tablespoons honey
1 teaspoon lemon peel, grated
2 tablespoons lemon juice

½ teaspoon salt
Dash cayenne pepper
½ cup salad oil

Soften cheese. Blend in all ingredients except salad oil in electric blender. Add salad oil, 1 tablespoon at a time, beating well after each addition. Chill. Yield: 1 cup.

Russian Dressing

Use the blender.

½ cup condensed tomato soup
6 tablespoons white vinegar
¾ cup salad oil
½ small clove garlic
½ small onion
½ cup sugar

1 tablespoon dry mustard
1 tablespoon salt
1 tablespoon Worcestershire
   sauce
½ teaspoon paprika

Put all ingredients into blender container. Cover and process until well blended. Yield: 2½ cups.

Applesauce Salad

3 ounces apple gelatin
1¾ cups water
1 cup applesauce
¼ teaspoon cinnamon, ground

⅛ teaspoon cloves, ground
⅛ teaspoon nutmeg, ground
½ cup raisins
½ cup pecans, chopped

Dissolve gelatin in hot water. Cool and add remaining ingredients. Pour into individual molds. Chill until firm. Serve on lettuce with mayonnaise. Yield: 6-8 servings.

Apricot Ribbon Ring

8 ounces crushed pineapple
2 envelopes unflavored gelatin
¼ cup cold water
12 ounces apricot nectar
¼ cup lemon juice
¼ teaspoon salt

7 ounces lemon-lime carbonated
  beverage, chilled
3 ounces cream cheese, softened
3 tablespoons salad dressing
Dash salt
⅓ cup celery, chopped
¼ cup pecans, chopped

Drain pineapple, reserving syrup. Soften gelatin in cold water and reserved pineapple syrup. Heat apricot nectar just to boiling; add to gelatin, stirring until gelatin is dissolved. Add lemon juice and ¼ teaspoon salt; cool to room temperature. To keep the bubbles of carbonated beverage, add by carefully pouring down side of bowl; stir gently with up and down motion. Chill until partially set. Add crushed pineapple, stirring gently with up and down motion. Fill a 5½ cup ring mold ⅓ full; chill until almost firm. Blend cheese, salad dressing and salt; stir in celery and pecans. Spoon over layer of firm gelatin, spreading evenly. Add remaining gelatin and chill until firm. Yield: 8-10 servings.

Autumn Apple Salad

20 ounces crushed pineapple
  with juice
⅓ cup sugar
3 ounces lemon gelatin
8 ounces cream cheese, softened

½-1 cup nuts, chopped
1 cup celery, chopped
1 cup unpeeled apples, diced
1 cup whipped topping

Combine pineapple with juice and sugar in saucepan. Bring to a boil and cook for 3 minutes. Stir in gelatin and cream cheese. Cool. Fold in nuts, celery, apples, and whipped topping. Pour into 9-inch square dish. Chill until set. Yield 12 servings.

"The flowers of tomorrow are in the seeds today."

Apricot Cheese Delight Salad

2 (3 ounces) orange gelatin
2 cups hot water
1 cup apricot juice

2 (17 ounces) apricots, drained
and chopped
1 large can crushed pineapple,
drained

Dissolve gelatin in hot water, add apricot juice. (Save pineapple juice for topping). Fold in apricots and pineapple. Chill until firm.

TOPPING
Pineapple juice
½ cup sugar
3 tablespoons flour
1 egg, slightly beaten

2 tablespoons butter or margarine
1 cup whipping cream, whipped
¾ cup cheddar cheese, grated

If necessary, add water to make 1 cup pineapple juice. Combine sugar and flour. Blend in egg and butter. Add pineapple juice and cook over low heat, stirring constantly until thickened. Cool. Fold in whipped cream and spread over APRICOT CHEESE DELIGHT SALAD. Sprinkle with grated cheese. Chill. Cut in squares and serve on lettuce. Yield: 12 servings.

Blueberry Salad

Eat til it ouches you!

6 ounces grape gelatin
2 cups hot water

1 large can crushed pineapple,
undrained
1 can blueberry pie filling

Dissolve gelatin in water. Cool. Add remaining ingredients. Congeal.

TOPPING
8 ounces cream cheese, softened
1 teaspoon vanilla extract
1 cup sour cream

¼ cup sugar
Nuts (optional)

Beat together all ingredients except nuts. Spread on top of congealed BLUE-BERRY SALAD. Sprinkle nuts over top. Yield: 8 servings.

Barbecue Salad Mold

3 ounces lemon gelatin
1¼ cups hot water
8 ounces tomato sauce
1½ tablespoons vinegar

⅓ teaspoon salt
Dash pepper
½ teaspoon horseradish
Onion to taste, minced

Dissolve lemon gelatin in hot water. Add remaining ingredients. Place in mold and congeal. Yield: 6-8 servings.

Bing A Ling Salad

Juice of 1 lemon
6 ounces cherry gelatin
2 cups grape juice

1 large can Bing cherries
1 cup nuts, chopped
1 small carton cottage cheese

Heat juice from cherries and lemon; add to gelatin. Cool. Add grape juice. Refrigerate. When this begins to thicken, add cherries, nuts, and cottage cheese. Yield: 8 servings.

Coca Cola Salad

6 ounces maraschino cherries,
    chopped
8 ounces crushed pineapple
3 ounces cherry gelatin

6½ ounces Coca Cola
3 ounces cream cheese
1 cup pecans, chopped

Drain juice from cherries and pineapple; reserve. Add water to the combined juices to make ¾ cup. Bring to a boil. Remove from heat and add gelatin. Dissolve well and add Coca Cola. Refrigerate for 8 minutes. Cut cream cheese into small blocks. Add cream cheese, cherries, nuts, and pineapple to gelatin. Pour into 8x8-inch glass dish and chill until firm. Yield: 8 servings.

Cranberry Eggnog Salad

1 envelope unflavored gelatin
8 ounces crushed pineapple, juice
    packed
3 tablespoons lime juice
1½ cups eggnog

1½ cups cranberry juice cocktail
3 ounces raspberry gelatin
14 ounces cranberry orange relish
½ cup celery, finely chopped

Soften unflavored gelatin in undrained pineapple and lime juice for 5 minutes. Heat gelatin mixture until gelatin dissolves. Cool. Stir in eggnog. Chill until firm. Heat cranberry juice to boiling; stir in the raspberry gelatin until dissolved. Chill until partially set. Fold in relish and celery. Carefully spoon atop eggnog mixture. Chill until firm. Cut into squares. Yield: 12 servings.

Cream Cheese And Fruit Cocktail Salad

28 ounces fruit cocktail, drained
1 envelope plain gelatin
2 tablespoons lemon juice
2 tablespoons fruit cocktail juice
3 ounces cream cheese

¼ cup mayonnaise
Dash salt
⅔ cup whipping cream, chilled
½ cup sugar
½ cup nuts, chopped

Drain fruit cocktail, soften gelatin in lemon juice and fruit cocktail juice, and dissolve over hot water. Blend cream cheese with mayonnaise and salt. Stir in gelatin. Whip cream until stiff; add sugar gradually. Fold in cheese mixture, nuts, and fruit cocktail. Place in favorite molds and chill until firm. Yield: about 12 servings.

Emerald Salad

3 ounces lime gelatin
¾ cup hot water
¾ cup cucumber, shredded and
    unpeeled

2 tablespoons onion, grated
1 cup cream style cottage cheese
1 cup mayonnaise
⅓ cup blanched almonds, slivered

Dissolve gelatin in hot water. Chill until slightly thick. Combine cucumber and onion; drain well. Add cottage cheese, mayonnaise, and almonds. Fold into gelatin. Pour into 8-inch square pan. Chill. Yield: 9 servings.

Cherry Salad

8 ounces crushed pineapple
Orange juice
½ cup sugar
1 can water pack pie cherries

3 ounces cherry gelatin
½ envelope unflavored gelatin
1 tablespoon lemon juice
½ cup nuts, chopped

Drain juice from pineapple; add enough orange juice to make 1 cup. Pour sugar over cherries and let stand. Heat juice and pour over cherry gelatin to dissolve. Dissolve unflavored gelatin in lemon juice and add to this mixture. Add cherries, stirring until sugar dissolves. Add crushed pineapple and nuts. Pour into oiled molds. Yield: 8-10 individual molds.

Cranberry Salad

1 pint cranberries
1 apple
1 orange
1 cup pecans

1 cup boiling water
3 ounces cherry gelatin
1 cup sugar

Chop cranberries, apple, orange, and pecans. Add 1 cup boiling water to gelatin and add to above mixture. Add sugar and mix well. Pour into a mold and refrigerate until set. Yield: 8 servings.

Fluffy Fruit 'N Cream Salad

Eat til it ouches you!

11 ounces mandarin orange
    sections
½ cup sugar
1 envelope unflavored gelatin
½ cup orange juice
¼ cup lemon juice

2 eggs, beaten
1 cup sour cream
3 ounces cream cheese, cubed and
    softened
1 medium banana, sliced
⅓ cup walnuts, chopped

Drain orange sections, reserving juice. Add water to syrup to make ¾ cup liquid. In saucepan, combine sugar and gelatin; add syrup mixture, orange juice and lemon juice. Heat until gelatin is dissolved. Gradually stir about half of the hot mixture into eggs; return all to saucepan. Cook and stir 2 minutes more. Remove from heat. Add sour cream and cream cheese; beat with mixer until smooth. Chill until partially set. Fold in orange sections, banana, and nuts. Pour into 5½ cup ring mold. Chill overnight. Yield: 8 servings.

Fellowship Salad

FIRST LAYER
3 ounces orange gelatin
3 ounces lemon gelatin
1 cup hot water
2 cups cold water

16 ounces crushed pineapple with
   juice
2 bananas, sliced
1 cup miniature marshmallows

Dissolve gelatins in hot water; add cold water, pineapple, and bananas; mix. Sprinkle top with marshmallows and chill until firm.

SECOND LAYER
2 eggs, beaten
1 cup sugar

6 tablespoons flour
2 cups pineapple juice

Mix all together in saucepan and cook until thick. Stir constantly. Cool. Spread on top of FIRST LAYER.

THIRD LAYER
8 ounces cream cheese
½ small whipped topping

Cheddar cheese, grated
Pecans, chopped

Mix cream cheese and whipped topping together. Spread on top of SECOND LAYER. Sprinkle with cheese and nuts. Yield: 24 servings.

Frosted Melon Mold

Lovely for a special occasion.

3 ounces lemon gelatin
1 package unflavored gelatin
White seedless grapes or other
   fruit

1 large cantaloupe
Cream cheese
Heavy cream

Make a fruit gelatin using lemon gelatin and 1 package of unflavored gelatin. Add small white seedless grapes or any other fruit. Peel the melon; cut slice from end and remove seeds. Fill center with gelatin and fruit mixture. Prop melon up in refrigerator until center congeals. Replace slice cut from end. Frost the entire melon with cream cheese thinned by heavy cream. Return to refrigerator and chill 24 hours. Serve on an aspic tray garnished with grape leaves and white grapes. Slice all the way through and serve with French dressing. Yield: 6-8 servings.

Gala Cherry Salad

16 ounces sour pie cherries,
  undrained
½ cup water
1 cup sugar
6 ounces cherry gelatin

16 ounces crushed pineapple,
  undrained
1 cup cola beverage
½ cup nuts, chopped

Pour cherries into saucepan. Add water and sugar; bring to a boil. Add to gelatin and stir until gelatin dissolves. Stir in pineapple, cola, and nuts. Pour into an oiled mold. Refrigerate to set. Yield: 12-15 servings.

German Style Perfection Salad

6 ounces mixed vegetable salad
  gelatin
2 cups boiling water
1 tablespoon vinegar

12-15 ice cubes
¼ cup green onion tops, sliced
1 pimento, chopped
1 pound sauerkraut, drained

DRESSING
1 cup mayonnaise

1 teaspoon horseradish

Dissolve gelatin in boiling water. Add vinegar. Stir in ice cubes and continue to stir for three minutes. Remove any unmelted ice. Add green onions, pimento, and sauerkraut. Pour into loaf pan. Chill. Unmold. Combine mayonnaise and horseradish and serve as DRESSING. Yield: 6-8 servings.

Holiday Cranberry Salad

1 cup sugar
1 cup raw cranberries, ground
3 ounces lemon gelatin
½ cup boiling water
¾ cup orange juice

2 teaspoons orange rind, grated
8 ounces crushed pineapple,
  drained
½ cup pecans, broken
1 cup celery, chopped

Mix sugar and cranberries together and let stand several hours. Add gelatin to boiling water and stir until dissolved. Add orange juice and rind; stir. Then add cranberries and other ingredients and pour into mold. Serve on lettuce and garnish with mayonnaise. Yield: 8 servings.

Grapefruit Salad

Eat till it ouches you!

3 large grapefruits
8 ounces crushed pineapple
Juice of 1 lemon
3 (3 ounces) lemon gelatin

1 teaspoon sugar
1 teaspoon salt
4 cups mixed fruit juices

Cut grapefruit into halves lengthwise. Scoop out fruit with a spoon reserving shell. Drain off juice and use it mixed with pineapple juice, lemon juice, and water to make 4 cups of liquid. Heat liquid and dissolve gelatin, sugar, and salt. Let cool until mixture begins to set. Add grapefruit sections and crushed pineapple. Put mixture in grapefruit shells and chill. To serve, cut each half into two wedges and spoon on GRAPEFRUIT SALAD DRESSING.

GRAPEFRUIT SALAD DRESSING

⅔ cup sugar
2 tablespoons flour
2 egg yolks, beaten slightly
Juice of 1 lemon

Juice of 1 orange
½ cup pineapple juice
½ cup heavy cream, whipped

Combine sugar, flour, and egg yolks. Add fruit juices and cook in double boiler, stirring constantly until thick. Remove from heat and set aside to cool. Fold in whipped cream and serve on GRAPEFRUIT SALAD wedges. Yield: 12 servings.

Holiday Frosted Fruit Salad

3 ounces orange gelatin
3 ounces lemon gelatin
2 cups hot water
1½ cups cold water
Juice of 1 lemon
12 ounces crushed pineapple
2-3 bananas
1 cup miniature marshmallows

2 tablespoons flour
½ cup sugar
1 egg, beaten
1 cup pineapple juice
2 tablespoons butter
1 box whipped topping mix
Nuts, chopped

Dissolve gelatins in 2 cups of hot water. Add 1½ cups cold water and juice of lemon. Chill until slightly thickened. Add drained pineapple, diced bananas, and marshmallows. Chill until firm. FROSTING: Mix and cook flour, sugar, egg, and pineapple juice in double boiler until thick. Remove from heat and add butter. Let stand until cold. Make whipped topping according to package directions. Add frosting mixture and pour over gelatin. Sprinkle with nuts. Yield: 10 servings.

Lime Cottage Cheese Salad

20 ounces crushed pineapple
½ cup lemon juice
Boiling water
6 ounces lime gelatin
1 cup walnuts, chopped

2 tablespoons lemon rind, grated
2 cups cottage cheese
1 cup celery, finely chopped
2 teaspoons prepared horseradish
½ teaspoon salt

Drain syrup from pineapple into 4 cup measure and save for next step. Add lemon juice and enough boiling water to make 3 cups liquid; add gelatin and stir until dissolved; chill mixture until syrupy. Spoon about 1½ cups syrupy gelatin into a medium-sized bowl; fold in drained pineapple, walnuts, and lemon rind; pour into lightly greased 9x5x3-inch loaf pan; chill until just firm. Keep remaining syrupy gelatin at room temperature. When layer in mold is firm; beat syrupy gelatin until fluffy; blend in cottage cheese, celery, horseradish, and salt; spoon over layer in pan; chill until firm. Unmold onto serving plate; garnish with avocado slices, if desired. Serve with BANANA-NUT DRESSING.

BANANA-NUT DRESSING

½ cup mayonnaise or salad
   dressing
1 banana

½ cup walnuts, chopped
3 tablespoons heavy cream
1 tablespoon lemon juice

Blend all ingredients in electric blender. Yield: 1 cup dressing.

Luscious Lime Salad

3 ounces lime gelatin
1½ cups boiling water
1 tablespoon lemon juice
½ teaspoon salt
1 cup creamed cottage cheese
1 cup cucumbers, grated

½ cup almonds, toasted and
   chopped
½ cup mayonnaise
½ cup heavy cream, whipped
¼ cup pickle relish
1 cucumber, thinly sliced

Dissolve gelatin in boiling water. Add lemon juice and salt. Chill until thick but not set. Fold in all remaining ingredients except cucumber slices. Cut slices in half and arrange in bottom of loaf pan. Pour in gelatin mixture. Chill until firm. Unmold on lettuce cup. Yield: 12 servings.

"Our deeds determine us as much as we determine our deeds."

Marshmallow Salad

2 eggs
1 tablespoon water
1 tablespoon vinegar
1 cup marshmallows
1 cup crushed pineapple

1 envelope plain gelatin
¼ cup pineapple juice
12 ounces evaporated milk, chilled
    and whipped
1 cup nuts, chopped

Beat eggs until light; put in double boiler with water and vinegar; cook until thick. Add marshmallows and crushed pineapple. Soak gelatin in pineapple juice and heat until dissolved, then add to egg mixture. Cool. Fold in whipped milk and nuts. Spoon into molds and chill in refrigerator until firm. Yield: 12 servings.

DRESSING
3 ounces cream cheese, softened
1 tablespoon honey

2 tablespoons lemon juice
½ cup oil

Cream softened cream cheese, honey, and lemon juice together. Gradually beat in oil. Serve on top of MARSHMALLOW SALAD.

Perfection Salad

2 envelopes unflavored gelatin
1 cup cold water
1½ cups boiling water
⅓ cup sugar
1 teaspoon salt
¼ cup vinegar
¼ cup lemon juice

¼ cup green pepper, chopped
¼ cup pimento, chopped
1½ cups cabbage, shredded
½ cup carrot, shredded
½ cup celery, diced
½ cup cucumber, chopped

Soften gelatin in cold water. Stir into boiling water. Add sugar, salt, vinegar, and lemon juice. Stir until gelatin is dissolved. Cool until slightly thickened. Add all chopped vegetables. Mix well. Pour into a ring mold or 8 (½ cup) individual molds or an 8-inch square pan. Chill until firm. Unmold on serving plate. Yield: 8 servings.

Orange Delight Salad

Easy to prepare.

3 ounces orange gelatin
12 ounces cottage cheese
15½ ounces chunk pineapple,
    drained

8 ounces non-dairy dessert
    topping
15 ounces mandarin orange slices,
    drained

Mix together gelatin and cottage cheese. Add remaining ingredients. Pour into 9x9-inch dish. Refrigerate for an hour. Yield: 8-10 servings.

Peardise Success Salad

Lovely for company!

3 ounces lime gelatin
1½ cups hot water
3 tablespoons lemon juice
6-8 Bartlett pear halves, canned
3-4 cherries

½ cup crushed pineapple, drained
1 cup cottage cheese
1 tablespoon crystallized ginger,
    chopped
Salad greens

Dissolve gelatin in hot water. Blend in lemon juice. Cool. Pour a thin layer (about ½ cup) into an 8-inch layer cake pan which has been lightly oiled. Allow to set. Cool remaining gelatin until slightly thickened. Drain pears and blot with paper towels. Arrange pear halves with cherry in cavity cut side down on layer of gelatin. Fold crushed pineapple, cheese, and ginger into remaining gelatin. Pour over pear halves and chill until firm. Unmold upside down and serve on salad greens. Garnish with mayonnaise. Yield: 6-8 servings.

Pineapple And Strawberry Molds

Beautiful red and green color.

8 ounces crushed pineapple
3 ounces lime gelatin
¼ cup lemon juice
8 ounces cream cheese

16 ounces frozen strawberries
3 ounces strawberry gelatin
½ cup nuts, chopped

Drain pineapple well. Add water to pineapple juice to make 1½ cups; heat to boiling and use to dissolve gelatin. Cool. Add 2 tablespoons lemon juice. Beat softened cream cheese with egg beater until light and fluffy and then beat into gelatin mixture. Add crushed pineapple and fill 10 individual molds half full. Chill until firm. Thaw strawberries and drain off juice. Add water to juice to make 1½ cups. Heat to boiling and use to dissolve gelatin. Chill until syrupy and then beat with egg beater until light and fluffy. Fold in 2 tablespoons lemon juice, strawberries, and nuts and fill molds. Chill until firm. Serve plain or with mayonnaise. Yield: 10 servings.

Pretzel Salad

CRUST
2½ cups pretzels, coarsely crushed
¾ cup butter, melted

3 tablespoons sugar

Preheat oven. Combine all crust ingredients in mixing bowl or food processor. Process or mix by hand until well mixed. Pat into a 13x9x2-inch pan. Bake. Cool. Temperature: 375 degrees. Baking Time: 8-10 minutes. Yield: 12 servings.

FILLING
8 ounces cream cheese
8 ounces non-dairy whipped
    topping

1 cup sugar

Combine filling ingredients in mixing bowl or food processor. Process or beat until mixture is light and fluffy. Spread evenly over cooled CRUST.

TOPPING
6 ounces strawberry gelatin
2 cups boiling water

20 ounces frozen strawberries,
    thawed

Make topping in a bowl, stir together gelatin and boiling water until dissolved. Add berries and chill until partially set. Pour over FILLING. Chill overnight. Cut into squares and serve. Yield: 12 servings.

Surprise Salad

3 ounces orange gelatin
¾ cup plus 2 tablespoons boiling
   water
2 cups orange sherbet

11 ounces mandarin orange
   sections, drained
¾ cup whipped topping

Dissolve gelatin in boiling water. Stir in orange sherbet until melted. Add orange sections and gently fold in whipped topping. Pour into a 8-inch square dish. Refrigerate overnight. Yield: 10-12 servings.

Waldorf Cranberry Molds

1 pint cranberry juice cocktail
3 ounces lemon gelatin
¼ teaspoon salt
1 cup apples, unpeeled and
   chopped

½ cup celery, chopped
¼ cup English walnuts, chopped
6 slices pineapple

Heat one cup cranberry juice to boiling point. Dissolve gelatin in this. Add remaining juice and salt. Chill until partially set. Stir in apples, celery, and nuts. Pour into six molds and let set. Unmold atop pineapple rings. Yield: 6 servings.

Wineberry Salad

Eat till it ouches you!

1 cup cranberry juice cocktail
3 ounces raspberry gelatin
¼ cup sugar
¾ cup red wine

8 ounces whole-berry cranberry
   sauce
1 cup whipping cream, chilled and
   whipped
½ cup pecans, chopped

Place cranberry juice in medium size bowl. MICROWAVE, HIGH, 2-3 minutes or until boiling. Add gelatin, stirring to dissolve. Mix in sugar, wine, and cranberry sauce. Chill 1 hour or until soft set. Fold in remaining ingredients. Pour into 6-cup mold. Chill 3-4 hours or until set. Unmold. Yield: 8 servings.

Banana-Sour Cream Jubilee

2 cups sour cream
¾ cup sugar
2 tablespoons lemon juice
8 ounces crushed pineapple
Salt to taste

3 tablespoons maraschino
    cherries, chopped
½ cup miniature marshmallows
1-2 bananas, mashed
⅓ cup nuts, chopped

Combine all ingredients in order, mix well. Pour into paper baking cups, freeze. Serve on lettuce. Garnish with additional cherries or nuts. Yield: 4-6 servings.

Dreamy Frozen Fruit

Great to have in freezer for unexpected guests!

2.6 ounces box (2 envelopes)
    whipped topping mix
2 (3 ounces) lite cream cheese,
    softened
¼ cup lemon juice

14 ounces sweetened condensed
    milk
1 cup pecans, chopped
15¼ ounces pineapple chunks,
    drained
21 ounces cherry pie filling

Prepare whipped topping according to package directions. Set aside. Combine cream cheese and lemon juice; beat until smooth. Stir in milk, pecans, and pineapple. Fold in whipped topping and pie filling. Spoon mixture into paper-lined muffin pans. Cover and freeze. Remove and store in plastic freezer bags. Yield: 24 servings.

Frozen Cranberry Salad

16 ounces cranberry sauce
2-3 tablespoons lemon juice
3 ounces cream cheese
¼ cup mayonnaise

¼ cup confectioner's sugar
1 cup nuts, chopped
2-3 cups non-dairy topping

Mix together cranberry sauce and lemon juice. Spread in a square 9-inch dish. Blend together cream cheese, mayonnaise, sugar, and nuts. Add the topping to this mixture. Spread this mixture over the cranberry layer. Freeze. Serve in frozen squares. Yield: 9 servings.

Frozen Cheese And Fruit Salad

2 (3 ounces) cream cheese
3 tablespoons cherry juice
⅓ cup mayonnaise
¾ cup pineapple slices, diced

¾ cup apricots, canned and sliced
¼ cup Maraschino cherries, diced
½ cup nuts, chopped

Soften cream cheese, add cherry juice and blend. Stir in mayonnaise. Fold in thoroughly drained fruits and nuts. Pour into freezing tray. Freeze. Slice and serve. Yield: 8 servings.

Frozen Date Soufflé Salad

8 ounces cream cheese, softened
¼ cup maple syrup
1 tablespoon lemon juice
1 banana, sliced
½ cup nuts, chopped

½ cup dates, chopped
8 ounces crushed pineapple, drained
8 ounces non-dairy whipped topping

Mix softened cream cheese, maple syrup, and lemon juice together. Add banana, nuts, dates, and pineapple. Fold in non-dairy whipped topping and put in 1½-quart shallow casserole. Cover and freeze. Let stand approximately 15 minutes at room temperature before serving. Cut into squares and serve on lettuce for a delightful salad. Yield: 6-8 servings.

Frozen Fruit Salad

8 ounces cream cheese
½ cup salad dressing
¼ cup confectioner's sugar
2 tablespoons lemon juice
½ teaspoon vanilla extract
1⅓ cups blueberries, drained

16 ounces peaches, sliced
20 ounces pineapple tidbits, drained
2 cups miniature marshmallows
2 cups whipping cream
Red food coloring

Combine cheese, salad dressing, sugar, juice, and vanilla; beat until smooth. Fold in fruits and marshmallows. Whip cream; add coloring; as needed to tint to a delicate pink. Fold cream into fruit mixture. Pour in individual paper baking cups placed in muffin pans. Freeze. Yield: 24 servings.

Frozen Strawberry Salad

9 ounces frozen whipped topping
1 cup frozen strawberries
1 cup miniature marshmallows

1 tablespoon mayonnaise
½ cup nuts, chopped
8 ounces crushed pineapple

Combine ingredients and freeze in 9x5x3-inch loaf pan or paper cups. Yield: 8 servings.

Fruit Salad

2 cups Concord grapes
2 stalks celery, chopped

1 apple, diced
¾ cup whipped topping

Cut grapes in half. Remove seeds. Combine grapes, celery, and apple; mix. Add whipped topping, toss until fruits are well coated. Yield: 4 servings.

Orange-Banana Salad
With Fresh Citrus Dressing

3 oranges
2 large bananas
Salad greens

⅓ cup nuts, chopped
3 tablespoons watercress, chopped

Peel and section oranges. Slice bananas in half lengthwise and cut into 2-inch pieces. Marinate orange and banana slices in FRESH CITRUS DRESSING for at least 30 minutes. Arrange fruit on salad greens; sprinkle with nuts and watercress. Serve with remaining marinade. Yield: 6 servings.

FRESH CITRUS DRESSING
¼ cup fresh orange juice
¼ cup fresh lemon juice
½ cup salad oil
¼ cup sugar
1 teaspoon salt

1 teaspoon paprika
1 teaspoon prepared mustard
½ teaspoon celery seeds
¼ teaspoon pepper
1 teaspoon onion, grated

Blend all ingredients. Yield: 1¼ cups.

Peachtree Salad

⅔ cup salad oil
⅓ cup wine vinegar
½ garlic clove
1 teaspoon sugar
½ teaspoon salt
⅛ teaspoon pepper

8 cups salad greens, torn and
  chilled
1 cup parsley, finely snipped
1 cup peaches, sliced
½ cup pecan halves

Combine first 6 ingredients in jar. Cover; shake vigorously. Chill to blend flavors. Remove garlic and shake again before tossing with salad greens, parsley, peaches, and nuts. Yield: 8 servings.

Poinsettia Salad

Makes a lovely Christmas salad that can be prepared ahead.

1 large can Bartlett pears
½ cup red cinnamon drops
3 tablespoons cider vinegar

Lettuce
¼ cup cheddar cheese, shredded

Drain syrup from pears into small saucepan. To syrup, add cinnamon drops and cider vinegar; bring to boil. Cut pear halves in half and simmer in mixture 45 minutes. Cool and refrigerate overnight. Before serving arrange pears on lettuce to form poinsettia. Sprinkle with cheddar cheese. Yield: 6 servings.

Summer Fruit Salad

Prepare ahead!

1 cantaloupe
2 bananas, sliced
2 peaches, sliced
Lemon juice
20 ounces pineapple chunks,
  undrained

1 unpeeled apple, cubed
1 cup strawberries, halved
6 ounce frozen orange juice
  concentrate

Peel cantaloupe and cut into ¾-inch cubes. Peel and slice bananas and peaches; dip in lemon juice. Layer fruits in large bowl in order given. Spoon undiluted orange concentrate on top. Cover and chill 6-8 hours. Yield: 8-10 servings.

Sweetheart Cherry Salad

1 can cherry pie filling
14 ounces sweetened condensed
　milk

8 ounces crushed pineapple,
　drained
8 ounces frozen whipped topping
¾ cup nuts, optional

Mix all ingredients together well. Refrigerate until firm. Yield: about 12 servings.

Twenty-Four Hour Salad

Great to make ahead!

1 egg
2 tablespoons lemon juice
2 tablespoons sugar
Pinch salt
½ cup heavy cream, whipped
12 marshmallows, quartered
1 cup pineapple tidbits, drained

1 cup orange, diced
1 cup seedless grapes
1 cup banana, sliced
8 maraschino cherries, quartered
½ cup toasted almonds, slivered
Crisp salad greens

In double boiler, beat egg with fork, stir in lemon juice, sugar, and salt. Cook, stirring constantly, over hot water about 5 minutes, or until mixture thickens. Remove from heat. Cool. Fold in whipped cream, marshmallows, and fruits. Chill overnight. To serve, fold in almonds and arrange on greens. Yield: 6 servings.

Winter Fruit Salad

2 bananas
2 medium apples, cubed
8 dried apricots or 4 dried
　peaches or nectarine halves,
　coarsely chopped
4 dried pitted prunes, coarsely
　chopped
½ cup raisins

3-5 heaping tablespoons plain
　yogurt
½ tablespoon honey
Dash nutmeg, ground
1-2 tablespoons orange liqueur or
　apple juice
2 tablespoons toasted almonds,
　coarsely chopped

Peel bananas, cut in halves lengthwise and then cut into 2-inch pieces. Combine first 8 ingredients in medium bowl and mix well. Mix in juice or liqueur to taste. Cover and chill. When ready to serve, gently mix in almonds. Yield: 4 servings.

Exotic Chicken Salad

2½-3 pound chicken, cooked and
    cubed
8 ounces water chestnuts, sliced
1 pound seedless grapes
2 cups celery, chopped
2-3 cups toasted almonds, slivered

2-3 cups mayonnaise
1 tablespoon curry powder
1 tablespoon soy sauce
2 tablespoons lemon juice
Lettuce, Boston or Bibb
20 ounces pineapple chunks

Combine first five ingredients, reserving ½ cup almonds for garnish. Combine mayonnaise, curry powder, soy sauce, and lemon juice; toss with chicken mixture and chill several hours. Spoon onto bed of lettuce or individual plates. Sprinkle with pineapple and rest of almonds. Yield: 6 servings.

Greek Island Salad

MICROWAVE.

1 pound ground beef
2 teaspoons parsley, snipped
1 teaspoon oregano
¼ teaspoon salt
¼ teaspoon garlic powder
¼ teaspoon thyme
Dash pepper
½ cup plain yogurt

¼ teaspoon dill weed
Dash salt
6 cups lettuce, torn
1 medium cucumber, coarsely
    chopped
1 medium tomato, chopped
¼ cup ripe olives, sliced

Crumble ground beef into 1-quart microwave safe casserole dish. MICROWAVE, HIGH, uncovered 5-6 minutes or until meat is no longer pink, stirring once. Stir to break into small pieces; drain. Mix in parsley, oregano, salt, garlic powder, thyme, and pepper. Cover and chill. Combine yogurt, dill weed, and salt; mix well. Refrigerate until ready to serve. Arrange lettuce on platter. Layer chilled meat mixture, cucumber, and tomatoes. Top with yogurt dressing and garnish with ripe olives. Yield: 6 servings.

Ham Salad

This superb ham salad is sure to be a winner.

5 ounces ham, baked or boiled
6 inch piece celery
⅓ cup mayonnaise

1 tablespoon Dijon mustard
2 ounces Swiss cheese, shredded
   (optional)

Cut ham and celery into 1-inch pieces. Using food processor bowl and chopping blade, chop celery with 2-3 pulses. Add ham to bowl and pulse 3-4 times. Add remaining ingredients and pulse 2-3 times more, scraping down bowl when needed. Swiss cheese can be stirred into salad before serving. Yield: 1 cup.

Hearty Supper Salad

3 cups elbow macaroni, cooked
12 ounces ham, cut into strips
¾ cup green pepper, diced
¾ cup green onions, thinly sliced
½ cup dill pickle, chopped
1 cup celery, diced

1½ cups cottage cheese
¼ cup pimento, diced
1½ cups mayonnaise
2½ tablespoons cider vinegar
¼ teaspoon salt
¼ teaspoon pepper

Combine cooked macaroni, ham, green pepper, onion, pickle, celery, cottage cheese, and pimento in a large bowl. Combine mayonnaise, vinegar, and seasonings. Add to mixture; mix well. Chill. Serve on lettuce cups, if desired. Yield: 6-8 servings.

Hot Chicken Salad

Eat til it ouches you!

1 small can mushrooms, diced
3 cups chicken, cooked and diced
2 cans cream chicken soup,
   undiluted
2 cups celery, diced
4 tablespoons onion, minced

1 cup mayonnaise
1 cup crackers, crushed
1 cup almonds, diced
½ teaspoon pepper
2 tablespoons lemon juice
6 hard-cooked eggs, diced

Mix in order and fold in eggs. Bake in greased casserole. Temperature: 350 degrees. Baking Time: 40 minutes. Yield: 12 servings.

Hot Seafood Salad

10¼ ounces shrimp soup, frozen
¼ cup milk or cream
¼ pound cheese spread
6 ounces can tuna, in large pieces

1 cup celery, chopped
¼ cup onion, chopped
¼ cup green pepper, chopped
Patty shells, rice or toast points

In saucepan place shrimp soup, milk, and cheese; heat until soup is melted. Add remaining ingredients, cover, and heat on low until heated thoroughly. (Vegetables should be tender crisp.) Serve in patty shells, over rice, or on toast points. Yield: 4-6 servings.

Hot Turkey Salad

2 cups turkey, cooked and diced
2 cups celery, chopped
½ cup salted almonds, chopped
2 tablespoons lemon juice

2 tablespoons onion, grated
1 cup (or less) mayonnaise
1 cup potato chips, crushed
1 cup sharp cheese, grated

Mix all together except potato chips and cheese which you sprinkle over top. Bake. Temperature: 400 degrees. Baking Time: 20 minutes. Yield: 8 servings.

Macaroni Salad

7 or 8 ounces macaroni, cooked
6 ounces can tuna or salmon
1 cup cheddar cheese, cubed
½ cup sweet pickle, chopped
½ cup celery, chopped

¼ cup onion, minced
½ cup mayonnaise
1 tablespoon prepared mustard
1 tablespoon sugar
1 cup peas, drained

Drain cooked macaroni, rinse in cold water. Add tuna, cheese, pickles, celery, and onion. Mix mayonnaise, mustard, and sugar. Combine the two mixtures. Add peas and salt to taste; mix well. Yield: 6 servings.

Meal-In-One Salad

Excellent for outdoor entertaining!

2 cups meat or poultry, thin strips
  cooked
½ cup peas, cooked
½ cup carrot, shredded
½ cup celery, diced
½ cup tart pickle or ripe olives,
  chopped

¼ cup French dressing
½ teaspoon curry powder
  (optional)
Salt to taste
Salad greens
Pickle beets, radishes, or tomatoes

Combine meats, peas, carrot, celery, pickle, French dressing, and seasonings with a fork. Use a light touch. Cover and keep in the refrigerator about 2 hours to chill and blend flavors. Spoon lightly onto shredded crisp salad greens. Garnish with sliced pickled beets, radishes, or tomatoes. Yield: 4 generous servings.

Salmon Salad Mold

Makes a great appetizer!

2 cups salmon, canned and
  drained
1 teaspoon salt
1½ tablespoons sugar
½ tablespoon flour
Dash cayenne pepper
1 teaspoon mustard

2 egg yolks
1½ tablespoons butter, melted
¾ cup milk
¼ cup vinegar
1 envelope unflavored gelatin
2 tablespoons cold water

Remove skin and bones from salmon and flake in small pieces. Set aside. Mix dry ingredients; add egg yolks, butter, milk, and vinegar. Cook in double boiler over simmering water until mixture thickens, stirring constantly. Soak gelatin in cold water and add gelatin to cooked mixture. Cool. Add salmon and blend well. Turn into a fish mold and chill until congealed and firm. Yield: 4 servings.

Taco Salad

A nutritious one-dish meal.

2 pounds ground beef
2 packs taco seasoning mix
1 pound bag corn chips
½ head lettuce, shredded

1 cup cheddar cheese, shredded
2 tomatoes, diced
½ cup onion, diced
8 ounces sour cream (optional)

Brown ground beef in electric skillet. Drain excess fat and add taco seasoning mix, with recommended amount of water. As the mixture simmers, layer ½ of the corn chips on the bottom of a large serving platter. Layer ½ of the lettuce, cheese, tomato, and onion over the chips. Then add ½ of the beef mixture. Continue to layer the other remaining ingredients over the beef and finish with the second half of ground beef and chips. Top with sour cream. Yield: 6-8 servings.

Curried Rice Salad

Good served with ham and hot rolls.

1½ cups rice, cooked
¼ cup onion, minced
1 tablespoon vinegar
2 tablespoons salad oil

¾ teaspoon curry powder
1 cup celery, chopped
2 cups peas, cooked
¾ cup salad dressing

Mix rice, onion, vinegar, salad oil, and curry powder together; marinate in refrigerator for at least three hours. Add celery, cooked peas, and salad dressing. Serve on crisp lettuce. Yield: 10 servings.

Million Dollar Rice Salad

8 ounces cream cheese
2 tablespoons sugar
1 tablespoon mayonnaise
1 large package miniature
    marshmallows

1 large can crushed pineapple,
    drained
2 cups regular rice, cooked cooled
1 small jar maraschino cherries
1 cup whipping cream
¾ cup pecans, chopped

Cream the cheese, sugar, and mayonnaise together until smooth. Add marsh-mallows, pineapple, rice, and cherries to cream cheese mixture and fold together. Fold in whipped cream and nuts. Pour into 9x13-inch pan. Chill. Cut in squares to serve. Yield: 18 servings.

Broccoli Salad

Eat til it ouches you! Add raisins to make a great combination.

1 bunch fresh broccoli, chopped
4 hard-cooked eggs, chopped
½ cup onion, chopped

¾ cup mayonnaise
¾ cup stuffed olives, chopped
Salt and pepper to taste

Mix all ingredients together in refrigerator overnight for flavors to blend. Yield: 4-6 servings.

Copper Pennies

A wonderful salad for an outdoor meal!

3 medium onions, sliced
2 pounds carrots, peeled, sliced, and cooked
1 medium bell pepper, diced
Salt and pepper to taste
1 can cream of tomato soup

¾ cup sugar
½ cup salad oil
¾ cup vinegar
1 teaspoon prepared mustard
1 teaspoon Worcestershire sauce

Slice onions and separate into rings. Place cooked carrots in large dish with bell pepper and onions in layers. Sprinkle each layer with salt and pepper. Mix remaining ingredients together and pour over carrots, pepper, and onions. Cover tightly and place in refrigerator. Let stand 12 hours before serving. Drain part of the dressing from the vegetables and serve either as a vegetable or as a salad on lettuce. Any dressing leftover is good on a tossed salad. Yield: 6 servings.

Crunchy Cauliflower Salad

2 cups raw cauliflower
¼ cup celery, chopped
3 hard-cooked eggs, chopped
½ cup mild cheddar cheese, diced
¼ cup green pepper, chopped
¼ cup sweet pickle, chopped

½ teaspoon salt
¼ teaspoon white pepper
½ cup mayonnaise
½ medium head lettuce, torn into bite size pieces

Combine all ingredients in large salad bowl, toss lightly. Chill well. Yield: 6-8 servings.

Carrot-Bacon Salad With Sour Cream

4-6 slices bacon
½ head lettuce, shredded
1 small onion, sliced
4 medium carrots, shredded
⅔ cup salad dressing
½ cup sour cream

Dash salt and pepper
½ teaspoon garlic salt
1 tablespoon parsley flakes
1 teaspoon celery seeds
¼-½ cup milk or cream

Fry bacon until crisp; crumble. In shallow dish, layer lettuce, onions, and carrots; set aside and mix the next seven ingredients, blending well. Spread over ingredients in dish; sprinkle with bacon. Yield: 6-8 servings.

Cauliflower-Broccoli Medley

Eat til it ouches you!

2 small onions
1 head cauliflower
1 bunch broccoli
½ cup mayonnaise
⅓ cup vegetable oil

⅓ cup vinegar
¼ cup sugar
½ teaspoon salt
¼ teaspoon pepper
2 slices bacon

Slice onions and separate into rings. Wash cauliflower and remove green leaves. Separate the cauliflower into flowerets, slicing the large ones into bite-size pieces. Trim off large leaves of broccoli. Remove tough ends of lower stalks and wash broccoli thoroughly. Cut into bite-size pieces. Combine vegetables in a large bowl. Combine remaining ingredients except bacon, add to vegetables tossing gently. Chill several hours or overnight. Fry bacon until crisp; crumble. Garnish with bacon. Yield: 6-8 servings.

Corn Salad

A great summer salad.

2 (11 ounces) whole white corn, drained
½ cup spring onions, sliced
½ cup celery, finely chopped
½ cup green pepper, finely chopped

2 ounces pimentos, chopped and drained
½ cup sugar
½ cup white wine vinegar
⅛ teaspoon garlic powder

Combine corn, onions, celery, green pepper, and pimentos. Mix well. Set aside. Combine sugar, vinegar, and garlic powder. Pour over vegetables, tossing gently. Cover and chill 8 hours or overnight. Yield: 8 servings.

Cucumber Salad

2 medium cucumbers
1 teaspoon soy sauce
1 tablespoon white vinegar
1 tablespoon sugar
2 teaspoons sesame-seed oil
¼ teaspoon Tabasco sauce
½ teaspoon salt

Peel cucumbers and cut in half lengthwise. Scrape the seeds out of each half, leaving hollow boatlike shells. Cut crosswise into ¼-inch slices. In a small bowl, combine soy sauce, vinegar, sugar, sesame-seed oil, Tabasco sauce, and salt; mix well. Add the cucumbers. Toss and coat each slice thoroughly with dressing. Chill slightly before serving. Yield: 4 servings.

English Pea Salad

Eat til it ouches you!

1 pound can petit English Peas,
    drained
1 medium white onion, chopped
1 small jar pimento, minced
1½ cups celery, diced
½ cup oil
⅔ cup vinegar
⅔ cup sugar
Salt and pepper to taste

Mix peas, onion, pimento, and celery together. Set aside. Mix oil, vinegar, sugar, salt, and pepper. Pour over vegetables. Marinade in refrigerator overnight. Yield: 8 servings.

Festive Tomato Wedges

⅔ cup salad oil
¼ cup white wine vinegar
¼ cup parsley, snipped
¼ cup green onion, thinly sliced
2 tablespoons mayonnaise or
    salad dressing
1 clove garlic, minced
1 teaspoon salt
1 teaspoon dill weed
1 teaspoon basil, crushed
¼ teaspoon oregano, crushed
¼ teaspoon pepper
6 medium tomatoes, cut in wedges
1 tomato, hollowed (optional)

In a screw-top jar, combine all ingredients except tomatoes. Cover and shake. Place tomato wedges in a bowl, pour marinade over all. Stir gently. Cover, chill several hours, stirring once. Use a slotted spoon to remove tomatoes, arrange on platter. Spoon remaining marinade into hollowed tomato cup. Yield: 8 servings.

German Potato Salad

Eat til it ouches you!

10-12 large potatoes
6-8 slices bacon
2 large onions, diced
¼ cup vinegar
½ cup sugar

½ cup water
Celery, parsley, hard-cooked eggs
(optional)
Salt and pepper to taste

Peel potatoes; cut in large squares. Boil in salted water until just tender. Do not overcook. Drain. Fry bacon until crisp; crumble. In drippings, fry onions until golden brown. Pour vinegar, sugar, and water into frying pan with onions, and bring to boil. Add potatoes and bacon. Toss together. Celery, parsley, and hard-cooked eggs may be added, if desired. Season to taste. Serve hot. Yield: 10-12 servings.

Gourmet Potato Salad

Slices of ham arranged around salad
make an appetizing and delicious main dish.

5 medium potatoes, cooked and
diced
2 teaspoons salt
1 teaspoon celery seeds
6 hard-cooked eggs
½ cucumber, chopped

½ small onion, chopped
1 teaspoon prepared mustard
¾ cup salad dressing
2 tablespoons vinegar
¾ cup sour cream

Toss together lightly the potatoes, salt, and celery seeds. Remove yolks from eggs. Dice egg whites and add to potato mixture. Blend cucumber, onion, mustard, salad dressing, vinegar, and egg yolks in electric blender. Fold sour cream into this mixture and fold this dressing into potatoes. Chill well. Serve on crisp salad greens.

Hot Bean Salad (Sweet And Sour)

4 slices bacon	1 teaspoon salt
1 medium onion, minced	1/8 teaspoon pepper
1/2 teaspoon flour	20 ounces kidney beans, drained
1/4 cup vinegar	1/4 cup parsley, snipped
1 tablespoon sugar	1/2 cup celery, chopped

Fry bacon until crisp and set aside. Add onion to drippings and sauté until tender. Stir in flour and vinegar. Add sugar, salt, pepper, and beans. Cook gently until beans are hot. Add parsley, celery, crumbled bacon. Toss and serve. Yield: 4 servings.

Ham And Spinach Layered Salad

Make ahead! It's wonderful to take to a covered dish meal.

6 cups fresh spinach, torn	10 ounces frozen green peas,
3 hard-cooked eggs, sliced	thawed
4 ounces boiled ham, cut in	3/4 cup mayonnaise
julienne strips	1/3 cup sour cream
1 small red onion, thinly sliced	1 1/2 cups Swiss cheese, cubed
	5 slices bacon

In large salad bowl, layer half the spinach, all the eggs and ham, the remaining spinach, onion, and peas. In small bowl, combine mayonnaise and sour cream, spread over the top of the salad, sealing to the side of the dish. Sprinkle with cheese. Cover and chill 24 hours. Fry bacon until crisp and sprinkle with crumbled bacon and serve. Yield: 6 servings.

Marinated Cole Slaw

Eat til it ouches you!

1 large head cabbage, shredded	1 cup vinegar
1 large onion, chopped	1 teaspoon dry mustard
1 large green pepper, chopped	1 teaspoon celery seeds
1 cup sugar	1 tablespoon salt
3/4 cup salad oil	

Place cabbage in large bowl. Add onion, then peppers on top. Sprinkle sugar on top. Bring to boil the salad oil, vinegar, dry mustard, celery seeds, and salt. Pour over other ingredients while hot. Do not stir mixture until it has been refrigerated several hours or overnight. Drain to serve. Keeps for days.

Layered Tossed Salad

A wonderful make ahead dish!

1 head lettuce, shredded
1 onion, sliced and separated into rings
3 celery stalks, chopped
1 can water chestnuts, sliced thin
10 ounces frozen green peas, thawed and uncooked
3-4 hard-cooked eggs, sliced
3 tomatoes, cut in small pieces
2 cups salad dressing
Bacon bits or ½ pound boiled ham, chopped
Cheese, grated (optional)

Layer ingredients in a 9x13-inch dish in order given. Spread dressing over the top of the salad, sealing to the side of the dish. Sprinkle with bacon, ham, or cheese. Cover and refrigerate for 24 hours before serving. Yield: 10-12 servings.

Oriental Salad

1 cup frozen peas
½ head cabbage
¼ cup sunflower seeds
½ cup almonds, sliced
1 package Oriental noodles, uncooked but broken up
4 green onions, sliced
⅓ cup sesame seeds

DRESSING
½ cup oil
¼ cup vinegar
1 seasoning packet from above noodles

Cook peas until tender and allow to cool. Shred cabbage and mix with remaining salad ingredients. Mix all dressing ingredients and add DRESSING and toss ORIENTAL SALAD to coat. Refrigerate for a few hours.

Sauerkraut Salad

Eat til it ouches you! This salad can be kept for over a year if refrigerated.

½ cup oil
½ cup vinegar
¾ cup sugar
2 pounds sauerkraut, drained
1 cup celery, chopped
1 cup onion, chopped
1 cup green pepper, chopped
1 cup red pepper, chopped

Mix together oil, vinegar, and sugar; bring to a boil and pour over all salad ingredients. Mix well. Place in a covered glass bowl. Marinate overnight. Drain liquid when salad is served. Yield: 16 servings.

Orange And Carrot Salad

3 cups (¾ pound) carrots,
   shredded
2 medium oranges
3 tablespoons lemon juice

1 tablespoon sugar
1 teaspoon cinnamon, ground
Dash salt

Place shredded carrots in a medium bowl. Peel and section oranges over the bowl to catch juices. Halve orange sections. Add to shredded carrots along with lemon juice. In small bowl, combine sugar, cinnamon, and salt. Add to carrot mixture; mix well. Cover and chill several hours. Serve in a lettuce lined bowl. Yield: 4-6 servings.

Yankee Doodle Salad

Eat til it ouches you!

¾ cup vinegar
¾ cup sugar
4 tablespoons water
½ cup cooking oil
¼ cup onion, chopped
½ cup celery, chopped

1 teaspoon salt
1 tablespoon paprika
Dash pepper
1 large can French style green
   beans
2 cups English peas, canned

Mix all ingredients except peas and beans. Then add peas and beans and marinate 24 hours in refrigerator. Drain and serve on lettuce cups. Yield: 6-8 servings.

Zesty Macaroni-Vegetable Salad

Eat til it ouches you!

¾ cup Italian dressing
2 cups macaroni, cooked
1 cup celery, chopped
½ cup onion, chopped
¾ cup carrots, shredded

¾ cup green pepper, chopped
½ cup American cheese, shredded
1 cup sour cream
4 slices bacon
Salt and pepper to taste

Add Italian dressing to cooked macaroni and chill overnight. A few hours before serving, add celery, onion, carrots, pepper, and cheese. When ready to serve, fry bacon until crisp; crumble. Add sour cream, bacon, salt, and pepper. Yield: 10 servings.

Spreads
and Soups

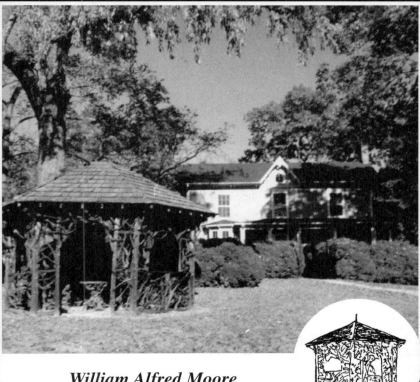

**William Alfred Moore
House**

WILLIAM ALFRED MOORE HOUSE

The Moore House, 202 Moore Avenue, Mount Airy, was built in 1860 and is the earliest known structure remaining in the town of Mount Airy. The house exhibits a combination of Victorian and Italianate stylistic features and on the interior, Greek Revival features.

Located in the front yard of the Moore House is an outstanding rustic hexagonal summer house, a very rare gazebo, circa 1865, constructed with 12 wood poles and intervening laurel root walls, and a wood shingle roof. The furniture inside the summer house includes a settee, chair, and table with plank top and laurel root vase.

Matthew Moore, William Alfred Moore's grandfather, served as a colonel in the Revolutionary War Militia. The Moore family was a well established family in the region prior to the establishment of Surry County in 1771 and neighboring Stokes County in 1789. Samuel Dalton Moore, William Alfred's father, married Matilda Carolina Franklin, daughter of Governor Jesse Franklin. Samuel Dalton was one of the village's pioneer merchants and was the first known owner of the Flat Rock, the world's largest open-faced granite quarry. William Alfred and his brother, Jesse Franklin, established the Greenhill Mills in 1869 which produced cotton and woolen goods and owned a grist mill. William Alfred also operated a general store on Main Street, Mount Airy.

William Alfred Moore married his cousin Rachel Martin, 1839-1882, from Stokes County. The education of their four children was most important. The house design included a large schoolroom located in a two-story shed roof rear ell. An elderly cousin who lived on the mountain came to town during the winter months and taught the younger children.

William was an educated and well-read man. His books formed a substantial library in the Moore House. Rachel Moore planted English boxwoods in the front yard which now almost obscure the house. Margaret, a daughter, expanded the shrubs and today several thousand boxwoods remain on the property.

The family enjoyed sharing their home and gardens with friends. They were active in Mount Airy's society and entertained often. The Christmas open house was a gala event and still continues to be observed by the Moore family.

In 1992, the home was purchased by the Mount Airy Restoration Foundation. Today, it is the setting for many weddings, receptions, dinners, and other gala social events.

Jamaican Sandwich

The combination of two breads make a beautiful and nourishing meal.

8 ounces cream cheese
2 tablespoons pineapple syrup
¼ teaspoon vanilla extract
Dash salt
¼ cup crushed pineapple, drained

¼ cup pecans, chopped
4 slices white bread
8 slices whole wheat bread
Butter or margarine

Combine cream cheese, pineapple syrup, vanilla, and salt. Stir in pineapple and pecans. Spread 4 slices white bread with PINK-PIG FILLING. Spread 4 slices whole wheat bread with butter or margarine, then spread evenly with cheese mixture. Top with remaining bread slices to complete the double-decker sandwich. Cut diagonally into halves. Garnish with ripe olives and pimento strips. Yield: 4 sandwiches.

PINK-PIG FILLING
8 ounces ham, cooked and
    coarsely ground
¼ cup pickle relish
2 teaspoons prepared mustard
2 teaspoons pimento, finely
    chopped

1 teaspoon green pepper, finely
    chopped
¼ teaspoon Worcestershire sauce
Dash pepper
2 tablespoons mayonnaise

Combine all ingredients and mix well.

Open-face English Muffin Sandwiches

Flour
Salt
Eggplant (2 slices per muffin)
English Muffins (1 per person)

Boiled ham slices
Tomato slices
Cheese Sauce

Split and toast English muffins. Lightly flour and salt slices of eggplant on both sides. Sauté until golden brown and tender. Layer on each half of muffin: 1 thin slice of boiled ham, 1 slice sautéed eggplant, 1 slice tomato, top with CHEESE SAUCE. Yield: 6 servings.

CHEESE SAUCE
2 tablespoons butter
2 tablespoons flour
1½ cups milk
1 cup cheddar cheese, grated

1 teaspoon salt
½ teaspoon Worcestershire sauce
¼ teaspoon paprika

Melt butter and blend with flour. Cook 1 minute. Add milk slowly, stirring constantly. When thick, add remaining ingredients.

Open-face Crab Supreme

8 slices bread, lightly toasted	1 teaspoon Worcestershire sauce
Tartar sauce	1 tablespoon lemon juice
2 cups crab meat, flaked	¼ cup mayonnaise
Dash hot sauce	1 cup sharp cheese, grated

Spread toast with tartar sauce. Combine crab meat, hot sauce, Worcestershire sauce, lemon juice, and mayonnaise. Spread bread evenly with crab mixture. Top with grated cheese. Place under broiler until cheese is melted. Serve with lemon wedges. Yield: 8 sandwiches.

Stuffed Picnic Rolls

Great to make ahead and freeze for a cookout.

1 pound hamburger	1 tablespoon Worcestershire
2 tablespoons fat	sauce
1 onion, chopped	1 cup cheese, shredded
Salt to taste	1 teaspoon mustard
⅓ cup catsup	

Combine hamburger, fat, and onion and cook in frying pan until meat looses its red color. Add salt, catsup, Worcestershire sauce, and cheese. Cook slowly ten minutes. Chill. Split buns and hollow out the inside. Spread surface with mustard. Fill each bun with mixture. Wrap in aluminum foil. Store in vapor-moisture resistant wrap and freeze. At serving time, heat, and serve rolls wrapped in foil. Heat over an open grate or in oven.

Tuna Burgers

6 hamburger buns	¾ cup American cheese, grated
Butter or margarine	½ cup stuffed green olives,
7 ounces can tuna, flaked	chopped
½ cup celery, chopped	¼ cup mayonnaise
1 small onion, minced	Dash black pepper

Split and butter hamburger buns. Mix tuna, celery, onion, cheese, olives, mayonnaise, and pepper. Fill buns with tuna mixture. Bake. Temperature: 350 degrees. Baking Time: 15-20 minutes. Yield: 6 servings.

"Good friends are cheaper than therapy."

Aloha Sandwich Spread

This is delicious on rounds of nut bread and it will freeze well too.

3 (3 ounces) cream cheese
3 tablespoons milk
¾ cup crushed pineapple, drained
2 tablespoons lemon juice

¾ teaspoon ginger, ground
3 ounces coconut, about 1 cup
¾ cup pecans, chopped

Soften cheese with milk. Drain pineapple and mix with cheese. Add remaining ingredients and mix well.

Colorful Cheese Spread

16 ounces sharp cheddar cheese,
   shredded
2 (8 ounces) cream cheese
20 ounces crushed pineapple,
   drained

¼ cup green pepper, finely
   chopped
6 slices bacon
Crackers or breads

Combine softened cheddar cheese (not melted) and softened cream cheese, mixing well until smoothly blended. Fry bacon until crisp, crumble. Add remaining ingredients, mix well. Chill. Serve with an assortment of crackers or breads. Yield: approximately 5 cups.

Create-A-Spread

3 ounces cream cheese, softened

OPTIONS

2½ ounces deviled ham
¼ cup crushed pineapple, drained
½ cup cheese, shredded
1-2 tablespoons bacon, cooked
   crisp and crumbled
1-2 tablespoons green pepper,
   chopped

1-2 tablespoons pickle, chopped
   and drained (dill, sweet or
   relish)
1-2 tablespoons olives, chopped
1-2 tablespoons pimento, chopped
1 tablespoon steak sauce
1 teaspoon prepared mustard

Add one or more of the above options in softened cream cheese. Add a few drops milk or cream, if necessary. Mix well. Spread on crackers or use as filling for finger sandwiches.

"We keep the best of that we give away."

Curried Turkey Spread

2 cups cooked turkey, finely diced	**½ teaspoon fresh lemon peel,**
¾ cup mayonnaise	**grated**
2 tablespoons capers	**1 teaspoon fresh lemon juice**
1 teaspoon curry powder	

Combine ingredients and mix well. Spread on bread or crackers. Yield: 2 cups.

Date Mint Sandwich

2 cups creamed cottage cheese	**Butter**
½ cup nuts, chopped	**Mint jelly**
½ cup dates, chopped	**Bread**

Mix cottage cheese, dates, and nuts together. Add enough butter to blend mixture. Spread on one slice of bread. Spread mint jelly, which has been heated slowly over low heat, on top of sandwich. Put in refrigerator to congeal. After jelly has congealed, cut with shamrock or other special cutter.

Vegetable Sandwiches

2 stalks celery	**¼ cup boiling water**
1 cucumber, medium	**1 teaspoon salt**
1 onion, small	**1 tablespoon Worcestershire**
1 green pepper	**sauce**
2 carrots, peeled	**1 teaspoon dry mustard**
1 package plain gelatin	**1 cup mayonnaise**
¼ cup cold water	**Dash soy sauce**

Blend celery, cucumbers, onion, green pepper, and carrots in blender; drain. Soak gelatin in cold water. Mix well together the softened gelatin in hot water and remaining ingredients to make a sauce. When ready to make sandwiches, mix ½ of sauce with vegetables. (This sauce is enough to use with twice as many vegetables). Use for open-face or finger and sandwiches.

_____

Cut a sandwich in half by cutting from corner to corner. Your sandwich will stay together better and will be easier to eat.

Tuna Sandwich Spread

This delicious sandwich spread can be used to top open-face sandwich.

7 ounces can tuna	2 teaspoons lemon juice
6 slices crisp bacon, chopped	Tabasco sauce to taste
6 tablespoons mayonnaise	½ teaspoon salt

With a fork, break up tuna fish into very small pieces. Add bacon. Blend mayonnaise, lemon juice, Tabasco sauce, and salt with tuna. Chill thoroughly before using. Yield: 1½ cups.

Orange Cream Cheese And Nut Spread

6 ounces cream cheese, soft	¾ cup pecans
½ cup orange marmalade	Bread

Combine cheese and orange marmalade in blender. Cover, blend until mixed. Add pecans and push down into mixture. Cover and blend only until nuts are coarsely chopped. Yield: about 1¾ cups.

Creamy Potato Soup

Eat til it ouches you!

4 cups potatoes, peeled and cubed	1 cup whipping cream
1 cup celery, ¾-inch slices	3 tablespoons butter or
1 cup onion, chopped	margarine, melted
2 cups water	1 tablespoon parsley flakes
2 teaspoons salt	½ teaspoon caraway seeds
1 cup milk	⅛ teaspoon pepper

Combine potatoes, celery, onion, water, and salt in large Dutch oven. Simmer, covered, about 20 minutes or until potatoes are tender. Mash mixture once or twice with a potato masher, leaving some vegetable pieces whole. Stir in remaining ingredients, return to heat and cook, stirring constantly, until soup is thoroughly heated. Yield: 7 cups.

"Cooking your favorite foods for friends brings out the very best in you."

Cream Of Broccoli Soup
(Cauliflower Or Spinach)

This soup freezes well.

½ stick butter or margarine
4 tablespoons corn starch
2 cans chicken broth
2 pints half and half

2 cups cheddar cheese, grated
Salt and pepper to taste
10 ounces frozen broccoli,
    cauliflower or spinach, cooked

In a heavy pan, melt butter. Stir in corn starch. Mixture will be pasty. Add 1 can of broth at a time and stir until thickened over low heat. Add 1 pint of half and half at a time until thickened. Add cheese, salt, and pepper, stir. Add vegetables and stir. Let soup simmer one hour. Yield: 8-10 servings.

Clam Chowder Manhattan

¼ pound salt pork, cubed
2 medium onions, sliced thin
1⅓ cups raw potatoes, cubed
2½ cups fish stock or chicken
    consommé
Salt and pepper to taste

Pinch thyme
1 bay leaf
3 cups hard-shelled clams,
    chopped
1½ cups tomatoes, peeled and
    cubed

Fry pork cubes, add onions, and cook about 8 minutes. Add potatoes, stock, and seasonings. When potatoes are almost done, add the clams and tomatoes and boil about 10 minutes. Yield: 6-8 servings.

Green Pea And Potato Soup

1 large onion, chopped
¼ cup butter
6 medium potatoes, sliced
3 cups green peas, fresh or frozen

1½ quarts chicken stock
1 bay leaf
½ cup heavy cream
2 tablespoons butter

Sauté onion in ¼ cup butter until softened. Add potatoes, peas, chicken stock, bay leaf, salt, and pepper to taste. Bring to a boil, reduce heat, simmer 15-20 minutes. Discard bay leaf. Press soup through sieve or purée in blender. Add cream and remaining butter. Reheat before serving. Yield: 12 servings.

"What goes around, comes around."

Nine Bean Soup Mix

Two cups of soup mix and Nine Bean Soup recipe make a lovely gift.

1 pound barley peas, dried
1 pound black beans, dried
1 pound red kidney beans, dried
1 pound pinto beans, dried
1 pound navy beans, dried

1 pound Great Northern beans, dried
1 pound lentils, dried
1 pound split peas, dried
1 pound blackeyed peas, dried

Combine all beans. Divide into 10 (2 cups) packages.

Nine Bean Soup

Use the slow cooker.

2 cups Nine Bean Soup Mix
2 quarts water
1 pound ham, diced
1 large onion, chopped
1 clove garlic, minced

½-3¼ teaspoons salt
16 ounces tomatoes, canned, undrained and chopped
10 ounces tomatoes with green chilies, canned and drained

Rinse two cups bean mix. Place beans in slow cooker. Cover with water two inches above beans; soak overnight. Drain beans. Add two quarts water and next 4 ingredients. Cook on high in slow cooker for one hour. Reduce to low and cook for six hours or until beans are tender. Add remaining ingredients and cook on low for one hour. Stir occasionally. Yield: eight cups.

*"Bless, O Lord, we beseech Thee, this food to our use,
and us to Thy service, and make us truly thankful for all Thy mercies,
we ask in the name of Jesus Christ our Lord. Amen."*
PROTESTANT BLESSING

Poor Man's Soup

2 cups water
1 tablespoon margarine
4 medium potatoes, peeled and
    diced
2 medium carrots, sliced
1 large onion, chopped

8 ounces tomato sauce
22 ounces tomato juice
½ teaspoon salt
½ teaspoon pepper
1 pound ground round

Bring water and margarine to a boil. Add potatoes and carrots. Cook 20 minutes. Add onion, tomato sauce, tomato juice, salt, and pepper; bring to a boil. Crumble ground round into boiling mixture. Cook 10 minutes. Reduce heat and simmer until ready to serve. Yield: 3 quarts.

Savory Minestrone Main-dish Soup

Perk up your winter meals!

3 slices bacon, chopped fine
1 cup onion, chopped
½ cup celery, chopped
2 large garlic cloves, minced
1 teaspoon basil, crushed
1 can beef broth
1 can Bean w/Bacon soup
1½ soup cans water

16 ounces tomatoes, canned
½ cup small tube macaroni,
    uncooked
½ teaspoon salt
1 cup cabbage, cut in long thin
    shreds
1 cup zucchini, cubed (optional)

In large saucepan, brown bacon and cook onion and celery with garlic and basil until tender. Stir in soups, water, tomatoes, macaroni, and salt. Bring to boil; cover, reduce heat; simmer 15 minutes. Add cabbage and zucchini; cook 10 minutes more until done. Stir occasionally. Yield: 10 servings.

Vegetables

Gertrude Smith
House Museum

GERTRUDE SMITH HOUSE MUSEUM

The home at 709 North Main Street was built in 1903 by the Jefferson Davis Smith Family. The two-story frame house with a variety of late Victorian and Colonial Revival features multi-sided projecting bays on the main and side elevations, shingled pedimented gables, Queen Anne Style windows and lighting the gabled dormers, decorated braked with drop pendant at the eaves. There is a first-story porch carried by paired Doric Columns on granite plinths and a small second-story side porch with spindle frieze. In the interior, the house follows a center hall and is ornamental with a variety of Classical Revival and Victorian style mantels, wide fluted baseboards and robust molded crown molding.

Mr. Smith was a native of Greensboro, owner of the J. D. Smith General Store, and owned vast amounts of real estate. He married a Mount Airy native, Gertrude Gilmer and they had seven children. Gertrude, Cameron, and Robert never married and continued to live in the home.

In the 1930's Miss Gertrude Smith, an interior designer, studied at the Parson's School of Interior Design, New York City. She died in 1981 at 90 years of age. Miss Gertrude's trademarks were stamped brass cornice boards over the windows and pier gold gilded mirrors. They are used throughout the home. She enjoyed going to the mountains "antiquing". The home features a large collection of antique teapots and corner cupboards.

The library contains over 3,000 books from Dr. Robert Smith, an ophthalmologist. Dr. Robert loved to travel and Miss Gertrude collected art. The paintings were collected from all parts of the world by Dr. Robert and given to Miss Gertrude.

The home is unique with all original furnishings and is left as though it were still occupied by the Smith family. It is now used as a museum. Special events and exhibits are held in the home throughout the year.

Asparagus À La Goldenrod

Eat til it ouches you!
For Christmas, decorate top with a poinsettia made with pimento.

1 cup American cheese, grated
1 can cream of mushroom soup
20-30 asparagus spears, cooked
    and hot

6 slices buttered toast points
3 hard-cooked eggs, chopped fine

Fold cheese into soup; heat one minute or until hot. Arrange drained asparagus on toast points. Cover with cheese sauce. Garnish by sprinkling chopped egg over each serving. Heat until warm. Serve at once. Yield: 6 servings.

Asparagus Almondine

MICROWAVE.

4 tablespoons almonds, sliced
2 tablespoons butter or margarine
1 pound fresh asparagus spears,
    trimmed and pared

1 tablespoon water
½ teaspoon seasoned salt

MICROWAVE, HIGH, almonds and butter in small bowl, uncovered, 4-6 minutes, stirring several times. Place asparagus in 9x13-inch glass dish, arranging tips in center of dish. Add water and cover with plastic wrap. MICROWAVE, HIGH, until tender, 5-8 minutes. Drain. Sprinkle with toasted buttered almonds and seasoned salt. NOTE: Use any kind of nuts or add fresh lemon juice. Yield: 4-6 servings.

Deviled Asparagus

4 ounces deviled ham
1 tablespoon pimento, chopped
1½ cups medium white sauce
2 hard-cooked eggs, diced

1 tablespoon cooking sherry
1 can asparagus (18 spears)
Parmesan cheese

Combine deviled ham and pimento with white sauce; stir until smooth; add eggs and sherry. Pour mixture over hot asparagus and sprinkle with cheese. Garnish with eggs and pimento. Yield: 4-6 servings.

Asparagus With Lemon Butter Crumbs

2 slices bread, day old cubed
2 tablespoons butter or margarine

2 pounds asparagus spears,
canned
1 tablespoon lemon juice

Cut bread in tiny cubes and brown in butter; heat asparagus; drain and put in serving dish. Top with crumbs; sprinkle with lemon juice. Yield: 6 servings.

Three Bean Bake

MICROWAVE. A great recipe for outdoor entertaining!

5 slices bacon
Bacon drippings
15 ounces kidney beans
15 ounces lima beans
15 ounces pork and beans
1 large onion, chopped

⅓ cup green pepper, chopped
¾ cup brown sugar, packed
½ cup catsup
1 teaspoon dry mustard
1 teaspoon vinegar

In rectangular pyrex dish with rack, place 5 slices of bacon. Cover with paper towel. MICROWAVE, HIGH, until crisp, about 5 minutes. Break into small pieces. In 2½-quart casserole dish, add bacon, half of bacon drippings and all remaining ingredients. Cover with clear microwave-safe plastic wrap. MICROWAVE, MEDIUM, for 30 minutes, stirring every 5 minutes. Yield: 8 servings.

Green Bean And Sour Cream Casserole

Eat til it ouches you!

3 tablespoons butter, melted
2 tablespoons flour
1 teaspoon salt
1 teaspoon sugar
¼ teaspoon pepper

1 tablespoon onion, chopped
1 cup sour cream
32 ounces green beans, drained
1 cup sharp cheese, grated
¾ cup Corn Flake crumbs

Combine 2 tablespoons butter and flour. Cook slowly. Remove from heat and add seasonings and sour cream. Fold in beans. Place in casserole. Cover with cheese and add crumbs mixed with 1 tablespoon melted butter. Bake. Temperature: 350 degrees. Baking Time: 30 minutes. Yield: 6 servings.

Great Green Beans

Eat til it ouches you! The name says it all.

3 slices bacon
1 small clove garlic, finely
    chopped
4 cups green beans, cooked
1½ tablespoons soy sauce

½ cup chicken broth
2 tablespoons bean liquid
1 tablespoon flour
1 cup French onion dip

In frying pan, cook bacon until crisp; remove; add garlic to bacon fat and cook for about 2 minutes. Add beans, soy sauce, chicken broth, and bean liquid. Cover; cook about 5 minutes. Remove beans. Blend flour and onion dip; combine with broth mixture. Cook until thickened. Return beans. Heat only to serving temperature. Serve immediately, garnish with crumbled bacon. Yield: 6 servings.

Baked Lima Beans And Peas

2 (10 ounces) frozen baby lima
    beans
2 (10 ounces) frozen peas
1 teaspoon sweet basil
1 teaspoon salt

4 green onions with tops, minced
4 tablespoons butter
3 tablespoons water
Lettuce leaves

Thaw vegetables. Place in greased 4-quart shallow casserole with tight fitting cover. Stir in basil, salt, and green onions. Dot with butter and sprinkle with water. Place lettuce leaves over vegetables, cover and bake until vegetables are tender. Temperature: 350 degrees. Baking Time: 30 minutes. Yield: 6-8 servings.

French Green Bean Casserole

2 (10 ounces) frozen French
   green beans, cut
¾ cup vinegar

1 cup sugar
4 slices bacon
1 medium onion, sliced

Cook beans according to package directions and drain. Bring vinegar and sugar to a boil. Fry bacon until crisp, crumble, and add bacon drippings to sugar mixture. Put beans in casserole with sliced onions to top. Pour sugar mixture over this. Bake until onions are done; top with crumbled bacon. Temperature: 350 degrees. Baking Time: about 25 minutes. Yield: 6-8 servings.

Holiday Green Beans

1 large onion, chopped
½ cup margarine
¼ cup plain flour
1½ cups milk
¾ pound sharp Cheddar cheese,
   grated
Dash Tabasco sauce
2 teaspoons soy sauce

½ teaspoon pepper
1 teaspoon salt
30 ounces frozen French green
   beans, cooked and drained
4 ounces mushrooms
4 ounces water chestnuts, sliced
Almonds, chopped

Sauté onion in margarine. Add flour, then milk; cook until smooth. Stir in cheese, Tabasco sauce, soy sauce, pepper, and salt; cook until cheese melts. Add beans, mushrooms, and water chestnuts. Pour into 9x13-inch casserole and sprinkle with almonds. Bake until thoroughly heated and thickened. Temperature: 350 degrees. Baking Time: about 30 minutes. Yield: 12 servings.

Recipe For Making Christmas Happen Everyday

Take a quart of joy and gladness,
A peck of folks and kin,
A dash of Christmas spirit
And toss some laughter in.
Take a large amount of giving
And spread it generously.

Read directions in the Good Book,
And apply them carefully.
Garnish well with human kindness,
And crystal leaves of cheer,
And you will have a batch of Christmas
To last the coming year.

Sweet-Sour Beets

⅓ cup beet juice or water
⅓ cup vinegar
½ teaspoon salt

1½ tablespoons sugar
2 cups beets, cooked or canned

Mix ingredients and pour over beets in a casserole. Cover and bake. Temperature: 350 degrees. Baking Time: 10-12 minutes. Yield: 4 servings.

Beets And Carrots À La Orange

MICROWAVE.

2 cups carrots, sliced
    (2-3 medium)
¼ cup water
2 tablespoons brown sugar,
    packed
1 tablespoon corn starch

¾ teaspoon salt
½ cup orange juice
¼ cup butter or margarine
1 tablespoon vinegar
1 pound beets, canned, drained,
    and sliced

Combine carrots and water in 1-quart glass casserole. Cover. MICROWAVE, HIGH, 5-6 minutes or until just tender. Let stand 5 minutes. Combine brown sugar, corn starch, salt, and orange juice in 2-cup glass measure; mix well. MICROWAVE, HIGH, uncovered, 2-2½ minutes or until mixture boils and thickens. Stir in butter and vinegar. Drain carrots. Add beets to carrots. Pour sauce over vegetables. Mix lightly. Cover. MICROWAVE, HIGH, 1½-2 minutes or until heated through. Yield: 6-8 servings.

Broccoli Bake

Quick and easy!

20 ounces frozen broccoli spears
6 tomato slices
½ teaspoon salt
⅛ teaspoon pepper

2 tablespoons butter
1 can condensed cheese soup
1 tablespoon lemon juice

Cook broccoli as directed. Drain. Arrange in 10x6-inch baking dish. Place tomato slices along outside edge. Sprinkle with salt and pepper. Dot with butter. Blend soup and lemon juice until smooth. Pour into center of casserole. Bake. Temperature: 350 degrees. Baking Time: 20 minutes. Yield: 6 servings.

Broccoli Onion Deluxe

Eat til it ouches you!

20 ounces frozen broccoli	Dash pepper
2 cups whole small onions	1 cup milk
4 tablespoons butter or margarine	3 ounces cream cheese, cut up
2 tablespoons flour	1 cup soft bread crumbs
¼ teaspoon salt	¼ cup Parmesan cheese, grated

Cook broccoli according to package directions; drain. Cook onions in boiling salted water until tender, about 10 minutes; drain. In saucepan, melt 2 tablespoons butter; blend in flour, salt, and pepper. Add milk and cook until thick. Add cream cheese; stir in vegetables. Place in 1½-quart casserole. Bake 20 minutes. Melt remaining butter. Toss with bread crumbs and Parmesan cheese. Bake, 15-20 minutes longer. Temperature: 350 degrees. Baking Time: 35-40 minutes. Yield: 10 servings.

Bacon Broccoli

10 ounces frozen broccoli, chopped	1/16 teaspoon dry mustard
4 slices bacon	1½ tablespoons cider vinegar
½ tablespoon light brown sugar, packed	1 large scallion, thinly sliced

Cook the broccoli according to package directions, drain. Fry bacon until crisp; crumble. In electric skillet, combine sugar, mustard, vinegar, and scallion in bacon fat. Bring to a boil. Add the broccoli. Heat 10-20 minutes. Top with the crumbled bacon. Yield: 4 servings.

Dilled Broccoli

1 head broccoli	½ teaspoon dill weed
⅓ cup vinegar	¼ teaspoon salt
½ cup oil	¼ teaspoon pepper
1 teaspoon sugar	¼ teaspoon garlic powder

Cut broccoli into small flowerets. Mix remaining ingredients and pour over broccoli. Marinate in refrigerator 6-8 hours. Drain and serve. Yield: 6 servings.

Broccoli Casserole

10 ounces frozen broccoli
¼ cup onion rings, canned
1 can mushroom slices
⅓ cup cashew nuts
¼ cup cheese, grated

½ can mushroom soup
¼ cup water
4-6 crackers, crumbled
1 tablespoon butter or margarine

Cook broccoli as directed on package. Layer cooked broccoli, onion rings, and mushrooms in casserole dish. Sprinkle cashews and grated cheese over dish. Mix soup and water; pour over all. Top with cracker crumbs. Dot with butter. Bake. Temperature: 350 degrees. Baking Time: 20 minutes. Yield: 6 servings.

Broccoli California

20 ounces frozen broccoli
⅓ cup olive oil or butter
1 clove garlic, crushed

¼ cup almonds, chopped
   (optional)
⅔ cup pitted ripe olives, sliced
2 teaspoons lemon juice

Cook broccoli according to package directions. Drain and keep warm. Put olive oil and garlic in a small saucepan. Place over medium heat; cook 2 minutes, stirring occasionally. Add nuts, olives, and lemon juice; heat thoroughly. Sprinkle over the broccoli. Yield: 6-8 servings.

Broccoli Parmesan

20 ounces frozen broccoli spears
2 tablespoons butter
¼ cup onion, chopped

1 can cream of chicken soup
⅔ cup milk
⅓ cup Parmesan cheese

Cook broccoli in boiling water until tender. Drain. Melt butter in saucepan; add onion and cook until tender but not brown. Blend soup, milk, and cheese. Heat thoroughly. Serve sauce over hot broccoli, Yield: 6-8 servings.

"To plant a garden is to believe in tomorrow."

Cabbage Casserole

Eat til it ouches you!

1 stick margarine
2 cups Corn Flakes
6-7 cups cabbage, shredded
2 cups onion, chopped

1 can water chestnuts, sliced
  (optional)
2 cups cheddar cheese, grated

SAUCE
8 ounces sour cream or ½ cup
  mayonnaise
1 can cream of celery soup

1 cup milk
Salt and pepper to taste

Mix margarine and Corn Flakes. Place ½ of Corn Flake mixture in bottom of 9x13-inch dish. Spread cabbage over Corn Flakes and sprinkle with onions and water chestnuts. Mix all sauce ingredients and pour SAUCE over cabbage. Top with remaining Corn Flake mixture. Bake. Remove from oven. Top with grated cheese. Allow to melt before serving. Temperature: 350 degrees. Baking Time: 30-40 minutes. Yield: 8-10 servings.

Stir-fried Chinese Cabbage

The tender crisp cabbage is sure to be a winner. Add any leftover meat.

1 pound green cabbage or Chinese
  cabbage
2 tablespoons peanut oil
1 teaspoon salt

¼ cup chicken bouillon
⅓ cup cooked, chopped ham,
  sausage, chicken, or shrimp
1 teaspoon corn starch

Trim cabbage. Wash thoroughly. Cut into 2x½-inch pieces. Heat skillet or wok on moderate heat for about 30 seconds. Pour in oil and heat for another 30 seconds. Add cabbage. Stir-fry for about 1 minute to coat the cabbage with oil. Sprinkle with salt and add bouillon. Bring to a quick boil, cover and cook over moderate heat for about 3 minutes. Stir in chopped meat and corn starch mixed with 1 tablespoon cold water; stir until cabbage and meat are coated with a light clear glaze. Serve immediately. Yield: 4-6 servings.

*"Bless us, O Lord, and these thy gifts which we are about to receive
from thy bounty, through Christ our Lord. Amen."*
CATHOLIC BLESSING

Red Cabbage And Apples

A tasty addition to any meal!

1 tablespoon unsalted margarine
¼ cup onion, chopped
½ cup water
1 tablespoon white vinegar
¾ teaspoon caraway seeds

½ teaspoon sugar
⅛ teaspoon black pepper
2 cups red cabbage, shredded
1 small apple, chopped

Melt margarine in a medium-size saucepan. Add onion and cook for 3 minutes, stirring frequently. Add remaining ingredients; cover and cook for 5-7 minutes or until cabbage is tender. Yield: 4 servings.

Orange Glazed Carrots

Eat til it ouches you!

5 medium carrots
1 tablespoon sugar
1 teaspoon corn starch
¼ teaspoon salt

¼ teaspoon ginger, ground
¼ cup orange juice
2 tablespoons butter or margarine

Slice carrots crosswise at an angle, about 1-inch thick. Cook, covered in ¼ cup boiling salted water for 15 minutes or until just tender. Meanwhile, combine sugar, corn starch, salt, ginger, orange juice, and butter; pour over carrots. Cook, stirring occasionally, for about 8 minutes. Yield: 4 servings.

Carrot Casserole

2 medium cans carrots, drained
1 medium onion, chopped
1 green pepper, chopped
2 tablespoons butter

2 tablespoons cream
Salt and pepper to taste
Seasoned bread crumbs

Mash carrots. Sauté onion and green pepper in butter; add to mashed carrots. Add cream, salt, and pepper. Sprinkle crumbs on top and bake. Garnish with parsley. Temperature: 350 degrees. Baking Time: 30 minutes. Yield: 6 servings.

Creamy Carrot Casserole

MICROWAVE.

4 cups carrots, sliced
¾ cup mayonnaise or salad
    dressing
¼ cup onion, chopped
2 tablespoons prepared
    horseradish
¼ teaspoon salt

¼ teaspoon pepper
14 (½ cup) saltine crackers,
    crushed
1 tablespoon butter or margarine,
    melted
2 tablespoons parsley, snipped
½ cup American cheese, shredded

In a 1½-quart casserole dish, MICROWAVE, HIGH, carrots in 2 tablespoons water, covered for 6-8 minutes or until tender, stirring once. Drain. In a small mixing bowl, stir together mayonnaise, onion, horseradish, salt, and pepper. Add to carrots in casserole; stir to combine. In a small mixing bowl, toss together crushed crackers, butter or margarine, and parsley. Sprinkle cracker mixture over carrots. MICROWAVE, HIGH, uncovered, 3 minutes. Add cheese. MICROWAVE, MEDIUM, 1-2 minutes more or until cheese is melted and mixture is heated through. Yield: 6-8 servings.

Dill And Honey Glazed Carrots

1 package frozen carrots
1 slice lemon
1 stick butter, melted

½ cup honey
1 large sprig fresh dill

Cook carrots as directed on package. Place rest of ingredients in blender container to make glaze. Blend on medium speed for about 40 seconds. Pour the glaze over hot cooked carrots. Yield: 4 servings.

Hot Pickled Cauliflower

1 medium head cauliflower
2 tablespoons butter
2 tablespoons green pepper,
    chopped

¼ teaspoon salt
3 tablespoons wine vinegar
2 tablespoons pimento, diced
1 teaspoon sugar

Break cauliflower into flowerets; cook in small amount of boiling salted water for about 10 minutes; drain. Combine remaining ingredients in a small saucepan; cook over low heat for about 5 minutes. Pour over hot cauliflower. Yield: 6 servings.

Frosted Cauliflower

MICROWAVE. Eat til it ouches you!

1 head cauliflower	½ teaspoon dill weed
2 tablespoons water	1 teaspoon prepared mustard
¼ cup mayonnaise	¼ cup sour cream
½ teaspoon garlic salt	Paprika

Trim leaves from cauliflower, but leave head whole. Cut and remove a core-shaped section from center core to help the center cook. Place cauliflower stem side down in 2-quart glass casserole dish. Add water. Cover with lid or plastic wrap. MICROWAVE, HIGH, 8-10 minutes or until just about tender. Let stand 5-10 minutes. Combine remaining ingredients except paprika. MICROWAVE, HIGH, ½-1 minutes or until sauce is heated. Yield: 8 servings.

Cauliflower-Walnut Bake

1 medium cauliflower	1 teaspoon dry mustard
1 cup sour cream	⅓ cup walnuts, chopped
1 cup cheddar cheese, shredded	¼ cup dry bread, crumbs
1 tablespoon flour	1 tablespoon margarine, melted
1 teaspoon instant chicken bouillon	1 teaspoon marjoram, crushed
	1 teaspoon onion salt

Break cauliflower into flowerets and cook in salted water for 15 minutes. Heat together sour cream, cheese, flour, bouillon, and mustard. Drain cauliflower and place in casserole, top with heated ingredients. Mix walnuts, bread crumbs, margarine, marjoram, and onion salt. Add to top of the cream mixture. Bake. Temperature: 400 degrees. Baking Time: 20 minutes. Yield: 6 servings.

Crunchy Celery Casserole

4 cups celery, sliced
5 ounces water chestnuts, drained
   and sliced
½ teaspoon basil
10¾ ounces cream of celery soup,
   undiluted

¼ cup pimento, chopped
2 tablespoons butter or
   margarine, melted
½ cup soft bread crumbs
⅓ cup toasted almonds, slivered

Cook celery in small amount of salted water until tender but still crisp, about 8 minutes; drain well. Combine celery with water chestnuts, basil, soup, and pimento. Spoon into lightly greased 2-quart casserole. Combine butter, bread crumbs, and almonds; sprinkle over celery mixture. Bake. Temperature: 350 degrees. Baking Time: 35 minutes. Yield: 6-8 servings.

Baked Hominy With Cheese

3 tablespoons butter
6 tablespoons flour
1 teaspoon salt
⅛ teaspoon pepper
2 cups milk
1 teaspoon Worcestershire sauce

½ teaspoon onion, grated
½ pound American cheese, grated
½ teaspoon dry mustard
2 (20 ounce) cans hominy
⅓ cup dry bread crumbs

Melt butter, add flour, and seasonings; blend. Gradually add milk, cook over low heat until thick, stirring constantly. Stir in Worcestershire sauce, onions, cheese, and dry mustard. Place drained hominy in 1½-quart greased casserole and pour cheese sauce over this. Sprinkle crumbs on top. Bake. Temperature: 350 degrees. Baking Time: 30 minutes. Yield: 6 servings.

Corn À La Southern

1 can corn, drained
2 eggs
2 tablespoons butter, melted
2 cups milk, scalded

1 medium green pepper, chopped
1 teaspoon salt
⅛ teaspoon pepper

Mix ingredients in order given. Pour into buttered 1-quart casserole dish. Bake slowly until firm. Use fresh corn, if desired. Temperature: 350 degrees. Baking Time: 30 minutes. Yield: 4 servings.

Corn Gumbo

Eat til it ouches you!

1 pound tomatoes, peeled
2 tablespoons butter
1 tablespoon vegetable oil
¾ cup onion, chopped
1 large clove garlic, minced
1 pound okra

½ cup ham, slivered
Salt and pepper to taste
¼ teaspoon red pepper flakes
2 cups fresh or canned corn
½ cup bread crumbs
2 tablespoons butter

Coarsely chop tomatoes. Trim stems from okra and cut into ⅜-inch slices. Heat butter and oil in heavy skillet over moderate heat. Add onions, garlic, okra, and ham. Cook 5 minutes until lightly browned. Stir in tomatoes, salt, pepper, red pepper flakes, and corn. Cook about 3 minutes, stirring once. Reduce heat to low and simmer 3 minutes until vegetables are tender. Top with bread crumbs and butter. Broil until browned. Yield: 6 servings.

Baked Corn Custard With Cheese

2 green onions, finely chopped
3 tablespoons butter
3 tablespoons flour
½ teaspoon salt
Pepper to taste
2 cups milk
1 cup cheese, grated
1 teaspoon sugar

2 tablespoons pimento, minced
½ teaspoon marjoram
2 eggs
2 (20 ounce) cans whole kernel
  corn, drained
½ cup bread crumbs
Paprika

Sauté onions in butter; blend in flour, salt, and pepper. Add milk slowly, stirring constantly. Cook over medium heat until thickened. Blend in cheese; add sugar, pimento, and marjoram. Beat eggs slightly; add to sauce mixture, blending well. Add corn; stir until well mixed. Pour into shallow 2-quart casserole. Sprinkle top with crumbs and lightly with paprika. Bake. Temperature: 350 degrees. Baking Time: 35 minutes. Yield: 8 servings.

"God often allows our hearts to be broken, so that He can beautify our souls."

Baked Corn With Sour Cream

6 slices bacon
2 tablespoons onion, chopped
2 teaspoons margarine
2 tablespoons flour
½ teaspoon salt

1 cup sour cream
2 (12 ounce) cans whole kernel
    corn, drained
1 tablespoon parsley, snipped

Fry bacon until crisp; crumble. Cook onion in margarine; blend in flour and salt. Add sour cream gradually, stirring until smooth. Bring to a boil; add corn. Cook until heated through. Fold in half of the bacon, pour into a greased baking dish. Top with parsley and the remaining bacon. Bake until bubbly. Temperature: 350 degrees. Baking Time: 30-40 minutes. Yield: 6-8 servings.

Eggplant Crunch Casserole

1 pound eggplant, pared and
    cubed (about 2 cups)
1 cup celery, chopped
½ cup onion, chopped
½ cup green pepper, chopped
4 tablespoons butter

8 ounces tomato sauce
4 ounces sharp American cheese,
    shredded
1½ cups corn chips, coarsely
    crushed

In large skillet, cook eggplant, celery, onion, and green pepper in butter until tender, about 15 minutes. Stir in tomato sauce, cheese, and 1 cup corn chips. Bake in 1½-quart covered casserole. Before serving, cover with remaining corn chips. Temperature: 350 degrees. Baking Time: 25-30 minutes. Yield: 6-8 servings.

Vegetable Potpourri

A super way to use fresh garden produce!

2 slices bacon, cut in small pieces
¾ cup onion, chopped
10 ounces frozen whole kernel
    corn
4 medium zucchini squash, sliced
1½ teaspoons cumin, ground

½ teaspoon salt
⅛ teaspoon garlic powder
3 medium tomatoes, peeled and
    cut in wedges
2 ounces American cheese,
    shredded

In large skillet, cook bacon until crisp. Add onion and cook until tender but not brown. Add corn, zucchini squash, cumin, salt, and garlic powder to skillet. Cook covered for 15-20 minutes. Add tomatoes, heat through. Turn into serving dish and sprinkle with cheese. Yield: 8 servings.

Golden Vegetable Bake

Shredded carrots and cream-style corn
combine to make a delicious casserole.

2 tablespoons butter
2 tablespoons flour
2 tablespoons onion, chopped
1 cup milk, scalded
1 teaspoon salt
⅛ teaspoon pepper

¾ teaspoon paprika
2 eggs, beaten
1½ cups carrots, shredded
1 can cream style corn
⅓ cup green pepper, chopped

Melt butter, add flour and onion; blend. Gradually add milk; cook over low heat until thick, stirring constantly. Add seasonings. Stir a little hot sauce into eggs. Add egg mixture to sauce. Stir in vegetables. Pour into greased 1½-quart casserole. Bake. Temperature: 350 degrees. Baking Time: 55-60 minutes. Yield: 6 servings.

Hot Vegetable Platter

1 head cauliflower
1 pound carrots, cut in thin strips
2 tablespoons butter or margarine
20 ounces frozen Italian green
   beans

½ cup milk
8 ounces cheddar cheese
4 tomatoes, sliced thick
3 slices bacon

Cook whole cauliflower covered in boiling, salted water for 20 minutes. Cook carrots covered in small amount of water 20 minutes. Drain and stir in 1 tablespoon butter or margarine. Cook Italian green beans according to directions on package, and stir in remaining butter. Stir milk into cheese. Heat slowly until cheese is melted. Place cauliflower on platter. Surround with other vegetables. Dribble cheese sauce on cauliflower. Fry bacon until crisp, drain, and crumble. Sprinkle with bacon. Yield: 10-12 servings.

Mixed Vegetable Casserole

20 ounces frozen mixed vegetables
½ cup celery
½ cup onion, chopped
1 cup mayonnaise

1 cup sharp cheese, grated
1 stick butter, melted
1 cup cracker crumbs

Partially cook vegetables for 5 minutes, drain. Combine all ingredients except butter and cracker crumbs. Put in casserole. Top with cracker crumbs and butter. Bake. Temperature: 350 degrees. Baking Time: 20-30 minutes. Yield: 6 servings.

Lyonnaise Vegetable Casserole

10 ounces frozen mixed vegetables
10 ounces frozen cauliflower
1 cup onion rings
5 tablespoons butter
3 tablespoons flour
½ teaspoon salt

Dash pepper
1 cup milk
4 ounces American cheese, grated
1 tablespoon pimento, chopped
½ cup bread cubes

Cook mixed vegetables and cauliflower as directed on packages; drain. Meanwhile, sauté onion rings in 3 tablespoons butter until lightly browned. Blend in flour, salt, and pepper. Add milk gradually and bring to a boil over low heat, stirring constantly. Add cheese and pimento; stir until smooth. Remove from heat. Arrange mixed vegetables and cauliflower in a 1½-quart greased shallow casserole. Melt remaining 2 tablespoons butter, add bread cubes, and toast lightly. Pour cheese sauce over vegetables and top with toasted bread cubes. Bake until bubbly. Temperature: 375 degrees. Baking Time: 15 minutes. Yield: 6-8 servings.

Mediterranean Stroganoff

10 ounces frozen cauliflower
10 ounces frozen broccoli
1½ cups carrots, thinly sliced
3 cups fresh mushrooms, sliced
1 small onion, chopped
1 clove garlic, minced
3 tablespoons butter or margarine
2 tablespoons flour
2 cups milk

½ teaspoon instant chicken
    bouillon granules
⅓ cup olives, pitted and sliced
    (optional)
1 cup ricotta cheese
¾ cup sour cream
½ cup Parmesan cheese, grated
12 ounces linguine, cooked

Cook cauliflower, broccoli, and carrots, covered, in boiling salted water 5 minutes; drain. Cut up large pieces of cauliflower and broccoli. Set vegetables aside. Cook mushrooms, onion, and garlic in butter 5 minutes. Stir in flour. Add milk and bouillon granules. Cook and stir till bubbly; cook and stir 1 minute more. Stir in vegetables and olives. Combine ricotta, sour cream, and half of the Parmesan cheese. Gradually stir 1 cup of the hot vegetable mixture into sour cream mixture. Return all to pan. Heat through; do not boil. Toss hot pasta with vegetable sauce. Sprinkle with remaining Parmesan cheese. Yield: 6 servings.

Mushroom Casserole

½ pound bacon
1 small onion, thinly sliced
1 clove garlic, minced
1 pound mushrooms, cleaned and
    sliced

Juice of one lemon
½ cup seasoned bread crumbs
2 tablespoons parsley, chopped

Fry bacon until crisp; remove from pan, drain and crumble. Sauté onion and garlic in bacon drippings until limp. Add mushrooms and cook (approximately 2-3 minutes) until change of color occurs. Add juice of lemon, seasoned bread crumbs, and parsley. Add crumbled bacon. Put in baking dish. Bake. Temperature: 350 degrees. Baking Time: 20 minutes. Yield: 4-6 servings.

Swiss Vegetable Medley

An interesting combination of vegetables!

16 ounces frozen broccoli, carrots,
    and cauliflower combination,
    drained
1 can condensed cream of
    mushroom soup
8 ounces Swiss cheese, shredded

⅓ cup sour cream
¼ teaspoon black pepper
4 ounces pimento, drained and
    chopped (optional)
2.8 ounces can French fried
    onions

CONVENTIONAL: Combine vegetables, soup, ½ cup cheese, sour cream, pepper, pimento, and ½ can French fried onions. Pour into an ungreased 1-quart casserole. Bake, covered for 30 minutes. Top with remaining cheese and onions; bake uncovered, 5 minutes longer. Temperature: 350 degrees. Baking Time: 35 minutes. Yield: 6 servings.

MICROWAVE: Prepare as above. MICROWAVE, HIGH, covered, 8 minutes; turn halfway through. Top with remaining cheese and onions. MICROWAVE, HIGH, uncovered, 1 minute or until cheese melts. Yield: 6 servings.

"Bloom where you are planted."

Baked Stuffed Onions

Eat til it ouches you!

8 large Spanish onions
½ pound pork sausage
½ cup onion, chopped
1 cup soft bread crumbs
2 tablespoons parsley, snipped

7 ounces can whole kernel corn,
    drained
2 tablespoons butter, melted
½ teaspoon paprika

Peel onions, and cut a slice from top. Cook onions in boiling salted water about 12 minutes or until tender, but not mushy. Cool. Remove center of onions, leaving shells intact. Reserve onion centers for use in other recipes or mix onion centers with any leftover sausage and place around stuffed onions in casserole. Cook sausage until browned, stirring to crumble. Drain, reserving pan drippings. Sauté ½ cup chopped onion, bread crumbs, parsley, and corn. Fill onion shells with sausage mixture. Place in greased shallow pan. Combine butter and paprika, brush on onions. Cover and bake for 15 minutes. Remove cover and bake 5 more minutes. Temperature: 400 degrees. Baking Time: 20 minutes. Yield: 8 servings.

Glazed Onions

MICROWAVE.

1 pound pearl onions, peeled
2 tablespoons butter or margarine
1 tablespoon brown sugar, packed
½ teaspoon corn starch

¼ teaspoon salt
¼ teaspoon dry mustard
Dash pepper
1 tablespoon cider vinegar

In 1-1½-quart casserole dish, combine onions and butter. Cover. MICROWAVE, HIGH, 6-8 minutes, or until tender, stirring once. Drain, reserve liquid. In small bowl, combine brown sugar, corn starch, and seasonings. Stir in vinegar and reserved cooking liquid. MICROWAVE, HIGH, 45-60 seconds, or until clear and thickened. Pour thickened sauce over onions. Toss to coat. Yield: 4-6 servings.

Minted Green Peas And Onions

½ cup water
1½ pounds onions, halved
    lengthwise and sliced thin
20 ounces frozen green peas

Salt and pepper to taste
¼ cup fresh mint leaves, minced
4 teaspoons margarine

In saucepan, add all ingredients. Cook until onion and peas are tender. Yield: 6 servings.

Cabbage Topped Tarragon Potatoes

1½ cups potatoes, chopped
½ cup cabbage, shredded
2 eggs, beaten
2 tablespoons butter or margarine
1 tablespoon flour
1 teaspoon onion, minced
¼ teaspoon salt

⅛ teaspoon tarragon, crushed
⅛ teaspoon garlic powder
⅛ teaspoon pepper
½ cup cheddar cheese, shredded
Plain yogurt (optional)
Chives, chopped (optional)

Cook potatoes, covered, in boiling salted water 20 minutes or until tender; drain and mash (should have about 1⅓ cups). Cook cabbage, covered in small amount of boiling water 5 minutes or until tender; drain. In bowl, combine eggs, butter, flour, and seasonings. Add potatoes; beat until smooth. Generously grease four (6 ounce) custard cups; spoon ⅓ cup potato mixture into each. Top with cabbage and cheese. Bake. Serve with yogurt and chives. Temperature: 350 degrees. Baking Time: 30 minutes. Yield: 4 servings.

Gourmet Stuffed Potatoes

Eat til it ouches you! Freezes well. Wrap separately.

6 large baking potatoes
1 pint sour cream
1 cup sharp cheddar cheese,
    grated or pimento cheese
¼ stick margarine

1 small onion, grated
¼ cup parsley, snipped
1 teaspoon garlic salt
Salt and pepper to taste
Paprika

Bake potatoes until soft. Remove from oven. Mix rest of ingredients in a large bowl with an electric mixer. Cut warm potatoes in half lengthwise and scoop potatoes from their shell with a spoon. Add potatoes to the mixture and beat thoroughly. Spoon mixture into shells and sprinkle with paprika. Serve hot. Temperature: 350 degrees. Baking Time: 1 hour. Yield: 12 servings.

"Take time to count all the things you have that money can't buy."

Oven-Roasted Potatoes

4 medium potatoes
1 medium red bell pepper, seeded
2 teaspoons rosemary, crumbled
4 cloves garlic, minced

½ teaspoon salt
¼ teaspoon pepper
2 tablespoons olive oil

Cut potatoes into ½-inch wedges. Cut pepper into 1-inch squares. Preheat oven. Place potatoes and remaining ingredients onto a greased baking sheet with sides. Toss well. Arrange in single layer. Bake until potatoes are tender and lightly browned. Toss two or three times during baking. Temperature: 475 degrees. Baking Time: 30-35 minutes. Yield: 4 servings.

Pizza Potatoes

MICROWAVE. The king of the potatoes!

4 medium potatoes, sliced
¼ cup water
1 pound ground beef
16-24 ounces tomato sauce

¼ teaspoon oregano
4 ounces pepperoni, sliced
4 ounces Mozzarella cheese, shredded

Combine potato slices and water in 12x8-inch glass baking dish. Cover with plastic wrap. MICROWAVE, HIGH, 11-13 minutes or until tender, stirring once. Let stand covered. Crumble ground beef into 1-quart glass casserole. MICROWAVE, HIGH, uncovered, 5-6 minutes or until meat is no longer pink, stirring once. Drain. Stir in tomato sauce and oregano. Pour meat sauce over potatoes. Arrange pepperoni evenly on top. Sprinkle with cheese. MICROWAVE, HIGH, uncovered, 7-8 minutes or until heated through, rotating dish once. Yield: 5-6 servings.

Baked Spinach With Sour Cream

3 (10 ounces) frozen spinach, chopped

1 package onion soup mix
1 pint sour cream

Cook spinach and drain; Mix soup with sour cream. Pour into baking dish; cover and bake. Temperature: 350 degrees. Baking Time: 30 minutes. Yield: 8 servings.

Apple And Sausage Stuffed Squash

MICROWAVE.

¼ pound pork sausage
2 medium apples, peeled and
    diced

¼ cup brown sugar, packed
4 teaspoons butter
2 (1 pound) acorn squash

Crumble sausage in thin layer on plate. Cover with paper towel. MICRO-WAVE, HIGH, 3 minutes, stirring every minute. Set aside. Combine apple, sugar, and butter in 1-quart casserole dish. Cover and MICROWAVE, HIGH, 2 minutes, until apples are almost tender. Add sausage and stir. Cut squash in half lengthwise. Remove seeds and fibrous membranes. Place cut side down in 8x8x2-inch dish and cover with wax paper. MICROWAVE, HIGH, 6 minutes. Turn squash cut-side up. Sprinkle lightly with salt and evenly divide filling among halves. Cover with wax paper and MICROWAVE, HIGH, 6-8 minutes more until squash is tender. Let stand 5 minutes before serving. Yield: 4 servings.

Country Style Yellow Squash

MICROWAVE.

8 slices bacon
⅓ cup water
1 teaspoon salt
2 pounds yellow squash, cubed
¼ cup onion, chopped
¼ cup butter, melted

¼ teaspoon pepper
¼ teaspoon basil
3 slices fresh bread, cubed
½ cup cheddar cheese, shredded
1 cup sour cream

In rectangle glass dish, place paper towel, add bacon slices, and cover with paper towel. MICROWAVE, HIGH, 8 minutes or until crisp; crumble. In a 2-quart glass dish, place water, salt, squash, and onion. Cover. MICROWAVE, HIGH, 13-15 minutes, stirring after 7 minutes. Drain well and mash. To squash, add ½ of crumbled bacon, butter, pepper, basil, bread cubes, cheese, and sour cream. Mix well and place in lightly buttered 1½-quart casserole dish. Sprinkle with remaining bacon. Cover. MICROWAVE, HIGH, 6-8 minutes. Yield: 4-6 servings.

"Believe in yourself."

Simple Summer Supper

3 cups zucchini, ¼-inch slices
1 teaspoon salt
¼ teaspoon pepper
¾ teaspoon basil
¾ teaspoon oregano
¼ teaspoon garlic powder

2 medium tomatoes, ½-inch slices
1 large onion, thinly sliced
4 ounces Muenster, American, or
    Swiss cheese, grated
6 slices bacon

Preheat oven. Arrange zucchini in a 2-2½-quart casserole dish; sprinkle with about one-third of salt, pepper, basil, oregano, and garlic. Add tomatoes and a third of seasonings; top with onion and remaining seasonings. Cover and bake 30 minutes. Fry bacon until crisp, drain, and crumble. Uncover; add cheese and bacon. Bake 10 minutes longer until cheese is melted. Temperature: 400 degrees. Baking Time: 40 minutes. Yield: 4-6 servings.

Aunt Nell's Zucchini Casserole

1 large zucchini, sliced in circles
1 large onion, sliced, rings
    separated
14¼ ounces stewed tomatoes or
    fresh tomatoes, sliced

Sprinkle oregano
8 ounces sharp cheddar cheese,
    shredded

Preheat oven. In large glass casserole dish, layer the above ingredients in the order listed, ending with the cheese, Bake until tender. Temperature: 350 degrees. Baking Time: 30-40 minutes. Yield: 8 servings.

Ambrosia Sweet Potato Bake

1 lemon
1 orange
7 cups sweet potatoes, sliced and
    cooked
8 ounces crushed pineapple

½ cup brown sugar, packed
½ cup margarine, melted
½ teaspoon salt
½ cup coconut, shredded
1 small jar maraschino cherries

Thinly sliced lemon and orange; alternate with sweet potatoes (drained) in long baking dish. Combine pineapple, sugar, margarine, and salt. Pour over all. Sprinkle with coconut and garnish with cherries. Bake. Temperature: 350 degrees. Baking Time: 30 minutes. Yield: 8-10 servings.

Sweet Potato Casserole

Eat til it ouches you!

3 cups sweet potatoes, cooked and
   mashed
1 stick butter or margarine

2 eggs
2 teaspoons vanilla extract
1 cup sugar

Mix together sweet potatoes, butter, eggs, vanilla, and sugar. Pour into Pyrex baking dish.

TOPPING

5⅓ tablespoons butter or
   margarine
1 cup brown sugar, packed

2 tablespoons flour
1 cup pecans, chopped

Melt butter and add brown sugar, flour, and pecans. Crumble TOPPING on top of SWEET POTATO CASSEROLE. Bake. Temperature: 325 degrees. Baking Time: 30 minutes. Yield: 6 servings.

Cranberry Yam Apples

Makes a beautiful garnish!

3 cups yams, cooked and mashed
½ teaspoon cinnamon, ground
½ teaspoon nutmeg, ground
¼ teaspoon cloves, ground

⅓ cup light brown sugar, packed
1 egg yolk
16 ounces whole cranberry sauce
8 whole cloves

Beat yams until smooth. Blend in spices and brown sugar. Form mixture into 8 balls. Place in lightly greased pan. Beat egg yolk and brush over each ball. Bake for 20 minutes. Remove from oven. Cover each "apple" ball with cranberry sauce. Place whole cloves in top center of each for apple stem. Return to oven for 5 minutes. Temperature: 350 degrees. Baking Time: 25 minutes. Yield: 8 servings.

"To a friend's house, the way is never long."

Yams And Apple Casserole

Eat til it ouches you!

6 yams, cooked and sliced

6 tart apples, peeled and sliced

SAUCE
4 tablespoons corn starch
½ cup water
1 cup sugar

1 teaspoon salt
¼ pound butter or margarine
½ cup boiling water

Butter a large casserole. Layer the yams and apples. Dissolve the corn starch in cold water. Add rest of the ingredients. Stir into boiling water and cook until thickened. Bake. Temperature: 350 degrees. Baking Time: 1 hour. Yield: 10 servings.

Cheesey Escalloped Tomatoes

MICROWAVE.

16 ounces stewed tomatoes
¼ teaspoon oregano
⅛ teaspoon garlic salt

¾ cup unseasoned croutons or
    stuffing mix
⅓ cup mozzarella cheese,
    shredded

Place regular size, 10x16-inch, Brown-in-Bag in 1-quart casserole dish. Combine all ingredients in bag, turning bag to mix. Close bag, make six half-inch slits near closure. MICROWAVE, HIGH, 4-5 minutes turning once during cooking. Yield: 4 servings.

Summertime Fried Tomatoes

⅓ cup flour
½ teaspoon salt
¼ teaspoon pepper
4 medium green tomatoes, sliced

¼ cup margarine
1 can condensed cream of
    mushroom soup
⅓ cup milk

Combine flour, salt, and pepper. Dip tomatoes in flour mixture. Fry in margarine over low heat until lightly browned on both sides. Remove to heated platter. Stir soup and milk into skillet. Heat, stirring occasionally. Pour over tomatoes. Yield: 4-6 servings.

Spinach-Stuffed Tomatoes

8 medium tomatoes, unpeeled
Salt to taste
8 slices bacon
20 ounces frozen spinach,
chopped
¾ cup soft bread crumbs

Pepper to taste
Pinch nutmeg, ground
Pinch garlic powder
Butter, melted
Sour Cream

Cut thin slice from top of tomatoes, scoop out center pulp (reserve for vegetable soup stock). Sprinkle inside of tomatoes with salt and turn upside down to drain for about an hour. Cook bacon until crisp, drain, crumble, and set aside. Cook frozen spinach according to package directions, but only until just thawed. Drain thoroughly. Combine with bread crumbs, seasonings, and finely crumbled bacon. Stuff tomatoes with mixture; place in buttered baking dish. Drizzle a small amount of melted butter over tomatoes. Bake uncovered until tender when pricked with fork, but do not overbake. Top with a tablespoon of sour cream before servings. Temperature: 350 degrees. Baking Time: 20 minutes. Yield: 8 servings.

Apple-Cranberry Casserole

Eat til it ouches you!

3 cups apples, peeled
2 cups whole raw cranberries
1 cup sugar
1 cup oatmeal, uncooked

½ cup brown sugar, packed
⅓ cup flour
½ cup pecans, chopped
1 stick margarine or butter

Cut apples into bite-size pieces. Mix first 3 ingredients and put in casserole dish. Mix oatmeal, brown sugar, flour, and pecans; pour over the above. Cut margarine into pieces and place on top of casserole. Bake covered for 50 minutes; remove cover and bake for 10 minutes more. Temperature: 350 degrees. Baking Time: 60 minutes. Yield: 6-8 servings.

"Take time to smell the flowers."

Baked Apricots

Wonderful served as a side dish with chicken, turkey, or ham.

4 ounce stack Ritz crackers
5 (16 ounce) cans apricot halves

⅔ cup light brown sugar, packed
1 stick butter, melted

Roll crackers into crumbs. In a 3-quart casserole dish, alternate layers of apricots, crumbs, and brown sugar. Pour butter over top. Bake. Hint: Quantities can be reduced easily. Temperature: 300 degrees. Baking Time: 30-45 minutes. Yield: 12 servings.

Curried Fruits

An elegant accompaniment for that special occasion!

1 pound can peach halves
1 pound can pear halves
1 pound can apricot halves
1 pound can pineapple chunks

⅓ cup margarine
¾ cup brown sugar, packed
2 teaspoons curry powder

Drain canned fruits and place in 3-quart baking dish. Melt butter; add sugar and curry powder. Pour over fruits. Bake. Temperature: 350 degrees. Baking Time: 20 minutes. Yield: 10 servings.

Pineapple Au Gratin

The perfect accompaniment to baked ham.

20 ounces pineapple chunks, drained
1 cup sugar
6 tablespoons flour

2 cups sharp cheddar cheese, grated
Ritz Crackers, crumbled
1 stick butter

Mix together pineapple, sugar, flour, and cheese. Place mixture in greased 1½-quart casserole dish. Cover top with cracker crumbs. Drizzle with melted butter. Bake. Temperature: 350 degrees. Baking Time: 25 minutes. Yield: 6-8 servings.

"Love endures all things."

Index

*Central United
Methodist Church*

CENTRAL UNITED METHODIST CHURCH

"In the 'Hollow', the region between the Chestnut Ridge, Slate, Sauratown, Pilot, and the Blue Ridge Mountains, there was very little religion", according to Methodist history, when Bishop Asbury, that remarkable founder of American Methodism, came riding through Mount Airy in the late 1700's. Methodist societies began in homes.

From 1831 until 1858 among these pioneer churches was our Lebanon, which stood on the crest of "Lebanon Hill", on North Main Street near the water tank. Then in 1858, with Methodism growing and the population of Mount Airy shifting, the little church of Lebanon divided. Those members who oriented toward the north formed their own church, Salem, and those members living toward the south built their new church on South Main Street, called "Old Methodist", Main Street Methodist. The cemetery of this large white frame church still exists.

From 1894 until 1965, Central grew into a most prominent Methodist congregation. The Pseudo-Gothic church featured a beautiful imported French stained glass window. This beautiful round stained glass window of Jesus in the Garden of Gethsemane now enhances the chapel at Northern Hospital of Surry County on Rockford Street.

In 1966, the fourth church, 1909 North Main Street, was built, a stately edifice with magnificent French designed stained glass windows and with "Old Central's" bell still pealing from its tall steeple. The seven magnificent windows known as the Chancel or Apse windows tell the story of the six days of creation as found in the Bible, Genesis, Chapter 1. The seventh window represents God resting from all His work which He created. Climaxing this masterpiece of art series, there are reflections of the various items in other windows.

INDEX

A

B

Mrs. Betty C. Lyerly
125 Taylor Street
Mount Airy, North Carolina 27030

Please send _____ **autographed** copies of *The Best of Mayberry*

Please send _____ copy(ies) of *The Best of Mayberry*   @ $19.95 each _____

Postage and handling   @   4.00 each _____

North Carolina residents add 7% sales tax   @   1.40 each _____

TOTAL _____

Name _____

Address _____

City _____ State _____ Zip _____

Please make checks payable to *The Best of Mayberry*.

— —

Mrs. Betty C. Lyerly
125 Taylor Street
Mount Airy, North Carolina 27030

Please send _____ **autographed** copies of *The Best of Mayberry*

Please send _____ copy(ies) of *The Best of Mayberry*   @ $19.95 each _____

Postage and handling   @   4.00 each _____

North Carolina residents add 7% sales tax   @   1.40 each _____

TOTAL _____

Name _____

Address _____

City _____ State _____ Zip _____

Please make checks payable to *The Best of Mayberry*.

— —

Mrs. Betty C. Lyerly
125 Taylor Street
Mount Airy, North Carolina 27030

Please send _____ **autographed** copies of *The Best of Mayberry*

Please send _____ copy(ies) of *The Best of Mayberry*   @ $19.95 each _____

Postage and handling   @   4.00 each _____

North Carolina residents add 7% sales tax   @   1.40 each _____

TOTAL _____

Name _____

Address _____

City _____ State _____ Zip _____

Please make checks payable to *The Best of Mayberry*.